PEARSON EDEXCEL INTERNATIONAL GCSE (9–1)

ENGLISH LANGUAGE B

Student Book

Roger Addison
Samantha Brunner
David Foster
Peter Inson
Robert O'Brien
Pam Taylor

Published by Pearson Education Limited, 80 Strand, London, WC2R 0RL.

https://www.pearson.com/international-schools

Copies of official specifications for all Pearson qualifications may be found on the website: https://qualifications.pearson.com

Text © Pearson Education Limited 2017
Edited by Fleur Frederick and Claire Smith
Designed by Cobalt id
Typeset by Tech-Set Ltd, Gateshead, UK
Original illustrations © Pearson Education Limited 2017
Cover design by Pearson Education Limited
Picture research by Ann Thomson
Cover photo/illustration © gettyimages.co.uk: Atsushi Hayakawa

The rights of Roger Addison, Samantha Brunner, David Foster, Peter Inson, Robert O'Brien and Pam Taylor to be identified as authors of this work have been asserted by them in accordance with the Copyright, Designs and Patents Act 1988.

First published 2017

25

10

British Library Cataloguing in Publication Data
A catalogue record for this book is available from the British Library

ISBN 978 0 435 18257 1

Printed in Great Britain by Bell & Bain Ltd, Glasgow

Endorsement Statement

In order to ensure that this resource offers high-quality support for the associated Pearson qualification, it has been through a review process by the awarding body. This process confirms that this resource fully covers the teaching and learning content of the specification or part of a specification at which it is aimed. It also confirms that it demonstrates an appropriate balance between the development of subject skills, knowledge and understanding, in addition to preparation for assessment.

Endorsement does not cover any guidance on assessment activities or processes (e.g. practice questions or advice on how to answer assessment questions), included in the resource nor does it prescribe any particular approach to the teaching or delivery of a related course.

While the publishers have made every attempt to ensure that advice on the qualification and its assessment is accurate, the official specification and associated assessment guidance materials are the only authoritative source of information and should always be referred to for definitive guidance.

Pearson examiners have not contributed to any sections in this resource relevant to examination papers for which they have responsibility.

Examiners will not use endorsed resources as a source of material for any assessment set by Pearson. Endorsement of a resource does not mean that the resource is required to achieve this Pearson qualification, nor does it mean that it is the only suitable material available to support the qualification, and any resource lists produced by the awarding body shall include this and other appropriate resources.

INTRODUCTION TO THE COURSE

This book has been written to help all students taking the Pearson Edexcel International GCSE English Language B (**4EB1**) (first examination June 2018). It is designed to enable them to achieve their full potential during the course and in the exam. It is written for both students and teachers. There are two specifications for the International GCSE course, English Language A (4EA1) and English Language B (4EB1).

This book is written to support specification B. This book will prepare students for all aspects of the course.

STUDENTS

How will this book support you? We hope you will find it:

■ useful in terms of developing your skills and techniques fully for the Pearson Edexcel International GCSE in English Language

■ a support in preparing for unseen passages

■ a helpful guide to your study of transactional writing and imaginative writing.

This book will also assist you in planning your revision.

STUDENTS AND TEACHERS

The book goes through the requirements for specification B, with explanations, suggestions and questions. It also includes a large number of practical activities and examples. These are for practice and will also help you to appreciate how really good answers are written and structured.

> **HINT**
>
> Remember to plan your work. The sooner you organise yourself and your ideas, the easier you will find your preparation for every section of the exam! This book aims to give you confidence by improving your skills and techniques.

READ WIDELY

It is very important to make sure that you have a really good grasp of many different types of non-fiction passages. Make sure that you read widely. Every year, examiners read International GCSE scripts in which the candidates write in a way that shows that they do not understand, or have not prepared carefully for, the texts that are set. Use the relevant sections from this book to strengthen your ability to analyse and compare texts.

USE YOUR SOURCES

An important part of Paper 1 is the test of your ability to think quickly when confronted with unfamiliar (unseen) prose passages, to show that you have understood and responded to these passages, and that you can base your own writing on the ideas that you have met in these passages. Work through the 'Types of text' section in order to ensure that you are ready to read and analyse a variety of unseen passages in Paper 1.

KNOW AND APPLY YOUR TECHNICAL TERMS

Like other subjects, English has a number of technical terms which you may need to use. It is important that you know how to use the correct term and that you can spell it. Refer to the subject vocabulary within the margins of this book or the Glossary on pages 202–203 to help you. Even more importantly, you need to know how to explain why a particular device is used by looking at the writer's intentions. In your exams, you will always be given credit for explaining the effects of a word or phrase, whether or not you use the technical terms, but accurate use of the correct terms will make your writing more fluent and concise.

> **HINT**
>
> Make lists of technical terms and write out what you think they mean, then check your definitions against the glossary at the back of the book or the subject vocabulary in the margins.

IMPROVE THE STRUCTURE AND ORGANISATION OF YOUR ANSWERS

Look closely at the model answers that are given at various points throughout this book. This will help you to write detailed, successful responses.

PRESENT YOUR WORK EFFECTIVELY

The way in which you set out your own writing is important. You should practise producing writing that is:

- neat, regular and clear
- correctly punctuated
- spelled accurately
- set out in clear paragraphs.

Doing this will give you the following benefits.

- Examiners will form a positive impression of your work.
- Examiners will be able to read your answer easily; they will not be able to do so if your handwriting is poor or if it is not written in proper sentences.
- How you write, as well as what you write, will be considered when your work is marked.
- Good writing is useful for applications for jobs or college courses.
- Many jobs require the ability to write clearly, accurately and precisely.

KNOW YOUR OWN STRENGTHS AND WEAKNESSES

It is an excellent idea to keep a checklist of your most common errors in spelling, punctuation and grammar, since these are assessed in all specifications. When you receive a piece of work back from your teacher, read it through and make sure that you understand any comments or corrections.

- Keep a sheet of paper at the front or back of your folder, on which you can write out the correct spelling of words you have misspelled.
- Refer to this before handing in your work to make sure you have not made the same mistakes as before.
- Take some time to learn the spellings on your list.

▼ REMEMBER!
- Make the best use of lesson time.
- Make sure you know what you have to do in class.
- Be sure you understand what the homework is.
- Be sure that you understand what you will be asked to do in the exam.

▼ MAKE NOTES!
- Write down key points from: teachers; books you read; class work; articles or worksheets.
- For International GCSE Specification B: annotate the texts that you are given carefully.
- Add points missed onto the end of your homework or practice questions when they are returned to you.

▼ SEEK HELP!
- Ask teachers to explain if you are unsure.
- Discuss with friends.
- Look things up using dictionaries, encyclopaedias and the internet.

▼ TAKE PART!
- Ask questions in class.
- Answer questions in class.
- Contribute to discussions.
- Be fully involved in group work. Don't let others do all the talking!

▼ KEEP UP!
- Hand in your work on time.
- Keep files or exercise books up to date.
- Make sure you do not get behind with your homework.
- Do not leave work unfinished. It is always difficult to remember what has been missed unless you amend it at the time.
- Check off completed work in your records.

▼ BE ORGANISED!
- Have a clear filing system for your work.
- Present your work neatly.
- Set yourself targets.
- Stick to deadlines.

HINT
Use a system such as different coloured cards or sticky notes to write down the **key points** on each text.

ABOUT THIS BOOK

This book is written for students following the Edexcel International GCSE (9–1) English Language B specification and covers both years of the course. The specification and sample assessment materials for English Language B can be found on the Pearson Qualifications website.

The course has been structured so that teaching and learning can take place in any order, both in the classroom and in any independent learning. The book contains five chapters: Reading Skills, Writing Skills and Section A, Section B and Section C.

The Reading Skills and Writing Skills chapters cover fundamental areas of these two key areas of English Language.

Activities
A wide range of varied activities to encourage understanding and embed understanding as an individual, as well as in larger groups to establish cross-peer learning and communication.

Key points
Easy to understand, core points to be taken away from sections or texts.

The following reproduces a sample spread (pages 62–63) from the book.

62 SECTION A — NON-FICTION TEXTS

ACTIVITY 3 | A01 | A02 | SKILLS — CRITICAL THINKING, ANALYSIS, INTERPRETATION

▼ **IDENTIFYING TECHNIQUES IN OBITUARIES**

Obituaries are often sympathetic accounts of someone's achievements.

► How does the writer of the Mandela extract begin to influence the reader's sympathies?
► What makes these extracts more appropriate for obituaries than for biographies?

Copy and complete the following table, finding examples of the methods and techniques in the two extracts and commenting on their effect. Now identify some methods for yourself, remembering to back them up with evidence from the text and comment on their effect.

▼ METHOD OR TECHNIQUE	▼ EXAMPLE	▼ COMMENT ON EFFECT
Formal register		
Focus on factual information		
Conciseness of writing		

SUBJECT VOCABULARY
register the type or style of vocabulary used according to the situation

SPEECHES

Speeches can be given for many different reasons. Lawyers make speeches in court for the defence or the prosecution. People make speeches in debates or after formal dinners to entertain an audience. However, the most famous speeches are those made by politicians as part of campaigns. The purpose of such speeches is often to rally supporters and give listeners a sense of purpose and inspiration.

The following speech was made by the American civil rights campaigner, Martin Luther King Junior, who was later assassinated for his beliefs and his work on behalf of black Americans.

As you read the speech, think about how Martin Luther King shows his listeners that he is fighting for a better and fairer society in America, using techniques such as:

- repetition of key words
- repetition of the beginning of sentences
- reference to particular individuals
- use of geographical references (i.e. different parts of the United States)
- describing the difficulties black people have faced over the years
- the idea of bringing all people together
- the use of words from a patriotic song.

▲ Martin Luther King at the March on Washington rally in August 1963

SECTION A — NON-FICTION TEXTS — 63

all men are created equal A quotation from the US Declaration of Independence, written just before the start of the war against Great Britain.

Georgia Southern American slave-owning state before the American Civil War.

colour of their skin but by the content of their character Note the alliteration of the sound /k/ five times.

let freedom ring Part of a patriotic American song.

New York New York State, which is very large.

Alleghenies A range of hills

the old Negro spiritual A traditional hymn-like song of the Afro-Caribbeans, many of which originated during the era of slavery.

KEY POINT
Look at the way an author has used the technical devices of language to persuade the reader of a certain viewpoint.

HINT
Although you will be given credit for knowing and identifying techniques, many more marks go to good explanations of their effects and of why they are used, than to mere technique-spotting.

SUBJECT VOCABULARY
alliteration the use of several words together that begin with the same sound or letter
onomatopoeia where a word sounds like the noise it makes
simile a description that says that an object is like an image
metaphor describing something by comparing it to an image which it resembles, in a way that says the object is the image
personification when something which is not human is made to seem human by attributing human qualities to it
emotive language language that produces an emotional reaction

▼ 'I HAVE A DREAM' BY MARTIN LUTHER KING AT WASHINGTON DC, AUGUST 1963

I have a dream…

I have a dream that one day this nation will rise up and live out the true meaning of its creed: 'We hold these truths to be self-evident, that all men are created equal.'

I have a dream that one day on the red hills of Georgia, the sons of former slaves and the sons of former slave owners will be able to sit down together at the table of brotherhood.

I have a dream that my four little children will one day live in a nation where they will not be judged by the colour of their skin but by the content of their character.

I have a dream today!

And this will be the day – this will be the day when all of God's children will be able to sing with new meaning:

My country 'tis of thee, sweet land of liberty, of thee I sing.

Land where my fathers died, land of the Pilgrim's pride,

From every mountainside, let freedom ring!

And if America is to be a great nation, this must become true.

And so let freedom ring from the prodigious hilltops of New Hampshire.

Let freedom ring from the mighty mountains of New York.

Let freedom ring from the heightening Alleghenies of Pennsylvania…

Let freedom ring from every hill and molehill of Mississippi.

From every mountainside, let freedom ring.

And when this happens, when we allow freedom ring, when we let it ring from every village and every hamlet, from every state and every city, we will be able to speed up that day when all of God's children, black men and white men, Jews and Gentiles, Protestants and Catholics, will be able to join hands and sing in the words of the old Negro spiritual:

Free at last! Free at last!

Thank God Almighty, we are free at last!

The art of persuasive writing and speaking is called rhetoric. Rhetorical devices include many techniques used in poetry, since they can make all kinds of writing more memorable. These techniques include alliteration, onomatopoeia, figurative language (similes, metaphors and personification), emotive language and word choices.

Subject vocabulary and General vocabulary
Useful words and phrases are colour coded within the main text and picked out in the margin with concise and simple definitions. These will support understanding of key subject terms and support students whose first language is not English.

Hint
Useful support and advice addressing common mistakes or difficult content.

They build on and reinforce what students already know and develop essential skills that will allow them to succeed on this course. These chapters can be used to teach these reading and writing skills in blocks at the start of the course or integrated into relevant sections of the texts being studied.

The chapters on Sections A, B and C covers all of the content required by the course, mirroring the exam paper.

For each section, information is interspersed with activities in order to put learning into practice and exam-style questions to help you prepare and practise for the exam. Other features help to expand students' knowledge and reinforce their learning.

You can find more information about the English Language B course, including the Specification and the Sample Assessment Materials, on the Pearson Edexcel website.

Learning objectives
Chapters and Units are carefully tailored to address key assessment objectives central to the course.

Pearson Progression
Sample student answers have been given a **Pearson Step** from 1 to 12. This tells you how well the response has met the criteria in the **Pearson Progression Map**.

Exam-style questions
Questions tailored to the Pearson Edexcel specification to allow for practice and development of exam writing technique.

---

196 SECTION C — IMAGINATIVE WRITING

LEARNING OBJECTIVES
This lesson will help you to
- take greater control over your writing
- think about the use of the senses when writing
- make clear what you want to say about characters, actions and locations.

PUTTING IT INTO PRACTICE
In the exam, you will need to demonstrate the following points in your imaginative writing.
- Ideas that are communicated effectively and imaginatively. This is what you will have to plan before you start.
- Writing that is clear and accurate. This is what you will have to check after you finish.

EXAM-STYLE QUESTION

A04
A05

SKILLS — CRITICAL THINKING, ANALYSIS, CREATIVITY, INNOVATION

Write a story (true or imaginary) entitled 'An Unexpected Event'. **(30 marks)**

It was a warm summer's day and we set off from the farmyard to round up some sheep. Early in the summer all the sheep were rounded up so that they could be dipped, pushed one at a time through a long narrow bath that contained an insecticide that would protect them from flies that would burrow into their flesh and lay their eggs in the wounds that they had created. The condition is called fly-strike. The sheep we were looking for had spread themselves over the moor and across to an open area of land between the road and the sea. With us we had two sheep dogs. Once we had crossed the road we sent the dogs round in wide sweeping paths to move the sheep together into a flock that we could move across the road and back to the farm.
Ahead of us we could see the dogs, their heads up as they looked from side to side for sheep that were standing still as if wondering whether to move or not. They moved on, and left us to follow, pushing the flock up towards the road. Then, as the ground sloped more steeply away beneath our feet, we could see them no longer. Below us, to our left, we could hear the sea crashing into the rocks at the foot of the cliffs. Suddenly, from ahead of us, came the blare of a fog horn.
We hadn't noticed the clouds that had come up behind us. They had yet to blot out the sun and we were more aware of the growing flock to our right that was moving slowly towards the road. Ahead of us the dogs were barking furiously now and we stepped forwards to see what was troubling them. Again the fog horn blared, this time almost above us.
Suddenly, the fog had surrounded us; damp and chill, it had been blown up behind us as the breeze had lifted. We could see nothing of dogs or sheep, but we could hear them and the rocks that were directly below us. To one side we leant on the round wall of the tower that housed the fog horn, built into the cliff. Around us sheep and dogs continued to move carefully, but we two-legged creatures were far less stable on the cliff face and so we waited until the breeze dropped and the fog slid away off the cliff and moved slowly, back down to the water.

The condition is called fly-strike. A long, detailed description is followed by a short sentence to vary pace.

we sent the dogs round in wide sweeping paths The vocabulary is fairly straight forward, but chosen precisely to create a vivid image.

Below us, to our left, we could hear the sea crashing into the rocks at the foot of the cliffs. Suddenly, from ahead of us, came the blare of a fog horn. Adding these sensory details makes the scene feel more real and also creates suspense.

Ahead of us the dogs were barking furiously now and we stepped forwards to see what was troubling them The description of the clouds, and then the dogs barking 'furiously', increases tension.

Suddenly, the fog had surrounded us; damp and chill, it had been blown up behind us as the breeze had lifted. Use of a semicolon to link together descriptions of the fog is very effective.

EXAMINER'S COMMENTS
This is a highly effective piece of imaginative writing. A vivid scene is created through precise use of vocabulary, which shows it's not always necessary to use lots of figurative language to describe effectively. The atmosphere becomes increasingly tense, showing the student has a good grasp of how to structure a piece of writing. There is a good balance of longer, more detailed sentences and short sentences for effect.

SECTION C — IMAGINATIVE WRITING — 197

COMMENTARY
This is an explanation of how this sample answer was written. Try following this process in your own imaginative writing.

PLANNING THE PLOT
The planning of this piece is focused on the fog surrounding the two characters who were caught unawares. The rounding up of the sheep provides a context, a background or explanation as to why the characters were on the sloping cliffs where fog was more of a danger, a sense of drama that could be used to a lesser or greater extent by the writer.
As the gathering of the sheep proceeds, the task becomes a distraction for the characters as they watch the sheep, rather than the weather behind them. As the drama develops you can feel the slope of the cliffs, see the dogs disappear from sight, somewhere ahead, then you hear the waves and the sudden burst of the fog horn. The reader's senses are used to create the drama.

CHECKING
This is where you must read the passage aloud or, under exam conditions, imagine the sound of a voice reading it aloud. This is the most effective way of checking your writing. If the punctuation is poor, you will find yourself unable to read the passage fluently, and if there are lapses in the grammar then the sense of the writing will not be clear. If this happens, ask yourself, 'What is the subject of this sentence?' and 'What am I told about the subject?'. These questions should help you to clarify the sentence.

EXAM-STYLE QUESTIONS

A04
A05

SKILLS — CRITICAL THINKING, ANALYSIS, ADAPTIVE LEARNING, CREATIVITY

KEY POINT
Engaging your audience is crucial. Remember that good writing usually involves something that the author wants to say. If the author wants something to be read, the reader must be given a reason to start and encouragement to keep reading.

Write approximately 400 words on one of the following:
EITHER
1 'Competing is good but winning is better.' Discuss. **(30 marks)**
OR
2 Write a story (true or imaginary) entitled 'Victory'. **(30 marks)**
OR
3 Describe a game that has made an impression on you. **(30 marks)**
Exchange your finished piece with a partner, then read each other's work and exchange comments. Try to suggest ways of improving each other's work rather than simply finding faults.

▲ The reader's senses are used to create the drama

Student answers
Higher- and lower-level written answers annotated with marker comments to encourage understanding of the marking criteria.

Skills
Each activity and set of questions has been assigned with the key skills gained from undertaking them, allowing for a strong focus on particular academic qualities.

ASSESSMENT OVERVIEW

The following tables give an overview of the assessment for this course. You should study this information closely to help ensure that you are fully prepared for this course and know exactly what to expect in each part of the assessment.

▼ PAPER 1	▼ PERCENTAGE	▼ MARKS	▼ TIME	▼ AVAILABILITY
READING AND WRITING Written exam paper Paper code 4EB1/01 Externally set and assessed by Pearson Edexcel Single tier of entry	100%	100	3 hours	January and June exam series First assessment June 2018

ASSESSMENT OBJECTIVES AND WEIGHTINGS

▼ SECTION	▼ ASSESSMENT OBJECTIVE	▼ DESCRIPTION	▼ % IN INTERNATIONAL GCSE
READING	AO1	Read and understand a variety of texts, selecting and interpreting information, ideas and perspectives	15%
	AO2	Understand and analyse how writers use linguistic and structural devices to achieve their effects	20%
	AO3	Explore links and connections between writers' ideas and perspectives, as well as how these are conveyed	15%
WRITING	AO4	Communicate effectively and imaginatively, adapting form, tone and register of writing for specific purposes and audiences	32%
	AO5	Write clearly, using a range of vocabulary and sentence structures, with appropriate paragraphing and accurate spelling, grammar and punctuation	18%

RELATIONSHIP OF ASSESSMENT OBJECTIVES TO UNITS

▼ UNIT NUMBER	▼ ASSESSMENT OBJECTIVE				
	AO1	AO2	AO3	AO4	AO5
PAPER 1	15%	20%	15%	32%	18%

ASSESSMENT SUMMARY

▼ PAPER 1	▼ DESCRIPTION	▼ MARKS	▼ ASSESSMENT OBJECTIVES
READING AND WRITING PAPER CODE 4EB1/01	**Structure** Paper 1 assesses 100% of the total English Language B qualification. There will be three sections on the paper. Students must answer all questions in Section A, the question in Section B and one question from a choice of three in Section C.		
	Section A: Reading Students will study and analyse selections from a range of non-fiction. Students must: ■ develop skills to analyse how writers use linguistic and structural devices to achieve their effects ■ explore links and connections between writers' ideas and perspectives.	40	Questions will test the following Assessment Objectives: AO1 – 5% AO2 – 20% AO3 – 15%
	Section B: Reading and Writing Students will explore and develop transactional writing skills. Students must: ■ develop transactional writing skills for a variety of purposes and audiences and to engage the reader ■ use spelling, punctuation and grammar accurately.	30	Questions will test the following Assessment Objectives: AO1 – 10% AO4 – 12% AO5 – 8%
	Section C: Writing Students will explore and develop discursive, narrative and descriptive writing skills. Students must: ■ develop imaginative writing skills for a variety of purposes and audiences and to engage the reader ■ use spelling, punctuation and grammar accurately.	30	Questions will test the following Assessment Objectives: AO4 – 20% AO5 – 10%
	This is a single-tier exam paper and all questions cover the full ranges of grades from 9–1. The assessment duration is 3 hours. Closed book: texts are not allowed in the examination. However, students will be provided with any relevant extracts in the examination.	The total number of marks available is **100**	

金玉君子
茶庄
清潔其風
神明之胄
茶
欢迎团购
免费品尝
本店经营
湖南各大名茶
经营项目
电话：15307432396
染
DIY
现场制作
中国非物质文化遗产
苗族蜡染简介
蜡染的工艺流程
免费品尝

READING SKILLS

Assessment Objective 1

Read and understand a variety of texts, selecting and interpreting information, ideas and perspectives

Assessment Objective 2

Understand and analyse how writers use linguistic and structural devices to achieve their effects

Assessment Objective 3

Explore links and connections between writers' ideas and perspectives, as well as how these are conveyed

This chapter focuses on some core reading skills that you can apply to all parts of the English Language B course. Working through these lessons and activities will help you to develop the reading skills that you will need for the exam.

The chapter is split into the following sections:
- Text analysis
- Use of language.

In the reading sections of your exams you will need to be able to meet the Assessment Objectives AO1, AO2 and AO3.

LEARNING OBJECTIVES

This lesson will help you to:

- understand the main ideas that a writer is communicating
- summarise the key points of a text quickly
- build confidence in independent reading.

KEY POINT

Skimming and scanning are important reading techniques. Skimming is reading quickly to get a general sense of a text. Scanning involves looking through a text for specific information.

HINT

To skim effectively, you don't read everything. What you read is more important than what you skip. Try to:

- highlight key points
- rephrase the main point of each paragraph in your own words
- underline any unfamiliar words.

SKIMMING AND SCANNING

It can be difficult to know where to start when approaching a text for the first time. You need a methodical approach that allows you to understand the main ideas that are being communicated.

Skimming and scanning are two important reading techniques. They are often confused with one another, but they are very different skills. However, both help you to achieve the same aim: to read more quickly and effectively.

SKIMMING

Skimming is useful when you want to quickly get a general idea of what a text is about. When you skim, you read through the text three to four times faster than when you read each word in order to get a sense of the topic, ideas and information being conveyed.

WHEN SHOULD I SKIM?

- When you have a lot to read in a short space of time.
- When revising topics to identify key information.
- When locating a passage in a text.
- When finding relevant material when planning an essay.

SCANNING

Scanning refers to reading through material to find specific information. When you scan, you run your eyes over the information in a text and pull out specific words, phrases or pieces of information. You may not realise that you scan through different texts every day, from television guides to football results.

WHEN SHOULD I SCAN?

- When looking for specific pieces of information quickly.
- When locating a relevant quotation or section in a text.

ACTIVITY 1   SKILLS ▸ DECISION MAKING

▼ SKIMMING OR SCANNING?

Read the following examples and identify which describes the process of skimming and which describes scanning.

1 You flick through a financial report to find a particular set of data.
2 You quickly go through a 20-page report in a few minutes to determine the overall subject, tone and a few key points.
3 You pick up a newspaper at a coffee shop, look over the first few pages and gather some general information about the events happening in the world.

SUBJECT VOCABULARY

topic sentence the first sentence in a paragraph, often used to explain the key idea

chronologically organised in linear time

flashback when the narrator of a story jumps out of the present in order to describe an event which happened in the past (often in the form of memories)

STRATEGIES FOR SKIMMING

- Read the **topic sentence**. This will give you a good sense of the ideas and structure of the whole text.
- Read the first and last paragraphs.
- Use chapter names, headings and subheadings as a guide.

STRATEGIES FOR SCANNING

- For scanning to be successful, be sure of your purpose. Think about what information you are looking for before you begin to scan the text.
- Consider how the text is structured. Is it arranged alphabetically, by category, **chronologically** or does it use other devices such as **flashback**?
- Use your index finger to help you, such as when scanning a timetable for a train time. Move your finger down the text at the same time as your eyes to help you to maintain focus.

ACTIVITY 2   **SKILLS** ▸ CREATIVITY, INNOVATION

▼ SKIMMING AND SCANNING RACE

▶ **How fast are you at finding the information you need?**

You need a dictionary, a pen, a piece of paper and a partner. Follow the instructions below carefully.

STEP 1	STEP 2	STEP 3	STEP 4	STEP 5
Open the dictionary at any page.	Write down the page number in the margin of the piece of paper.	Close your eyes and place your finger somewhere on the page of the dictionary.	See what word you have chosen. Write down its (first) definition, but NOT the word itself.	Repeat steps 1–4 until you have ten definitions on your page.

STEP 6	STEP 7
Now swap pieces of paper with your partner. See who can complete the written list with all the words first.	Now write a paragraph that is as short as possible and that uses all your partner's words.

ACTIVITY 3   **SKILLS** ▸ INITIATIVE

HINT

Use your own words in a summary wherever possible. Simply repeating sentences from the original text does not show that you have understood what the writer is communicating.

▼ SUMMARISING INFORMATION

Once you are confident that you understand the text, you need to be able to summarise the key points that the writer makes. A good summary phrases these points in a **concise** and **clear** style. Choose an extract and write a summary of it.

LEARNING OBJECTIVES

This lesson will help you to:
- interpret the information and ideas in a text
- read between the lines to work out what the text implies.

SUBJECT VOCABULARY

infer read between the lines

KEY POINT

Explicit meaning is where the writer **ex**plains their ideas.
Implicit meaning is where the writer **im**plies their ideas; you have to **in**fer and **im**agine based on what you know.

EXPLICIT AND IMPLICIT MEANING

To be a good reader, you need to understand both what a text tells you directly, or explicitly, and to **infer** based on what you think the writer indirectly, or implicitly, suggests in their text. This may be about the writer's views, character or theme.

▲ A couple on their wedding day

EXPLICIT MEANING

The picture shows a woman in a dress holding flowers and standing close to a man in a suit.

IMPLICIT MEANING

You may be able to **infer** that this is a wedding photograph because you have experience of seeing this type of image being related to weddings.

▼ AN EXTRACT FROM *A WALK IN THE WOODS* BY BILL BRYSON

We hiked till five and camped beside a tranquil spring in a small, grassy clearing in the trees just off the trail. Because it was our first day back on the trail, we were flush for food, including perishables like cheese and bread that had to be eaten before they went off or were shaken to bits in our packs, so we rather gorged ourselves, then sat around smoking and chatting idly until persistent and numerous midgelike creatures (no-see-ums, as they are universally known along the trail) drove us into our tents. It was perfect sleeping weather, cool enough to need a bag but warm enough that you could sleep in your underwear, and I was looking forward to a long night's snooze – indeed was enjoying a long night's snooze – when, at some indeterminate dark hour, there was a sound nearby that made my eyes fly open. Normally, I slept through everything – through thunderstorms, through Katz's snoring and noisy midnight pees – so something big enough or distinctive enough to wake me was unusual. There was a sound of undergrowth being disturbed – a click of breaking branches, a weighty pushing through low foliage – and then a kind of large, vaguely irritable snuffling noise.

▶

Bear!

I sat bolt upright. Instantly every neuron in my brain was awake and dashing around frantically, like ants when you disturb their nest. I reached instinctively for my knife, then realized I had left it in my pack, just outside the tent. Nocturnal defense had ceased to be a concern after many successive nights of tranquil woodland repose. There was another noise, quite near.

"Stephen, you awake?" I whispered.

"Yup," he replied in a weary but normal voice.

"What was that?"

"How the hell should I know?"

"It sounded big."

"Everything sounds big in the woods."

This was true. Once a skunk had come plodding through our camp and it had sounded like a stegosaurus.

ACTIVITY 1

SKILLS   CRITICAL THINKING, ANALYSIS, INTERPRETATION

▼ INFERRING FROM A TEXT

Read the extract from *A Walk In the Woods* by Bill Bryson. In pairs, choose a paragraph each and consider the following questions.

▶ **What does the narrator tell you about his thoughts and feelings?**

▶ **Which words and phrases allow you to infer his thoughts and feelings?**

Draw a table with two columns, one for each question, and pick out the key words and phrases from your paragraph which convey **explicit** and **implicit** meaning.

SUBJECT VOCABULARY

narrator a character that tells the story in a novel, play, poem or film
explicit expressed in a way that is very clear and direct
implicit suggested or understood without being stated directly

KEY VOCABULARY

SUBJECT VOCABULARY

synonyms words that share the same meanings as other words; for example, 'quick' might be a synonym for 'fast'
connotations ideas linked to words; ideas that have become associated with particular words

Writers use a lot of similar phrases to convey meaning. Don't just use 'shows'; using some of these **synonyms** could improve your writing.

- highlights
- suggests
- is redolent of
- has **connotations** of
- exposes
- denotes
- illustrates
- conveys
- introduces
- portrays
- demonstrates
- emphasises
- signifies
- reflects
- implies
- represents
- reveals
- infers
- connotes.

POINT-EVIDENCE-EXPLAIN (P-E-E)

When writing, it is important to express points in a clear and structured way, so you should organise your writing into paragraphs. Each paragraph should be self-contained and make sense on its own. It should be constructed of a group of sentences which all link to the same idea, theme or topic.

MAKING THE PERFECT POINT

The P-E-E chain stands for **Point-Evidence-Explain**. This is the order in which you should organise the information in each paragraph that you write.

1 State your basic **point** clearly and concisely. Your point should be relevant to the task or question that you have been set.

2 Demonstrate how you can support your opening statement with reference to a specific part of the text that you are writing about. Quotations can be used as **evidence** to support what you are saying and to help you to make your point. Try to select words or phrases from the text that precisely support your point and keep them as brief as possible. Use inverted commas, also known as quotation marks, to indicate where you have used words directly from another text.

3 Add an **explanation**. The first step is to explain how your quotation supports the point that you have made so that your reader knows why you have included it. In English Language, it is often useful to consider the use of language, going into some detail about the writer's choice of words (this is also known as diction) and considering any linguistic devices or techniques which have been used.

PERFECT PUNCTUATION

Short quotations of a single line or part of a line should be incorporated within quotation marks as part of the running text of your essay, 'just like this'. Quotations of two or more full lines should be indented from the main body of the text and introduced by a colon, like this:

> 'this is how you would quote a longer piece of text, but make sure that it is all relevant.'

PARAGRAPH SANDWICHES

You can think of your paragraph like a sandwich or burger, with three separate parts.

Top bun: opening topic sentence. Introduces the paragraph and your main idea.

Fillings: supporting sentences. This is the main part. Describe and explain your main point, using quotations and evidence to complement and support it.

Bottom bun: closing sentence. A concluding sentence to bring everything together

ACTIVITY 1   SKILLS   PROBLEM SOLVING, ANALYSIS, REASONING

▼ SUMMARISING WITH P-E-E

Read this chain paragraph, summarising the extract from *The Men Who Stare at Goats* by Jon Ronson (page 135). Copy the paragraph and colour code or label each part of the P-E-E chain. Each part of the chain may be more than one sentence.

> This extract forms the opening scene of *The Men Who Stare at Goats* and serves to acquaint the reader with the mysterious character of Major General Albert Stubblebine. Ronson gives the scene an air of mystery by not explaining key statements, such as why going into the next office is something that Stubblebine 'needs to do' and that 'frightens him'. The repetition of the words 'the next office' keeps drawing the reader's attention to the fact that they do not know what is significant about the next office. Instead, Ronson describes the scene in a way that ensures that the reader comes to understand what is going on through reading about Stubblebine's thoughts and actions, rather than being told by the narrator.

ACTIVITY 2   SKILLS   CRITICAL THINKING, PROBLEM SOLVING, ANALYSIS, INTERPRETATION

▼ WRITING P-E-E-RFECT PARAGRAPHS

Using a text that you have encountered in your English Language studies, write your own question and P-E-E chain paragraph about a theme or character. The following questions are examples to help you to construct a question based on your own reading.

▶ **What is the main theme of the text?**

▶ **What meaning is the writer trying to convey in the text?**

▶ **How does the opening set the scene for the text as a whole?**

▶ **Are there any characters in the text and, if so, how are they portrayed?**

Give your question and paragraph to a partner and check each other's work. Consider the following questions and clearly label examples of each within the paragraph.

Does the paragraph include the following?

- A **point**?
- Some **evidence**: a quotation or example?
- An **explanation**: an exploration of the quotation and what it shows? This may include:
  - some comment on the **language** used
  - some understanding of the **writer's attitude**
  - a **personal response** to the characters or themes of a text.

LEARNING OBJECTIVES

This lesson will help you to:

- approach a non-fiction text critically
- recognise fact and opinion and follow an argument
- build confidence in responding to a text
- understand how writers use language to influence their readers.

EVALUATING A TEXT

This section will help you to prepare for **Paper 1 Section A**, which will test your reading and critical skills. There will be questions on unprepared non-fiction reading passages. They will be drawn from a range of contemporary non-fiction, including autobiography, travel writing, reportage, media articles, letters, diary entries and opinion pieces. You will find additional information on this section of the exam on pages 56–137.

EVALUATING A TEXT: A GUIDE

SUBJECT VOCABULARY

rhetorical device using language in a certain way to achieve an effect

When you read a text, you form an opinion. Understanding how writers present ideas is key to understanding how texts work. You need to be aware of a variety of ways in which writers use language to influence their readers.

The devices used tend to be linked to the purpose of the text. So a text that tries to persuade a reader of a particular opinion will use rhetorical devices, while a text that describes another country is likely to use a wide range of descriptive and figurative devices to establish a vivid sense of place.

When you read a new piece of non-fiction, you should first try to understand what points are being made.

▼ 'IT'S SO OVER: COOL CYBERKIDS ABANDON SOCIAL NETWORKING SITES' FROM *THE GUARDIAN*

From uncles wearing skinny jeans to mothers investing in ra-ra skirts and fathers nodding awkwardly along to the latest grime record, the older generation has long known that the surest way to kill a youth trend is to adopt it as its own. The cyberworld, it seems, is no exception.

The proliferation of parents and teachers trawling the pages of Facebook trying to poke old schoolfriends and lovers, and traversing the outer reaches of MySpace is causing an adolescent exodus from the social networking sites, according to research from the media regulator Ofcom.

The sites, once the virtual streetcorners, pubs and clubs for millions of 15- to 24-year-olds, have now been over-run by 25- to 34-year-olds whose presence is driving their younger peers away.

Although their love of being online shows no sign of abating, the percentage of 15- to 24-year-olds who have a profile on a social networking site has dropped for the first time – from 55% at the start of last year to 50% this year. In contrast, 46% of 25- to 34-year-olds are now regularly checking up on sites such as Facebook compared with 40% last year.

Overall, 30% of British adults have a social networking profile, against 21% in 2007 when Ofcom first did the research. Half the UK's online population have a Facebook profile and spend an average of nearly six hours a month on the site compared with four hours in May 2008.

"There is nothing to suggest overall usage of the internet among 15-to 24-year-olds is going down," said Peter Phillips, the regulator's head of strategy. "Data suggests they are spending less time on social networking sites."

James Thickett, director of market research at Ofcom, said that while older people seemed to be embracing social networking sites, Facebook and MySpace remained immensely popular with children under 16.

▶

"Clearly take-up among under 16-year-olds is very high … so we cannot say for certain whether this is people in a certain age group who are not setting up social networking profiles or whether it's a population shift which is reflecting people getting older and having a social networking profile that they set up two years ago," he said. "The main point is the profile of social networking users is getting older."

The arrival of the 25- to 34-year-old age group, meanwhile, also appears to be behind the explosion in usage of Twitter.

ACTIVITY 1 | **SKILLS** | CRITICAL THINKING, ANALYSIS, CREATIVITY, INNOVATION

▼ RECOGNISING FACT AND OPINION AND FOLLOWING AN ARGUMENT

Read the article taken from *The Guardian* newspaper. Complete two lists: one listing the facts used in this article and one listing the opinions. How do the use of the facts and opinions influence you?

Next, pull out the key arguments of this article and re-write each point in your own words. Summarise the article in five or six key points.

▼ 'SOCIAL WEBSITES HARM CHILDREN'S BRAINS' FROM *MAIL ONLINE*

Social networking websites are causing alarming changes in the brains of young users, an eminent scientist has warned.

Sites such as Facebook, Twitter and Bebo are said to shorten attention spans, encourage instant gratification and make young people more self-centred.

The claims from neuroscientist Susan Greenfield will make disturbing reading for the millions whose social lives depend on logging on to their favourite websites each day.

But they will strike a chord with parents and teachers who complain that many youngsters lack the ability to communicate or concentrate away from their screens.

More than 150 million use Facebook to keep in touch with friends, share photographs and videos and post regular updates of their movements and thoughts.

A further six million have signed up to Twitter, the 'micro-blogging' service that lets users circulate text messages about themselves.

But while the sites are popular – and extremely profitable – a growing number of psychologists and neuroscientists believe they may be doing more harm than good.

Baroness Greenfield, an Oxford University neuroscientist and director of the Royal Institution, believes repeated exposure could effectively 'rewire' the brain.

Computer games and fast-paced TV shows were also a factor, she said.

'We know how small babies need constant reassurance that they exist,' she told the Mail yesterday.

'My fear is that these technologies are infantilising the brain into the state of small children who are attracted by buzzing noises and bright lights, who have a small attention span and who live for the moment.'

Her comments echoed those she made during a House of Lords debate earlier this month. Then she argued that exposure to computer games, instant messaging, chat rooms and social networking sites could leave a generation with poor attention spans.

'I often wonder whether real conversation in real time may eventually give way to these sanitised and easier screen dialogues, in much the same way as killing, skinning and butchering an animal to eat has been replaced by the convenience of packages of meat on the supermarket shelf,' she said.

▶

Lady Greenfield told the Lords a teacher of 30 years had told her she had noticed a sharp decline in the ability of her pupils to understand others.

'It is hard to see how living this way on a daily basis will not result in brains, or rather minds, different from those of previous generations,' she said.

She pointed out that autistic people, who usually find it hard to communicate, were particularly comfortable using computers.

'Of course, we do not know whether the current increase in autism is due more to increased awareness and diagnosis of autism, or whether it can – if there is a true increase – be in any way linked to an increased prevalence among people of spending time in screen relationships. Surely it is a point worth considering,' she added.

Psychologists have also argued that digital technology is changing the way we think. They point out that students no longer need to plan essays before starting to write – thanks to word processors they can edit as they go along. Satellite navigation systems have negated the need to decipher maps.

A study by the Broadcaster Audience Research Board found teenagers now spend seven-and-a-half hours a day in front of a screen.

Educational psychologist Jane Healy believes children should be kept away from computer games until they are seven. Most games only trigger the 'flight or fight' region of the brain, rather than the vital areas responsible for reasoning.

Sue Palmer, author of Toxic Childhood, said: 'We are seeing children's brain development damaged because they don't engage in the activity they have engaged in for millennia.

'I'm not against technology and computers. But before they start social networking, they need to learn to make real relationships with people.'

ACTIVITY 2

SKILLS ▶ REASONING, INTERPRETATION, DECISION MAKING

▼ DIFFERING WRITING SKILLS

Read the article 'Social websites harm children's brains', from *Mail Online*. Analyse it using the same steps as in Activity 1. What are the similarities and differences in the way that the two articles present ideas?

HOW WRITERS USE LANGUAGE TO INFLUENCE THEIR READERS

SUBJECT VOCABULARY

bias not fair; a particular point of view influenced by one's own or someone else's opinions
emotive language language that produces an emotional reaction

Once you have established the main ideas being communicated in a piece of non-fiction, you should consider whether the article is showing an opinion or **bias**. Look out for the following:

- use of biased language
- use of **emotive language**
- stating of opinion as fact
- use of quotations or the reported views of others
- use of unsupported claims
- the given facts
- an argument.

ACTIVITY 3

SKILLS ▶ ANALYSIS, INTERPRETATION, COLLABORATION, INTERPERSONAL SKILLS

▼ PICKING OUT KEY INFORMATION AND RECOGNISING BIAS

Look back at the two articles from *The Guardian* and *Mail Online* again. In groups, answer the following questions, carefully considering how language has been used.

1 What view of teenagers are given and what are the main arguments raised in each article?
2 How are facts and opinions used in each article?
3 How is scientific research used to put across the main points of view in each article?
4 What linguistic devices have been used to present the point of view more powerfully in each article?

▲ They need 'a warm, dry, comfortable place for snoozing'.

ACTIVITY 4   SKILLS ▸ ANALYSIS

▼ RHETORICAL DEVICES

Rhetorical devices are often used in texts that seek to present a particular point of view or opinion. Match the following rhetorical devices with the correct example sentence.

Emotive language	Kittens need a warm, dry, comfortable place for snoozing.
Personal pronouns	These vulnerable, weak kittens need our help.
Repetition	Over 100,000,000 cats need re-homing every week.
Rule of three	You can help us make a difference; all we need is £2 a month.
Hyperbole	Every year the number of cats on the streets increases, every year it is up to us to rescue them.

SUBJECT VOCABULARY

emotive language language that produces an emotional reaction
personal pronoun a word used instead of a noun, such as 'I', 'you' or 'they'
repetition saying the same thing more than once to highlight its importance
rule of three where three things are linked or something is repeated three times in order to emphasise them and ensure they are memorable
hyperbole exaggerating for effect
direct address using second person pronouns 'you' or 'your'
imperative verbs verbs that give an instruction or command
rhetorical questions questions that are asked to make a point rather than to get an answer

ACTIVITY 5   SKILLS ▸ PROBLEM SOLVING, ADAPTIVE LEARNING, INNOVATION

▼ WRITING PERSUASIVELY

Write a letter to persuade an organisation to ban the use of animal fur in its products.
Include the following rhetorical devices in your letter:

- direct address
- rule of three
- emotive language
- imperative verbs
- repetition
- rhetorical questions.

Your letter must be at least three paragraphs long and should follow all the conventions of a normal letter.

ACTIVITY 6   SKILLS ▸ CRITICAL THINKING, ANALYSIS, REASONING, INTERPRETATION

▼ ANALYSING IDEAS

Read the following article, 'Myth of the Teenager' by Lucy Maddox, and answer the question.

▶ **How does Lucy Maddox present teenagers in this article?**

Your answer should:

- reflect on audience and purpose (that is, how and why language has been used for effect)
- show a detailed understanding of the article and the points that the writer is making
- identify a wide variety of devices used by the writer and analyse the effect in as much detail as possible
- use appropriate terminology throughout.

After answering the question, write a one-paragraph summary in which you say how your understanding of the topic has developed or changed as a result of reading this article. What impact has it had on you and why?

GENERAL VOCABULARY

ABSOs court orders used in the UK to restrict anti-social behaviour

hug a hoodie a slogan used to make fun of British politicians who attempt to engage with disaffected young people

stigmatised unfairly discriminated against or disapproved of

vilified discussed or described in a very negative way

SUBJECT VOCABULARY

stereotypes fixed and generalised ideas about particular types of people or groups

syntax the way in which words and phrases are arranged into sentences

'MYTH OF THE TEENAGER', BY LUCY MADDOX

Teenagers often get a bad press. There are easy stories to be mined here: ASBOs, underage drinking, "hug a hoodie," drug use–even, recently, the teenager who drugged her parents to access the internet.

These are not new stereotypes. As a shepherd in Shakespeare's *A Winter's Tale* puts it, "I would there were no age between 10 and three-and-20, or that youth would sleep out the rest; for there is nothing in the between but getting wenches with child, wronging the ancientry, stealing, fighting." Change the syntax, and this description could easily fit in many newspapers today.

Are the stereotypes fair? Is the idea of wild adolescence rooted in evidence? There are two sorts of arguments. On the one hand, neuroscientific evidence seems increasingly to suggest that this is a true developmental phase of its own—teenagers behave differently because their brains are different. On the other, some argue that teenagers behave differently because they are learning to handle so many new situations, and if we hold stereotypical ideas about their behaviour, we risk underestimating them.

Take the latter argument first. Philip Graham, a professor of psychiatry who has written extensively on what he perceives to be a misconception, believes that although hormonal and physical changes are occurring, most teenagers are not risky or moody. Graham sees teenagers as a stigmatised group, often highly competent yet treated as if they were not. He argues that teenagers need to be acknowledged as potentially productive members of society and that the more independence and respect they are given, the more they will rise to the challenge.

"Once young people reach the age of 14, their competence in cognitive tasks and their sexual maturity make it more helpful to think of them as young adults," says Graham. "Media coverage is almost uniformly negative. Adolescence is a word used to describe undesirable behaviour in older adults. Young people of 14, 15 or 16 are thought to be risk-takers… they are people who are experimenting. They are doing things for the first time and they make mistakes. Would you call a toddler who is learning to walk and who falls over all the time a risk-taker? These people are just beginning something."

Graham places less importance on the conclusions of research into risk-taking and on adolescent brain changes – "Not to say there are not a small minority who do take dangerous risks but I think the results have been over-generalised to justify the stereotype."

Instead, Graham argues that the way teenagers make decisions is related to encountering situations they haven't dealt with before. "If they are moving into new types of social situation they do need more help with that." He likens it to learning to drive, something you need expert help with at any age.

However, neuroscientific evidence suggests a basis for the teenage stereotype. Sarah-Jayne Blakemore, a professor at University College London, has specialised in researching the adolescent brain using a variety of techniques, including functional brain scanning. Although also concerned that teenagers can be vilified in the media, Blakemore rejects the idea that adolescence is entirely a social construct: "If you look throughout history at the descriptions of adolescence they are similar, and also in different cultures. Of course this is not to say that all adolescents are the same, but there is quite a lot of evidence that during this period of life there's an increase in risk-taking, peer influence

▶

▲ Adolescents often struggle to find their own identity.

and self-consciousness." Blakemore's research suggests that during the teenage years the brain is still developing the capacity for certain sophisticated skills, including problem-solving, social skills and impulse control.

Blakemore and other researchers describe a gradual development of brain areas related to planning, inhibiting inappropriate behaviour and understanding other points of view. They also suggest a less linear development of the system in the brain that recognises and responds to rewards. "Teenagers tend to be more self-conscious," said Blakemore. "They show more risk-taking when their peers are present." Their social brain is changing and so is their ability to plan, inhibit impulses and make decisions.

"Research by Laurence Steinberg at Temple University in the US has shown that adolescents tend not to take into account future consequences of actions. For example, if you offer them a choice between having £10 now and £100 in six months, whilst adults tend to wait for the larger amount, most adolescents are more likely to go for the lower value now. Life in the future doesn't hold so much importance."

It might make sense, then, that a teenager trying to decide whether to tell a lie in order to go out, or to try an illegal drug, might be influenced more by the reward of the night out or the novel experience, or peer congratulation, than by longer-term negative consequences. "It's not that teenagers don't understand the risks," says Blakemore. "It's just that for some teenagers, in the moment, this understanding goes out of the window."

Despite their different views, both academics conclude that teenagers could benefit from being treated according to their development. Graham suggests friendly advice-giving. It is important to "recognise their desire for autonomy," he says. "They want to do more than they can. We should treat them differently because they are inexperienced… and first experiences are important. A bad experience can put you off something for a long time."

He does not advocate tolerating too much difficult behaviour, though: "Adolescents are influenced by the stereotype as well. If they expect to get away with being 'bolshy' for example… I don't think we should be particularly tolerant of bad behaviour in adolescence."

Blakemore thinks that we should adjust the way we try to motivate teenagers: "Anti-smoking campaigns, for example, might be more effective if they used short-term social negatives like bad breath as a disincentive, rather than longer-term health consequences. And we perhaps expect too much. "We expect them to act like adults but their brains aren't yet completely like an adult brain. Maybe we should be more understanding. Teaching adolescents about how their brains develop might be helpful."

Whether you attribute adolescent differences in decision-making to brain development or lack of experience, educational aims could include the handling of social dilemmas. Parents might be able to help by being explicit about the pros and cons of a situation, considering other people's views or negotiating in a transparent way. We should also bear in mind that teenagers are often uniquely affected by economic and political challenges such as high unemployment levels.

In my view, adolescence is a tricky time, where individuals often struggle to find their own identity in the face of a sometimes hostile outside world, whilst needing peer support. Both Blakemore and Graham are more phlegmatic. "Every time's a tricky time," says Graham. "You try being my age."

LEARNING OBJECTIVES

This lesson will help you to:
- identify the main parts of speech
- consolidate your understanding of the function of each.

WORD CLASSES

Words may be divided into groups called parts of speech. Words are classified as one of nine parts of speech:

- verb
- noun
- pronoun
- adjective
- adverb
- preposition
- conjunction
- interjection
- determiners.

PARTS OF SPEECH

SUBJECT VOCABULARY

verb a word that describes actions

noun a word that represents a person, place, object or quality

pronoun a word that is used instead of a noun

adjective a word that describes a noun or pronoun

adverb a word that describes a verb or an adjective

preposition a word that is used before a noun or pronoun to show time, place or direction

conjunction a word that joins parts of a sentence

interjection a word used to express a strong feeling

determiner a word used before a noun in order to show which thing is being referred to

Each part of speech signifies how the word is used, not what a word is. This means that the same word can be a noun in one sentence and a verb or adjective in the next. For example, the word 'book' in the following sentences.

- Books are made of ink, paper and glue.
  (In this case, 'books' is a noun and is the subject of the sentence.)
- Deborah waits patiently while Bridget books the tickets.
  (In this case, 'books' is a verb and the subject of the sentence is Bridget.)

If you were asked to describe the following photograph, you might say, 'The happy lady was laughing'.

▲ The sentence 'The happy lady was laughing' contains a noun, verb and adjective.

This sentence is made up of different parts of speech.

This is a **noun**. It is a **naming word**.

This is a **verb**. It is a word that describes **actions**.

The happy lady was laughing.

This is an **adjective**. It is a **describing word**. It tells you more about the **noun**.

ACTIVITY 1   SKILLS ANALYSIS

▼ IDENTIFYING PARTS OF SPEECH

In the following sentences, circle the adjectives, tick the nouns and underline the verbs.
1 I tripped over the uneven floor.
2 The silly boy crashed his new bike.
3 When the old lady reached her house, she sat down.
4 We saw wild horses in the forest.
5 The large crowd cheered as the skilful player scored.
6 The giggling girls annoyed the teacher.
7 A prickly hedgehog snuffled in the dry leaves.
8 The lazy man was sleeping under the tall tree.

PROPER NOUNS

Nouns that name particular things are called proper nouns and begin with capital letters. The names of people and places, days of the week, brand names, company names and titles of films are all proper nouns, e.g. Yara, France, Thursday, Google, Ford, *Avatar.*

PREPOSITIONS

A preposition tells you the position of one thing in relation to another.

Altamash hid **behind** the tree.

You cross **over** a bridge.

ACTIVITY 2   SKILLS ANALYSIS

▼ USING PARTS OF SPEECH

Write a suitable word in the gap in each of the following sentences. In the brackets after each sentence, write down what part of speech it is.
1 Sam put the _____ suitcase on the floor. (_____)
2 Athens is the capital of _____. (_____)
3 The mountaineers _____ to the summit. (_____)
4 The children sang loudly at the _____. (_____)
5 The cat's _____ was soft and silky. (_____)
6 The helicopter _____ over the motorway. (_____)

LEARNING OBJECTIVES

This lesson will help you to:
- explore and develop your interpretations of language
- considering the associations that words hold and how they can be used to create meaning in a text.

SUBJECT VOCABULARY

denotation what something literally is or shows

KEY POINT

Words and images can have a range of connotations that influence meaning and interpretation.

CONNOTATIONS

Connotations are the associations and ideas which a particular word or image suggests to a reader. It is important to consider the connotations implied by a text in order to explore its effects in detail.

ACTIVITY 1   SKILLS ▶ INTERPRETATION

▼ CONNOTATIONS OF IMAGES

Copy and complete the table, writing down the denotation and the connotation for each image. On a piece of paper, draw your own example of a sign or image. Ask a partner to look at your image and identify its denotation and connotation.

▼ IMAGE/SIGN	▼ DENOTATION	▼ CONNOTATION
	Skull and crossbones	Pirates, poison, danger

ACTIVITY 2   SKILLS   ANALYSIS, INTERPRETATION

▼ CONNOTATIONS OF WORDS

Your local newspaper runs a weekly column called 'Why I love…', in which a guest writer is asked to write a short article to inform readers of a personal interest. Read the following extract, from a piece called 'Why I love reading', and consider the connotations of the highlighted words, and then answer the question.

> I love reading because I love getting to know new characters. They become friends: I inhabit their lives while I read and when I finish that book, I take a part of them with me. Reading gives me an escape from reality: it's my magic carpet that I can fly on whenever I choose, soaring off on adventures all over the world, from past to present, over the vast terrains of human history. I can see all of the colours of life as I go. They say you never read the same book twice: reading a new book makes me feel slightly new myself because I know something different; I've experienced something more. Reading makes me a bigger, better, smarter version of myself.

▶ **What ideas and attitudes to reading are suggested in the extract?**

Copy and complete the following table, considering the connotations of the highlighted words and phrases used in the extract. Then choose another quotation from the extract and consider its connotation.

▼ PHRASE	▼ CONNOTATION
'new characters… become friends'	By describing characters as 'friends', the writer demonstrates the emotional connection they feel with books and the companionship they get from reading.
'it's my magic carpet'	The metaphor describes reading as a 'magic carpet'. This has connotations of adventure and implies the fantastic experiences that the writer enjoys in reading books. The 'magic carpet' also has connotations of freedom and flight: books give this reader the wings to explore worlds which might otherwise be inaccessible to them.
'Reading makes me a bigger, better, smarter version of myself.'	

KEY POINT

Connotations are how writers are able to convey their ideas to readers. Inferring information from a text is a critical skill in understanding what message and ideas the author wants to convey to readers.

SUBJECT VOCABULARY

metaphor describing something by comparing it to an image which it resembles, in a way that says the object *is* the image

ACTIVITY 3   SKILLS   PROBLEM SOLVING, ADAPTIVE LEARNING

▼ CREATING YOUR OWN CONNOTATIONS

Using the extract 'Why I love reading' as a model, write two paragraphs of your own, entitled 'Why I love…' and 'Why I hate…'. Choose something that you will enjoy writing about: it can be anything from motorbikes to a particular website. Use bias, emotive language and connotations to create a positive or negative description of your chosen subjects. You may choose to use similes, metaphors and other figurative language to help you to do this.

LEARNING OBJECTIVES

This lesson will help you to:
- identify the main sentence types.

DIFFERENT SENTENCE TYPES

A sentence is a group of words that are put together in such a way as to mean something. It is a basic component of communication. Clumsy sentence structure leads to writing that is grammatically incorrect. Poor sentence structure will also prevent your ideas flowing in a coherent and logical way and make it much more difficult for the reader to understand what you are trying to convey. A writer's use of sentence structure often helps to convey meaning in a text. It is important to be able to identify and comment on this in the reading sections of the exam.

TYPES OF SENTENCES

'Friend, car, France holiday' is not a sentence as it doesn't make sense.

'I am driving my friend to France for a holiday' is a sentence. You can understand what it means as it makes sense on its own.

Sentences come in different forms.

- A **declarative** (or statement) **conveys** information.

  My car is red.

- An **interrogative** (or question) **asks** for information.

  Does it go fast?

- An **imperative** (or command) **tells** someone to do something.

  Get in.

- An **exclamation** shows that someone **feels strongly** about something.

  It's great!

HINT

Remember the conjunctions that you can use to create a compound sentence by using the acronym FANBOYS:
For, And, Nor, But, Or, Yet, So.

ACTIVITY 1	SKILLS ANALYSIS

▼ SENTENCE TYPES

Match the sentences with the sentence types.

1	The door is open.	statement
2	Go and have a wash.	question
3	What a lovely surprise!	command
4	Have you seen my shorts?	exclamation

SIMPLE SENTENCES

SUBJECT VOCABULARY

clause a group of words that make up part of a sentence, built around a finite verb

A **simple sentence** contains a single subject, a verb and an object. This is also known as a clause.

The boy ate the chocolate.

Simple sentences may contain other elements or parts of a clause, but they only express one thing.

PARTS OF A CLAUSE

A sentence must contain the following parts.

- The **subject** identifies the topic of a clause or, in other words, what it is about. Every complete sentence contains two parts: a subject and a predicate. The subject is what or whom the sentence is about, and the predicate tells you something about the subject. In the following sentence, the predicate is enclosed in brackets ( ), while the subject is **in bold**.

    My hockey teacher and his dog (go running every morning).

- The **verb** identifies the action of a clause or, in other words, what happens.

    Her boyfriend **gave** her a bunch of flowers.

- The **object** identifies who or what is directly affected by the action of the verb. This is always a noun or pronoun. Two kinds of objects follow verbs: direct and indirect objects. 'Her boyfriend gave her a bunch of flowers', contains a direct object ('Her boyfriend') and an indirect object: in this case the recipient of the direct object ('her').

Not all verbs are followed by objects:

    After work, David usually **walks** home.

Verbs that take objects are known as **transitive** verbs. Verbs not followed by objects are called **intransitive** verbs. Some verbs can be both.

A sentence may also contain the following components.

- The **complement** gives extra information about the subject or object.
- The **adverbial** gives additional information about a situation: when, where and how it happened.

ACTIVITY 2 SKILLS ANALYSIS

▼ PARTS OF A SENTENCE

Find the subject, verb and object in the following sentences. Can you find any adverbials as well?

1 Last week, Peggy redecorated the pub.
2 Are you hungry yet?
3 Martin, be quiet.
4 Tuesday was very rainy and cold.

▲ Last week, Peggy redecorated the pub.
'Last week': an adverbial phrase

COMPOUND SENTENCES

A compound sentence consists of two simple sentences (clauses) joined by a **conjunction**. A conjunction is a joining word. It may be used to join two sentences together.

    It was raining. I put up my umbrella. (two sentences)

    It was raining **so** I put up my umbrella. (one sentence with a conjunction)

SUBORDINATE CLAUSES

Subordinate clauses are often present in a sentence. They are called subordinate as they are second to the main action in the sentence; they are additional information that the sentence doesn't need to function.

    After his Dad gave him some pocket money, Andrew went to the cinema.

'After his Dad gave him some pocket money' is a subordinate clause. Anything between commas, dashes or brackets would be subordinate clauses too.

COMPLEX SENTENCES

A **complex sentence** contains a main sentence and one or more subordinate clauses that contribute to the meaning of the statement.

LEARNING OBJECTIVES

This lesson will help you to:

- use a full range of sentence structures
- control and vary sentence structure for effect in your writing.

SENTENCES FOR EFFECT

When sentence structure is repetitive and boring, writing is less interesting to read. Learning how to use sentence structure for effect will help you to engage your reader.

If writing contains little variety in sentence structure, it will be less interesting for the reader than if it contains a variety of sentence types that are handled well.

Little variety in sentence structure ➡ Skilful control in the construction of varied sentence forms

EDINGLY OPENERS: VARYING SENTENCE STARTERS FOR IMPACT

EDINGLY openers consist of words ending in -ED (verbs), -ING (verbs) and -LY (adverbs). They can be an engaging way to begin sentences.

▶ **How could you change these sentences using this technique?**

1 I walked through the dark alley and suddenly a hand reached out and grabbed my shoulder.
2 I was breathing deeply as I crept through the deep, dark wood.
3 I was trapped and could not see a way out.

HINT

Use a comma or exclamation mark after the opener.

ACTIVITY 1 **SKILLS** CRITICAL THINKING, ANALYSIS, INTERPRETATION

▼ EXPLORING SENTENCE TYPES

What is suspense? How do writers build suspense? Why do readers like a good mystery? What do you expect from a suspense story?

Read the following extract and see how many sentence types you can identify. Does it create a sense of suspense?

The window shattered, sending glass cascading in all directions. Flames exploded into the room. I ducked, keeping my body as low as I could, desperately trying to avoid the smoke that was rapidly streaming across the ceiling. I scanned the room for other exits and was glad to see a small window on the far wall. The smoke was getting denser and started to expand, the cloud reaching down from the ceiling to the floor. My brain shouted, 'Move!' Frozen. Taking a deep breath of clean air, possibly my last, I pushed away from the wall to safety. As I struggled to open the window, I felt my heart pounding. My lungs screamed for air. The smoke descended and I worked blind, my eyes stinging. I pulled frantically at the catches, felt them give and tumbled out onto the ground below. I felt the heat escaping from the open window above and started to crawl slowly away.

▲ The sentence 'Grasping the handle, she turned it slowly' helps to build suspense.

KEY POINT

Sentence structure can be used for particular effect. For example, short, simple sentences can be used to build suspense or a sense of actions, whilst longer, complex sentences may be helpful in creating a layered character description.

ACTIVITY 2

SKILLS ▸ ANALYSIS, INTERPRETATION, DECISION MAKING

▼ CREATING SUSPENSE

Compare the two extracts below and consider how effectively each has created a feeling of suspense. The first is written using short simple sentences and the second uses long complex sentences. Compare the two passages and then copy out and add to the table that follows, writing down the effects of using each type of sentence.

EXTRACT 1

Running. Faster. Faster. She grabbed the handle and turned it. Pushing the door open, she moved inside. No one was there. She turned and fled in the opposite direction.

EXTRACT 2

Jane stood in the doorway collecting her thoughts, delaying her decision until the last possible moment. As she plucked up her courage, she studied the door in front of her. It was crafted from an ancient-looking wood, the handle a simple metal ring. Jane glanced down at her shaking hand as she stretched out to turn the handle. She took two deep breaths, brushing her fringe from her pale face with nervous fingers. She stood a while, thoughts racing through her mind. Then, at last, she was ready. Grasping the handle, she turned it slowly; pushing the heavy door in front of her, she stepped into the hallway.

▼ SHORT, SIMPLE SENTENCES	▼ COMPLEX, LONGER SENTENCES
Develop tension	Give a detailed picture of the action

ACTIVITY 3

SKILLS ▸ INTERPRETATION, ADAPTIVE LEARNING

▼ ADAPTING SENTENCE TYPES FOR EFFECT

Re-write the following extract as three sentences. What is the effect?

Ryan stood as still as stone, listening intently, but the faint rustling continued from inside the bedroom, so putting his good eye to the keyhole, he peered into the dimly lit room.

Re-write the following extract as five sentences. What is the effect?

He squinted through the gloom of the interior, which was quite deserted, with a single candle burning near the altar, thinking that it was sad to see an empty church on Christmas Eve, but, shrugging the thought away, he began a careful inspection of the places where the statue might have been concealed.

Col di Pra - Taibon
Per Passo della Fradusta 6.30 709-708-707
Buse Alte - Forcella Miel

Rif. Canali - Treviso
Per Passo della Fradusta 4.00 709-708-707
e Passo Canali

Rif. Rosetta   2.40 709-703
Rif. Mulaz
per Passo di Pradidali Basso 6.30

Cant del Gal
709 Villa Welsperg   1.45
                            2.15
Primiero   3.30

S. Martino di Castrozza
715-702 Per Passo di Ball   3.30
Col dei Bechi

Passo di Ball   1.10
S. Martino di Castrozza   3.00
Rif. Rosetta   3.00

Rifugio
Pradidali
2278 m

WRITING SKILLS

Assessment Objective 4

Communicate effectively and imaginatively, adapting form, tone and register of writing for specific purposes and audiences

Assessment Objective 5

Write clearly, using a range of vocabulary and sentence structures, with appropriate paragraphing and accurate spelling, grammar and punctuation

This chapter focuses on some core writing skills that you can apply to all parts of the English Language B course. Working through these lessons and activities will help you to develop the writing skills that you will need for the exam.

The chapter is split into the following sections:
- Vocabulary
- Sentences
- Structure
- Punctuation and spelling.

In the writing sections of your exams you will need to be able to meet the Assessment Objectives AO4 and AO5.

LEARNING OBJECTIVES

This lesson will help you to:

- appreciate a writer's choice of words
- develop your own choice of words.

CHOOSING THE RIGHT VOCABULARY

Your words need to attract the attention of a reader and keep them engaged so that they will continue to read what you have written. Choosing the correct vocabulary is central to achieving this.

Words that engage the senses are particularly effective for this purpose. Look at the following opening sentences.

- It exploded in her face. (**sight**)
- Something was scratching under the door. (**sound**)
- From the kitchen came a reminder of the garlic that she loved. (**smell**)
- He pulled a face as if he had swallowed sour milk. (**taste**)
- The wind brushed his skin. (**touch**)

ACTIVITY 1

SKILLS ▶ INNOVATION

▼ ENGAGING THE SENSES

Work with a partner and write two opening sentences using each of the senses: sight, sound, smell, taste and touch.

PRECISION

Your choice of words can be very important, especially when you write. When you speak, the person who is listening can ask you to explain yourself if anything you say is not clear. However, when you write, your reader will probably not be able to ask for an explanation so you have to get things right first time.

There are times when you need to be precise in your choice of words. Compare the following sentences, then answer the question.

Some sort of animal could be seen approaching along the side of the road.

A cat could be seen walking cautiously along the gutter.

▶ **Which of these two sentences is clearer and more precise? Which words and phrases bring about this effect?**

Next, compare the following sentences.

Here at summer camp you will be under the supervision of a residential nurse and a medical practitioner who is available at any time.

Welcome to summer camp where we hope you will enjoy being cared for.

You could read either of these sentences at the start of a stay at a summer camp and they would make sense. However, one immediately informs you of the medical precautions that have been taken and this suggests that there might be a need for medical supervision. The second sentence simply provides a more appropriate, warmer welcome that expresses a hope that things go well.

Finally, compare the following sentences.

> Put dirty cutlery into the basket on the left and leave dirty crockery next to the sink on the right, taking care that no uneaten food is dropped carelessly onto the floor.

> Please leave your dirty cutlery and crockery in the places indicated; your keeping this area clean and tidy will help our staff who will appreciate your cooperation. Thank you.

The first sentence simply instructs you what to do and anticipates that you will be careless. The second example contains three very important words, 'please' and 'thank you'. This shows that the writer is addressing the reader with respect and consideration by showing why the reader's taking care will be appreciated by other people.

▶ **Which of these two sentences will encourage better cooperation?**

These examples show the impact that individual words can have and their significance in how a sentence is read.

ACTIVITY 2   SKILLS ▶ CRITICAL THINKING, ANALYSIS, INTERPRETATION

▼ PRECISION IN ACTION

This extract is from an account of the sinking of the *Titanic*. The *Titanic* had been described as unsinkable, and so its sinking caused widespread shock in 1912. Read the following extract carefully, noticing the choice of language used to convey the witness's shock and horror. Then copy and complete the table, selecting key words and phrases that the writer uses to convey what they can see.

> In a couple of hours, though, she [the *Titanic*] began to go down more rapidly. Then the fearful sight began. The people in the ship were just beginning to realise how great their danger was. When the forward part of the ship dropped suddenly at a faster rate, so that the upward slope became marked, there was a sudden rush of passengers on all the decks towards the stern. It was like a wave. We could see the great black mass of people in the steerage sweeping to the rear part of the boat and breaking through into the upper decks. At the distance of about a mile we could distinguish everything through the night, which was perfectly clear. We could make out the increasing excitement on board the boat as the people, rushing to and fro, caused the deck lights to disappear and reappear as they passed in front of them.

▼ KEY WORD OR PHRASE	▼ WHAT IT CONVEYS
Fearful	This word conveys the pitiful state of the panicking passengers who were still on the ship.

▲ RMS *Titanic*

GENERAL VOCABULARY

stern rear of a boat
steerage the lower decks where the cheapest accommodation was provided

KEY POINT

The bigger your vocabulary, the more words you have to choose from and the easier it is to express yourself clearly. The best way to improve your vocabulary is by reading and taking an interest in the words that other people use.

LEARNING OBJECTIVES

This lesson will help you to:

- consider the effect of words and phrases
- demonstrate an ability to use words and phrases to good effect.

VOCABULARY FOR EFFECT

The words you use come from the vocabulary that you know and can use confidently and comfortably. Some words – *the, some, is, what,* for example – do not have the effect of other words such as *revolting, splendid, monster* and *eliminate.* Here you are going to look at the way writers choose words.

CONNOTATIONS

SUBJECT VOCABULARY

referend the thing or idea to which a word refers

connotations ideas linked to words; ideas that have become associated with particular words

GENERAL VOCABULARY

nauseous feeling sick

A word means more than just its referend. For example, the word 'grease' denotes or refers to an oily material often used to lubricate machinery or carry medication. Sometimes, however, the word is used to indicate distaste or revulsion, allowing the word's connotations, such as 'nauseous', 'slimy' and 'sticky', to come into play.

Some words have positive or negative connotations, such as 'success' or 'regrets'.

> They talked all morning about her **success.**

In the first sentence, the use of the word 'success' means that you know that whatever she had done was approved of or appreciated as something positive.

> Now she was left only with her **regrets.**

However, in the second sentence, the use of the word 'regrets' lets you know that the subject now wishes that she had not done something which is seen in a negative light.

ACTIVITY 1

SKILLS ANALYSIS, INTERPRETATION, INNOVATION, COLLABORATION

▼ CHOOSING VOCABULARY IN PRACTICE

1 Work in small groups and discuss the effect of the following words and phrases:

traitor	magic	cool	on the brink
totally helpless	awesome		readily available
desperate	cruel	adorable	

2 Write complete sentences using each of the words and phrases listed in question 1.

3 Read the following extract and choose some of the words and phrases in it that have a particular effect on you as a reader. Then copy and complete the table that follows, adding your own ideas. Try to find at least another six examples.

> Once upon a time it was said that three trolls lived in a forest. Local people lived in fear of them and avoided at night the twisting path that wound its way between the trees. From time to time late-night travellers would find themselves lost in the forest, alone and bewildered, and they would imagine the sound of a foot snapping a twig or catch in the corner of their eye something moving in the shadows.
>
> These close encounters with the trolls were reported widely and fed the imaginations of the locals. None of them realised that nobody had ever been harmed in any way by these trolls, but that did not

▶

restrain those people who really enjoyed terrifying their fellow citizens with outrageous tales of a death that could so easily catch up with them in the woods around the town.

The truth of the matter was that the three trolls were very shy. However, they craved the company of other beings and would approach them warily in the forest and then, before they could introduce themselves, their courage would fail and they would scuttle back into the undergrowth, safely out of sight.

▼ QUOTATION	▼ WHAT EFFECT IT HAS
Once upon a time…	This expression is frequently used to start fairy tales and so its use here alerts the reader to the possibility that this story follows key features of the genre.
Bewildered	This word creates a strong sense of uncertainty.

4 Complete the following sentence stem with six different words or phrases, indicating the effect you are aiming for in each case.

When it rains we…

5 Write a brief paragraph to finish the troll story. Before you start, state the effect that you would like to achieve; perhaps you would like to amuse your reader or shock them. Make it clear what your intention is before you start.

SYNONYMS

A synonym is a word that means the same thing or nearly the same thing as another word. They can be used to echo or widen your understanding of a word or to reinforce an idea.

The young tree, **the sapling**, was the place chosen by the blackbird to build its nest.

Here the word 'sapling' provides a synonym for the tree. It helps to develop the referend (tree) by supplying more detail and further connotations.

'Sapling' provides a synonym for 'tree'. Can you think of any other synonyms?

LANGUAGE FOR DIFFERENT EFFECTS

As you read you become aware of the different ways in which language is used, and you might form preferences. When you read for a particular purpose, such as when looking for information on a holiday destination, you quickly learn to recognise the sort of material for which you are looking. This means that when you write something you should aim to make clear the purpose of the writing and the effect you want to achieve. It also helps to have examined and understood how other writers achieve different effects.

ACTIVITY 1   SKILLS ▶ PROBLEM SOLVING, ANALYSIS

▼ TYPE OF EFFECT IN WRITING

Visit a library and look for examples of written material that is informative, transactional, emotive, persuasive, discursive, entertaining, inspirational, descriptive, ironic and advisory.

Record the source for each type and be aware that one source may include more than one of these types. If necessary, a librarian should be able to help you.

ACTIVITY 2   SKILLS ▶ CRITICAL THINKING, ANALYSIS, INTERPRETATION, CREATIVITY

▼ IDENTIFYING TYPES OF WRITING IN AN EXTRACT

1 Read the following extract and consider what effects the writer is trying to achieve. Look at some of the words used that indicate the writer's intentions. See if you can find and explain other ways in which the language is used to achieve important effects.

I expect that you will have often heard warnings about the dangers to your health of smoking. One of my teachers once described handling the lungs of a victim of lung cancer; they resembled, he said, an old leather rugby ball[1] and they sat in his hands, hard and rough like a large lump of coal[2].

Giving advice to young people is often difficult for parents and teachers[3]; it's part of growing up, to put aside advice and warnings from the older generation[4] and to trust your own judgement. One of the difficulties for young people, however, is "peer pressure," the need to fit in with their contemporaries, to meet their approval at least and, better still sometimes, to impress them. Daring to smoke, especially when it is forbidden, is part of this and it is probably as important for some young people as any pleasure to be gained from supposedly enjoying[5] a cigarette while watching nervously in case a teacher appears[6].

[1] Warning: this is what can happen to smokers.

[2] Description: shows the effects of smoking, to strengthen the warning.

[3] Information: plainly stated and aimed at readers who have yet to be parents or teachers.

[4] Explanation: rejecting adult advice is sometimes just a part of growing up.

[5] Ironic: suggests that the person is not really enjoying the cigarette when the purpose of smoking is supposedly to enjoy it.

[6] Description: shows the fear of a young person trying to show how grown-up he or she is.

Look at the following sentence.

Now stop.

Which of the two words in this sentence is emphasised? What is the effect of this?

If the order of the words is altered, something changes.

Stop now.

Instead of emphasising the action that is to be carried out, to stop, the emphasis is now on the timing of that action – it must be amended now, immediately.

The ordering of words in a sentence is important, particularly at the end of a sentence or before a pause. There is a brief moment before you hear the next word while the sound of the last word continues in your mind. Such a word is emphasised and brought to your attention.

Look at the following sentences. One is the first sentence of the extract in Activity 2, and the other is a re-ordered version. Consider the difference made by re-ordering the words. Which ending do you think is the more effective? Can you say why?

I expect that you will have often heard warnings about the dangers to your health of smoking.

I expect that you will have often heard warnings about the dangers of smoking to your health.

It may help you to analyse the phrases further by breaking them down into the following smaller phrases:

- about the dangers to your health / of smoking
- about the dangers of smoking / to your health.

There are three key words: 'dangers', 'health' and 'smoking'. Which of these should be most closely connected? Perhaps it would help to put the three words together like this: *Smoking endangers health.* Can you see now why smoking was left at the end of the original sentence?

ACTIVITY 3 | **SKILLS** INNOVATION, TEAMWORK

▼ OTHER LITERARY DEVICES

Look at the following literary devices. Can you think of an example of each? What effect do they have?

Rhetorical question

Contrast

Repetition

Direct address

Pattern of three

Hyperbole

Alliteration

Simile

Personification

LEARNING OBJECTIVES

This lesson will help you to:

■ understand the importance of your choices when writing

■ see how different choices can change meaning.

GENERAL VOCABULARY

clarity the quality of being expressed clearly

▲ Even relatively simple poems such as 'This is just to say' can create strong images.

WHY YOUR CHOICES MATTER

You must take care when choosing words, when arranging them and when you incorporate them into the speech and writing.

■ **Your choice of words** matters because it enables you to write with precision or exactness, clarity and an appropriate tone.

■ **Your ordering of words** matters because it allows you to phrase points in a way that is effective and clear.

■ **Your use of language and literary techniques** matters because it enables you to achieve particular effects with writing.

ACTIVITY 1 **SKILLS** ▶ PROBLEM SOLVING, ANALYSIS, INTERPRETATION, CREATIVITY, INNOVATION

▼ HOW ARRANGEMENT OF WORDS AFFECTS MEANING

1 William Carlos Williams was an American poet and doctor. Because his medical work took him into homes where families were facing emergencies, he was able to learn a lot about them. This is one of his most famous poems, 'This is just to say'.

> I have eaten   5
> the plums
> that were in
> the ice box
>
> and which   10
> you were probably
> saving
> for breakfast.
>
> Forgive me
> they were delicious   15
> so sweet
> and so cold.

It is not difficult to imagine 'This is just to say' as a hasty note of apology scrawled on a sticky note and stuck on a fridge door.

Now look at the words of the poem arranged as ordinary sentences.

> I have eaten the plums that were in the ice box and which you were probably saving for breakfast. Forgive me; they were delicious, so sweet and so cold.

▶

Work on your own and pick out key words in the poem which simply present clear facts. What words are left? What are the effects of these other words?

2 Work in a small group and consider the following questions.

▶ **Which words describe the plums? What effect does this description have? Does it simply help you to imagine what the plums were like?**

▶ **What happens to the tone or mood of the poem after the first sentence?**

▶ **Which word is crucial here? What is the effect of the rest of the last sentence: 'they were delicious | so sweet | and so cold'? What would be the effect of describing the plums in the first sentence?**

3 Write a cheeky note of mock apology along the lines of 'This is just to say'. For example, you could write an apology to a particular teacher for failing to do your homework.

4 Remember the different effects of, or purposes for, writing: informative, transactional, emotive, persuasive, discursive, entertaining, inspirational, descriptive, ironic and advisory. How many of these can you find in Williams's poem? Explain how these effects are brought about.

ACTIVITY 2   **SKILLS**   CRITICAL THINKING, ANALYSIS

▼ CHECKING WRITTEN MATERIAL

To practise checking your own work, it helps to read other people's material critically. Read the following extract and the critical analysis of the text to see an example of critical reading. Can you suggest any other changes that should be made to the text?

> For some time, it suited the British authorities to sentence troublesome people[1] to transportation. Unfortunate poor people, who had found themselves starving and who had stolen food simply to stay alive, turned up[2] in the colonies in the country that would become Australia. Along with others who had chosen to settle in this new country[3], they made a go of things[4] and now take on[5] the English at games such as rugby and cricket and sometimes win.

[1] 'Convicts' would be a more precise way of referring to them and technically correct, whether or not they deserved conviction.

[2] '…turned up' is vague. They were sent.

[3] The reference to 'others who had chosen to settle in this new country' is verbose. They were settlers.

[4] 'made a go of things' is slang and may not be clear to all speakers of English. They succeeded.

[5] 'now take on' is inaccurate. It is their descendants who now take on the English.

▲ Transportation was often used as an alternative punishment to execution.

SUBJECT VOCABULARY

verbose excessively wordy or long-winded

KEY POINT

To write effectively, you must make sure your intention is clear to the reader.

LEARNING OBJECTIVES

This lesson will help you to:
- understand the ways in which sentences can be assembled
- see the way that the meaning of a sentence is made effective.

SENTENCE TYPES

As you start to examine sentences it is important to remember what makes a sentence. A sentence is the most basic part of the written language and properly constructed sentences help you to communicate effectively, whatever your purpose.

A sentence is built around finite verbs, or action words, which indicate whether the action takes place in the past, present or future and which have some indication of the agent, the person or thing that carries out the action.

BUILDING SENTENCES

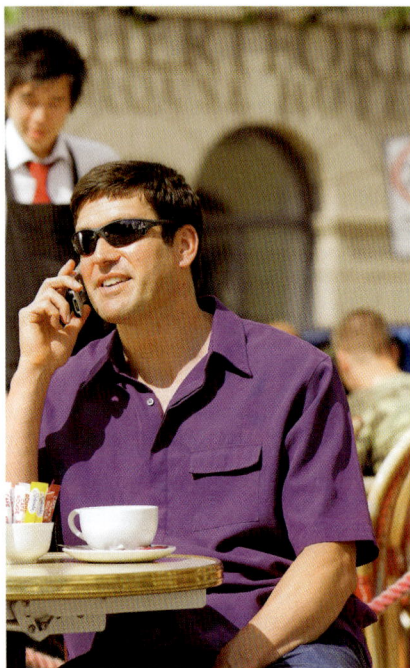

▲ 'They took their sunglasses and (they) enjoyed themselves' is a compound sentence.

First look at sentences in a mechanical way. Here is a simple sentence. It has one main verb, *took*.

They took their sunglasses.

To this you can add something more:

They took their sunglasses and (they) enjoyed themselves.

The original sentence has become a compound sentence. Two simple sentences have become joined by a conjunction: *and*. They have become two coordinate clauses in a compound sentence. Each coordinate clause has a main verb; in this case, *took* and *enjoyed*.

You can develop the sentence further:

They took their sunglasses and enjoyed themselves although it was raining.

To the compound sentence, with its two main verbs, a subordinate clause has been added: *although it was raining*. This clause also contains a verb, *was raining*; however, the clause, *although it was raining,* makes incomplete sense on its own. Without the main clause, you do not know what happened while it was raining.

This clause has to be joined to the main sentence with a subordinating conjunction, *although*. The sentence is now a complex sentence with two main verbs and a subordinate verb.

They took their sunglasses and enjoyed themselves although it was raining.

You could link two of the components in other ways to form complex sentences:

They took their sunglasses although it was raining.

Although it was raining they took their sunglasses.

Each sentence here has a main clause and a subordinate clause.

Finally, look at another sentence:

He looked at the menu which was badly written.

A simple sentence, *He looked at the menu,* has become a main clause to which a relative clause, *which was badly written* has been added. This relative clause has been linked with a relative conjunction, *which*, to form another complex sentence.

The purpose of examining sentences like this is to show you how you can build up ideas and communicate them effectively. By using subordinate, coordinate and relative clauses, you can add information without interrupting the flow of words and still indicate the most important aspects of what you are saying.

ACTIVITY 1   **SKILLS** ANALYSIS

▼ IDENTIFYING FINITE VERBS

Identify the finite verbs in these sentences and decide what kind of sentence it is.

1 We should try to smile and try to laugh.
2 The program, which she had spent weeks developing, crashed.
3 Whenever they can all cows eat grass because grass is good for them.

ACTIVITY 2   **SKILLS** ADAPTIVE LEARNING, INNOVATION

▼ VARYING SENTENCE TYPES

SUBJECT VOCABULARY

narrative the story or plot

Try to write a short narrative, describing a short sequence of events, using simple, compound and complex sentences. You could start with these two sentences:

'His parents stood immediately in front of him. From beyond the closed door there came the sound of someone shouting and he decided to tell the truth.'

MINOR SENTENCES

You will sometimes find groups of words punctuated as if they were ordinary sentences when they are not.

Good. (A reaction to something.)

Over here! (A demonstration, some information.)

The boyfriend I ditched last week. (An answer to a question.)

In speech, such minor sentences are much more common and the listener can usually ask for clarification if required. When you write, it is better only to use minor sentences in direct or quoted speech to show what is actually said.

KEY POINT

Words and phrases can be built up into different types of sentences. By varying the sentences you use, you help the reader to stay engaged and strengthen the effect of what you write.

OPENING SENTENCES

Choosing the very first thing that you want to write or say can sometimes make it difficult to start. However, once you have taken that first step, you can continue more easily.

Opening sentences are very important as they set the tone for the reader. They are mainly used to introduce but can also be used to explain, attract attention or pose questions.

ACTIVITY 1   **SKILLS** ▶ CRITICAL THINKING, REASONING

▼ OPENING SENTENCE STYLE

Here are some opening sentences. Where would you expect to find them? In a novel, a newspaper, a text book or a television broadcast?

1 It was a man in front of them, a man with a gun.
2 Before being despatched to you, the contents of this package were carefully checked.
3 Hot pools can be found in Rotorua, on New Zealand's North Island, evidence of volcanic activity.
4 The views here are fantastic; we can see from the car park a long gentle slope down to a beach where Pacific rollers crash and spread themselves across the sand.
5 Once upon a time there was a wild goat who lived in the forest.
6 And European ministers gathered today in Brussels to update their latest agreement.
7 In order to update their latest agreement, European ministers gathered in Brussels.

Work in groups and match each of these opening sentences to the explanations that follow.

i A newspaper article or an introduction to an item broadcast on radio or television. It's about an event that has already taken place, but is being reported very soon afterwards. The main point is conveyed early in the sentence to encourage the reader to continue to pay attention.

ii An information slip. The sentence tells you what has been done and gives an explanation that is designed to reassure the reader.

iii Travel writing. The reader is stopped by the drama of the opening which is followed by a description of a geographical feature.

iv A history book. The sentence begins with an explanation of why the event took place with the main point made briefly at the end of the sentence, as if it is of less importance.

▶

v   A narrative, the beginning of a novel or of a chapter in a novel. The reader is confronted with a simple but dramatic scene with only the bare essentials so that we are not distracted from the main image.

vi A geography book. The subject of the sentence is a geographical feature, introduced immediately and referred to as 'evidence', a matter of interest to geographers. This information is delivered in a straightforward manner.

vii A children's fairy story. The opening phrase is frequently used to introduce children's stories.

ACTIVITY 2

SKILLS ANALYSIS, INNOVATION, COMMUNICATION

▼ KEY WORDS

Work in groups to copy and complete the table below. Look again at the sentences in Activity 1 and consider the essential words in each opening sentence and what effects they create.

▼ ESSENTIAL WORDS	▼ THE EFFECTS THEY CREATE
1 'in front', 'man', 'gun'	There is drama because the writer is confronted by an armed man.

After completing the table, work on your own or with a partner. Write another introductory sentence to match each of the explanations in Activity 1. Swap your opening sentences with a partner or with another pair. Write a sentence of your own to follow the introductory sentence that has been passed to you.

KEY POINT

To start a piece of writing you can:

- use particular words or phrases
- present something that is obviously new
- refer to something that has already been mentioned before saying something new about it.

▲ The Charlemagne building – part of the EU in Brussels

LEARNING OBJECTIVES

This lesson will help you to:

- understand the ways that sentences achieve their effects
- understand the way in which a sentence is constructed around its main points.

SENTENCES FOR EFFECT

You have already seen the mechanical ways in which sentences can be built up. Now look at the ways in which sentences achieve their effects.

ANALYSING SENTENCES

▲ What is the main point of this image?

SUBJECT VOCABULARY

periodic sentence a sentence that is not complete until the final word or clause

Here's a sentence from a book for young children:

The cat sat on the mat.

To see how this sentence achieves its effect, consider the point of the sentence. What is it about? It's about the cat sitting on the mat. That is all you are told. This is a **periodic sentence**, a few simple words followed by a full stop (.) or, as it is called in American English, a period.

You can extend this sentence:

The cat sat on the mat and smiled.

This time the question is more subtle: what main point or points is the writer making? You are told two main points.

A compound sentence is a sentence with more than one subject.

ACTIVITY 1

SKILLS   ADAPTIVE LEARNING, INNOVATION, TEAMWORK

▼ PERIODIC SENTENCES

Write a few periodic sentences on individual slips of paper. Then work as a group and see how many balanced sentences you can form by joining the slips in pairs. You will probably need a few additional words.

Now look at a final development of the sentence.

With a huge grin on her face the cat sat on the mat while from next door there came the sound of a dog digging its way under the fence.

The main point is still *The cat sat on the mat.* All the other information is of lesser importance and the main point is inserted among this additional information. This is a 'loose sentence'.

Each person in the group now writes one short periodic sentence. Pass your sentence to another member of the group who should add further information in order to make a balanced sentence. This should then be passed onto the next member of the group to be turned into a loose sentence.

ACTIVITY 2   SKILLS ▸ ADAPTIVE LEARNING, INNOVATION, TEAMWORK

▼ CONSTRUCTING VARIED SENTENCES

Work on your own and write three sentences as follows:

1 A periodic sentence including one of the following:
   - an important piece of information
   - a description of something that you find attractive
   - something in which you believe very strongly.
2 A balanced sentence developing the idea from your first sentence in two main points.
3 A loose sentence developing your idea further.

Then, in groups or as a class, listen to each other's sets of sentences read aloud and see how quickly you can identify the points they are trying to make.

MOVING ON

Look at two aspects of these examples: their length and their ordering.

> It was late. He had left home early, caught the early bus, but the accident on the main road meant he was alone now, after dark, in an area that he did not know.

A short opening sentence establishes the time in a dramatic fashion and the following sentence builds up to the next dramatic revelation, that the character is alone. It is then that more drama is revealed: the darkness and his lack of familiarity with the area.

> These instructions should be followed carefully. Operatives who fail to do this will be dealt with severely.

Here a simple sentence conveys information coupled with a warning at the end where it is more noticeable, more emphatic. The warning tone is maintained in the second sentence with its final warning that severe treatment is in prospect for operatives who fail to head the instructions.

> What would you do? You come home to find your house broken open, your goods stolen, and all the plumbing smashed. Then the sergeant down at the police station asks you to stay calm. Stay calm?

Confronted with a disaster, someone asks why they should be expected to stay calm. A short question holds the reader ready to respond. 'You' introduces the second sentence, an attempt to lead the reader into imagining the writer's feelings and aspects of the disaster are listed to build up the force of the description. In the next sentence, the tension is eased as you are told of the police sergeant's reaction, ready to hear the anger of the final, minor sentence, a simple question that is all the more direct and challenging in its brevity.

KEY POINT

In a periodic sentence the main point is found at the end, in a balanced sentence there is more than one main point and in a loose sentence the main point is not at the end. You can use this variety of sentence types to help convey effectively the things you wish to say in writing.

LEARNING OBJECTIVES

This lesson will help you to:

- consider the purpose of sentences and the way you construct them to achieve your purposes.

SENTENCE PURPOSE

It is important to consider the purpose of sentences and the way in which they are constructed. By always being aware of this, it is possible to convey clear and strong ideas.

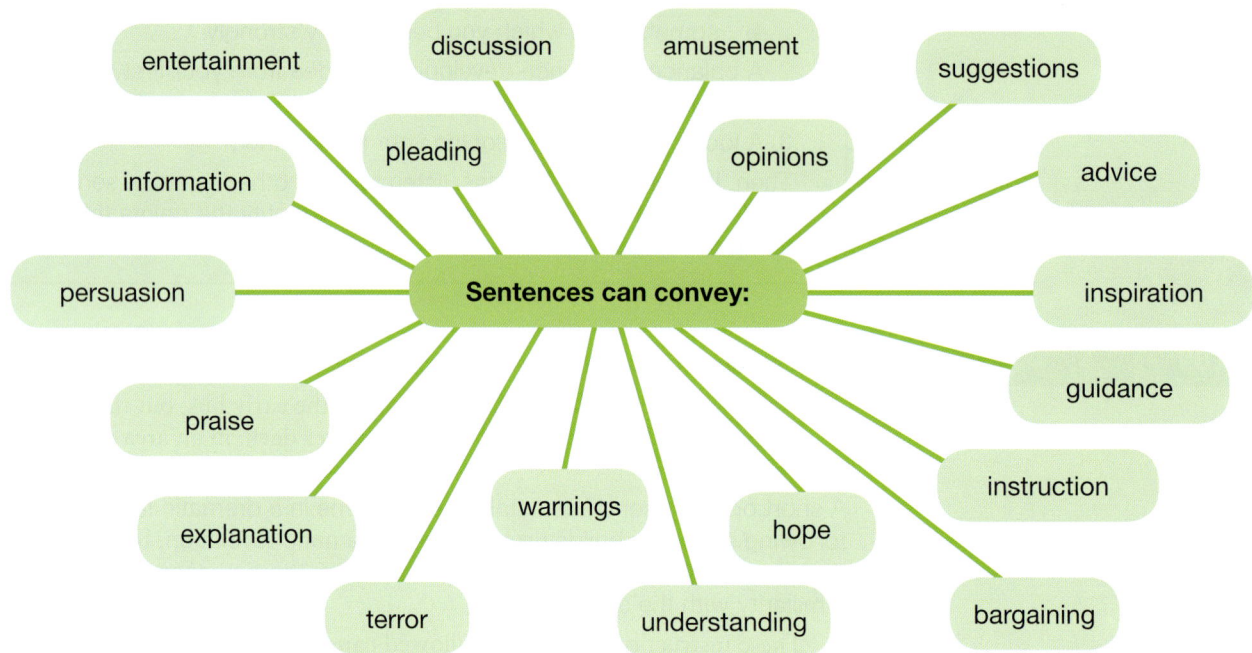

entertainment

discussion

amusement

suggestions

pleading

opinions

advice

information

Sentences can convey:

inspiration

persuasion

guidance

praise

instruction

explanation

warnings

hope

terror

understanding

bargaining

BASIC SENTENCE TYPES

There are three basic types of sentence: sentences that are informative, descriptive or discursive.

EFFECTS OF DIFFERENT SENTENCES

Here you will look at the effects that can be achieved in an opening sentence.

Look at the development of a simple sentence that provides information.

> Our pets' favourite sleeping place was the dog's bed.

Now some description has been added.

> Our pets' favourite sleeping place was the dog's bed, nestled in a woollen blanket next to the radiator.

And now some discussion has been added.

> Our pets' favourite sleeping place was the dog's bed, nestled in a woollen blanket next to the radiator, which was not fair on the two cats, the guinea pigs and the mice which used to hide there when they managed to escape from their cage.

▶ **Identify the key words that convey information, description and discussion.**

▶ **Divide this last sentence into three sentences, one informative, one descriptive and one discursive.**

KEY POINT

Remember to always consider your audience, whether you are speaking directly to them or leaving something in writing for them to read later.

COMMENTARIES

Here are two passages for you to consider. The first one is measured, with quite long sentences.

> The news had arrived and it was not good. For many people in the crowd it was not bad news that they were expecting, but something better, the prospect of better rations at least. Better still would be release from this strange land and transport back to the border, if not all the way home. However, once they had listened to the commandant's words, there was nothing for it but to make their way back to the barracks and try to get some sleep.

The first, balanced sentence provides two items of information; the second item provides a response to the first, a natural flow of ideas. The second complex sentence contrasts this bad news with what they had perhaps been hoping for, 'something better'. This sentence is extended here with the phrase, 'the prospect of better rations at least', an important descriptive detail. The idea of hope is also extended in a complex sentence where a group of three items remind of this: release, transport to the border and transport home. The first, subordinate clause in the final sentence kills off any prospect of hope and leads to a main clause in which the inevitability of this is brought home to the reader and the prisoners' attempts to sleep bring closure to this episode.

The second passage is rather more dramatic.

> The hand of the clock moves to the vertical, like a sentinel arriving at his post. Now the moment has come. The referee looks around the pitch, catches the eye of each linesman and then raises his whistle to his lips. Mahama's boot makes contact. There is the beginning of a roar. The ball reaches a winger. He turns and sends the ball back towards the keeper who picks it up, as if concerned for its safety. The ball bounces once in front of him and he kicks it forwards. Razak it is now. He moves forward. Modi joins him. One kick and the ball is bouncing in the net.

A longer opening sentence holds the reader at the moment before the game begins. A short sentence hurries you towards the start, increasing the sense of drama, but then you are held still as the next sentence, a compound one, lists the referee's three actions as he prepares to unleash the players. Three short, simple sentences propel the action forward, then a longer, complex sentence allows the goalkeeper to slow things down. The reader watches as the ball is taken under his control and returned, a balanced sentence holding back the excitement until a series of short sentences, pared of any surplus information, conveys the essentials and the scoring of the goal provides a natural end to the passage.

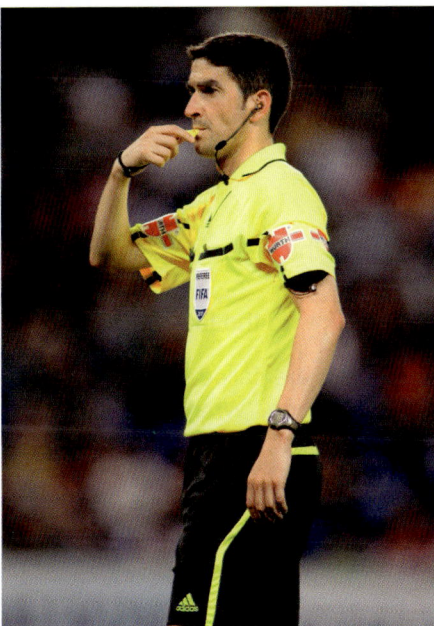

▲ Different types of sentences can determine how something is read, for example, in football commentary.

ACTIVITY 1   **SKILLS** ▶ ADAPTIVE LEARNING, INNOVATION, COMMUNICATION, TEAMWORK

▼ CONTROLLING YOUR WRITING

1 Work on your own and develop one of the following ideas into a paragraph of at least four sentences of varying length and complexity.

- The approach of a stranger.
- A glance from a window.
- A surprise around a corner.
- A clever idea.

2 Read this paragraph aloud, to your partner and ask them to comment.

LEARNING OBJECTIVES

This lesson will help you to:

- appreciate how you can structure or organise writing effectively, whether you are providing information, describing something, discussing something or providing entertainment.

PRINCIPLES OF STRUCTURE

When a piece of writing is judged by readers or marked by examiners, the purpose of the writing is considered, alongside the accuracy and clarity of the writing and with an overall sense of the writing's effectiveness.

Here you are going to consider the way that sentences and paragraphs are organised so that the structure of the writing is enhanced and made more effective.

UNDERSTANDING THE PRINCIPLES OF STRUCTURE

▲ The structure of a sentence can alter the meaning and impact. Compare 'Zlatan, look out!' with 'After school I need to speak to you Zlatan.'

Read the following sentence.

> Zlatan, look out!

There is an urgent call to one person, the first name you read: Zlatan. The most important word is placed at the start of the sentence. Now look at the following sentence.

> After school I need to speak to you, Zlatan.

Here a teacher is making an announcement and wants all the class to listen until the name of the student concerned is revealed at the end of the sentence.

If you ask what a sentence is about, you can identify its subject. The subject of each of these sentences has been highlighted.

1 **The ice cream** was hidden in the freezer.

2 Hidden in the freezer was **the ice cream**.

3 **The ice cream**, which her brother had hidden in the freezer, was discovered.

4 Hidden in the freezer, which had been turned off, was **the ice cream**.

Those parts of the sentence that are not the subject are called the predicate. The predicate can be discovered by asking the question, 'What am I told about the subject of the sentence?'

Apply this question to the four sentences above.

ACTIVITY 1   **SKILLS** ▶ INNOVATION, TEAMWORK

▼ PURPOSE AND PROGRESSION IN SENTENCES

Work in pairs and identify the key words and ideas in each of these sentences. Ask what seems to be the key ideas that link one sentence to another. Then look at the beginnings, middles and endings of these sentences.

> The ice cream was hidden in the freezer. Then the bananas were discovered in the bathroom and the marshmallows tucked away in Sophie's bedroom. Now there would have to be an inquiry.

Now identify the important stage in each sentence of this mini-narrative.

STAGES OF WRITING

The principle of stages in writing applies to any piece of writing that you create. Whether it is a brief email, a set of instructions for a piece of machinery, a text book or a novel, it will require an introduction, a middle section and an ending.

ACTIVITY 2

SKILLS   CRITICAL THINKING, ANALYSIS

▼ STAGE TRANSITIONS

Work with a partner and identify the key words that show the transition from introduction, to mid-section, to the ending in the paragraph that follows.

> The Turkish teacher met them at the airport and introduced her husband, a company lawyer. Soon they were hurrying along the freeway and then there was a turning off, followed by miles bumping along worn back roads. For a while he wondered just what he had let himself in for and then the car slowed. Away from the road there was a large timber house, set in a large garden. Then he sighed with relief for this was to be his home for the next six weeks.

Now use those same words in a paragraph of your own construction, to show shifts from the introduction, to the middle section, to the conclusion.

KEY POINT

You have looked at how sentences can have an introduction, a middle section and an ending. The same is true of a more substantial piece of writing, including books, essays and articles.

ACTIVITY 3

SKILLS   CRITICAL THINKING

▼ BREAKING DOWN STORIES

Work with a partner and identify any story that you know and that you think your classmates will know. It could be a television drama, a film you have watched, a story that you have read or a story that was read to you. Describe the three stages of the story (the introduction, the middle section and the ending) in three sentences.

Here is an example of three sentences that outline a well-known story (*The Cruel Sea* by Nicholas Montsarrat) in the same way.

> We meet Ericson, the captain of both the boats involved in the story, in a naval dockyard where the first of his two commands is still in the hands of the builders. Ericson's career, as captain of a warship that is sunk, and of another warship that survives the war, leads us through five years of naval warfare in what came to be known as *The Battle of the Atlantic*. At the end of this battle, Ericson finds himself in charge of captured submarines which are now incapable of threatening allied shipping any more.

PARAGRAPHING FOR EFFECT

There are no mechanical rules about the size or length of sentences or paragraphs, nor about the number of lines or words needed in each. The important thing is to ask yourself: how can I best organise sentences and paragraphs so that they are as clear as possible?

You have already looked at ideas that link sentences. Now, when you start a new paragraph you have to do two things: firstly, maintain contact with what you have already written and, secondly, develop ideas, sometimes by introducing new material, new ideas and new directions.

ACTIVITY 1   **SKILLS** CRITICAL THINKING, ANALYSIS, INTERPRETATION

▼ DEVELOPING NARRATIVES

Work with a partner or in groups and read the passage below. There are three key items in the first paragraph: the tea, the woman and the newspaper. Follow these items from the first paragraph into the second paragraph. How is each developed?

> The woman offered him another cup of tea. She had been very friendly since he had stepped into the house. The room seemed all right and now there was another cup of tea. There was something slightly odd about the taste, not enough to worry him and, anyway, he wanted to find out what the rent would be. While she waited for his answer she glanced down at the newspaper and folded it away, hastily, out of sight, behind one of the cushions.
>
> There was a knock at the front door. The woman got up and went into the hall to see who it was and he could hear a conversation get under way. From behind the cushion he retrieved the newspaper and read the headline: *Missing students – poisoner suspected*. He took another sip of his tea. This time he screwed up his face and put down the cup. From one side he picked up his coat and stood up.

▶ **What is new in the second paragraph?**

▶ **What changes about the young man in the second paragraph?**

There is a balance in these two paragraphs. You learn why the young man has come to the house and that information needs no further development. The hints about the tea in the first paragraph prepare you for the dramatic newspaper headline revealed in the second paragraph.

ACTIVITY 2

▼ KEY CONTENT IN PARAGRAPHS

Work with a partner or on your own and identify the key words or ideas in each of the following two paragraphs. Copy and complete the table, commenting on the links between these words and ideas.

> At the foot of the hill there is a large spread of woodland, pine trees – dark green, that swarm upwards, almost to the top of the hill. Local people love this place, to which they bring their dogs and their children; on most days, providing the weather is reasonable, you will see them dotted about on the parkland, clearly in no hurry, clearly enjoying this special space.
>
> Now the county council has announced plans to extend the city ring-road to accommodate industrial traffic to the new factory sites as well as the growing rush-hour traffic associated with the expansion of the university. Councillors are divided about the threats to local people's leisure and the need to move traffic quickly around the city. Protests are planned for next week and locals hope that the council will be sufficiently embarrassed and will re-think the transport committee's recommendations.

▼ KEY WORDS AND IDEAS	▼ LINKS
Woodland/ring-road	Different types of location introducing each paragraph and contrasting what exists and what is proposed.

▶ A new paragraph can be used to shift tone or ideas.

ACTIVITY 3

▼ DEVELOPMENT IDEAS

Work with a partner and develop the ideas listed below into sentences and paragraphs for a report in a newspaper. Remember to arrange the ideas in an order that suits the effect you want your report to have. Do you want to alert your readers, warn them or reassure them? Or something else completely?

> A burst water main, a busy road junction, freezing weather conditions, accidents and a busy hospital.

KEY POINT

As you move from one paragraph to another you should indicate clearly that you are either developing an idea or introducing a new one.

LINKING IDEAS

Good writing flows and is easy to read. Here you will see how a writer can organise the flow of ideas to maximise their effect.

UNDERSTANDING HOW IDEAS LINK TOGETHER

Read this article about Nevil Shute, a 20th century British author. His best-known novel was *A Town Like Alice*.

Not many people[1] who enjoyed Shute's novels realised that he had started out as an engineer in the early days of aero-engineering after the First World War, not with aeroplanes, but with airships[2]. It was while he was working as an engineer that he began to write[3].

Although well-qualified[4], with an engineering degree from Oxford University, Shute, whose full name was Nevil Shute Norway was a practical man[5], interested in the ways that people from different backgrounds could get along well. In *A Town Like Alice*, a brief encounter during the Second World War between a brash Australian prisoner of war and an English girl who had also been taken prisoner by the Japanese, developed into a romance as the Australian travels to England after the war to find the woman he had known as Mrs Bong[6].

It is in his non-fiction[7], his auto-biography, *Slide Rule*, that we learn how to build an air-ship and he describes the ladder-way inside the craft[8] that enables engineers to climb out onto the top of the balloon while it is flying to sit and chat[9]. While the engineers hold on to a safety rope, passengers in the cabin slung below the balloon travel in comparative safety[10]. Shute also wrote authoritatively about the economics of air-ship construction and the politics that drove a government-controlled industry to compete with a private one[11].

In this book we also learn of[12] his terrible sadness in his early teens when his older brother was killed in the trenches of the First World War[13], as a result of the enemy's tunnelling under the British trenches and packing the space with high explosive. Shute watched as his brother, Fred, took two weeks to die in hospital in France; Shute's parents, unlike most people, were in a position to drive across France to visit their dying son. When Shute eventually wrote about this he was forty and still missing his brother terribly[14].

ACTIVITY 1   **SKILLS**   CRITICAL ANALYSIS, ANALYSIS, REASONING

▼ IDEA PROGRESSION

Read through the passage about Nevil Shute. Then look at each of the numbered sections along with the table which shows how each of these sections moves the reader along through the ideas conveyed.

Try to see how the flow is maintained. For example, the first point concerns the movement from the idea of Shute as a well-known novelist to the less well-known fact that he began his professional life as an

▶

Writing that flows helps the reader to enjoy and follow a piece of writing. Look at the second sentence of the piece about Shute that refers first to engineering, which has already been established, but also to his writing, a theme that is taken up in the next paragraph.

aeronautical engineer. The next direction of the flow of this passage is provided by the information that he worked, not with aeroplanes, which is what you might expect of aeronautical engineers, but with airships. It might help you to see your reading of the passage as a series of steps that lead you from one idea to the next, so that you follow the writer and understand what it is that they want to say.

1 Engaging the reader	Contrast novelist/engineer, surprising information
2 Contrast – unexpected	'not with' / 'airships' rather than 'aeroplanes'
3 Moving along	From engineering to writing
4 Anticipation	'Although well-qualified…'
5 Comparisons	Educated but practical, engineering and people
6 Adding detail	Summary of a novel
7 Adding ideas	Non-fiction as well as fiction
8 Explanation	Intriguing detail
9 Illustration	Engaging the imagination
10 Contrast	Passengers at ease, 'a safety rope'
11 Adding information	Expanding a point: economics and politics covered
12 Adding information	'We also learn': preparing for a new topic
13 Explanation	Details to help the reader understand this topic
14 Final comment	Distanced: 'eventually'

ACTIVITY 2   SKILLS ▸ CRITICAL THINKING, CREATIVITY

▼ LINKING KEY POINTS AND IDEAS

Find a piece of writing about a topic that you like that is between one and two pages long. It could be on sport, music, IT, engineering, fashion, cooking, travel or a piece of fiction. Mark or identify each of the main points as they are introduced and make a list of them. Re-order the list if you think the flow of writing could be improved then re-write the piece in your own words, taking care to link your points.

▲ You could try structuring your writing around these images.

ENDING A SENTENCE

The way in which a sentence finishes can have a dramatic impact on its purpose and content.

Read this passage aloud.

> there are three ways of ending a sentence this is very important if you do not punctuate sentences accurately they are very difficult to read then the meaning will not be clear do you understand this it is extremely important

Now read this passage aloud.

> There are three ways of ending a sentence. This is very important. If you do not punctuate sentences accurately they are very difficult to read. Then the meaning will not be clear. Do you understand this? It is extremely important!

Three ways of signalling the end of the sentences have been used in the second passage. Unless you use a question mark for a question or an exclamation mark to stress something important or dramatic, you should use a full stop. In American English, full stops are called 'periods'.

ACTIVITY 1   SKILLS ▸ INNOVATION

▼ CHOOSING CLOSING PUNCTUATION

Work on your own and punctuate the following passage. If you cannot read the passage aloud, try to imagine the sound of your voice as you read it. Remember, each sentence must have at least one main verb.

> it was night over the hill they could see the stars they had been told of the dangers of the area but they had decided to continue anyway soon they reached the first of the houses where the street took a sharp turn to the right soon they would be back home

Questions must be finished with a question mark. They are formed in two ways. They may be formed with auxiliary verbs such as *would*, *should*, *do*, *does*, and so on. For example: *Should we leave?* or *Does he take sugar?*

Another way of forming questions involves the reversal of the subject/verb order in a statement. For example, *Is it theirs?* This form of question may include question words such as *why*, *what*, *where*, *who*, *whom* and *how*. For example, *How do you like your coffee?*

Exclamation marks can be used to represent strong emotions, emphasise points or suggest volume. They should be used sparingly so as to not lessen their impact.

LEARNING OBJECTIVES

This lesson will help you to:

■ understand that a comma is used to indicate a pause within a sentence.

COMMAS

Commas are essential for dictating the way in which sentences are read, spoken and understood. A single comma can change the entire meaning of a sentence.

Commas do the following:

■ indicate a pause, to leave clear a main clause:

While it was raining, they watched a film.

■ separate items in a list:

For breakfast he ate cereal, toast, baked beans and two apples.

■ clarify meaning by separating ideas:

His friend who had black hair was found with him. (*It was his friend with black hair who was found with him, not one of his other friends.*)

His friend, who had black hair, was found with him. (*This friend just happened to have black hair.*)

■ Look at this sentence:

The River Niger rises in the north of Nigeria, which takes its name from the river, to the north of Lake Oguta, and makes its way southwards towards the delta and out into the Gulf of Guinea.

The first and second commas separate information about the origin of Nigeria's name and the second and third commas separate further information, about the place where the river rises. These three commas enclose additional information that does not impede the main flow of the sentence. Without this information the main sections of the sentence would still flow together.

The River Niger rises in the north of Nigeria and makes its way southwards towards the delta and out into the Gulf of Guinea.

■ open and close direct speech (notice how the actual words that are spoken are enclosed in speech marks, or inverted commas):

'Come in,' said the doctor, 'do sit down.' The patient made himself comfortable and replied, 'Good to see you, doctor.'

'You know,' said the doctor, 'it's a good job you made this appointment.'

ACTIVITY 1   SKILLS ▸ INNOVATION

▼ USING COMMAS

Insert commas where required in the following passage.

It was raining. Slowly very slowly the puddles filled dull and grey under the dull light. Look out! shouted Henry but it was too late. I told you to look where you were going. You never pay attention ever. Further down the road half a kilometre away an old truck started up misfired once or twice and began a struggle up the hill towards them.

KEY POINT

It is easy to read quickly from the start to the end of a sentence, as long as commas are used correctly to make clear the writer's intentions.

APOSTROPHES

Apostrophes have two functions. They indicate the omission of one or more letters and, usually with the letter **s**, they indicate possession, meaning that something belongs to someone or something else. Like other punctuation marks, if they are used correctly, they help to make clear to the reader what the writer intended.

Read both these sentences aloud.

It's going to be a long night and there's nowhere to go.

It is going to be a long night and there is nowhere to go.

When you read the second sentence you have to make just a little more effort to read *It is* and *there is*. In speech people usually prefer to elide the *i* in *is*. That means the sound is suppressed or glided over for the sake of ease and speed. In writing, however, this is often seen as informal in style.

You can do this with other letters and, so long as you use the apostrophe, this will be clear to the reader. Here is another example.

We haven't a penny between us but she's got plenty.

This time the *o* and *ha* sounds have been missed.

When an apostrophe is used to indicate possession, the apostrophe usually appears before the *s* if the subject is singular and afterwards if the subject is plural.

Helen's mother hid all her brothers' bicycles.

With words that end in *s*, or words that do not take an *s* to show the plural there are two ways to punctuate possession, for example, *Chris' bike* and *the children's clothes*. Alternatively, an additional *'s* can be added to names ending with an *s*: *Chris's bike*. However, ensure that you remain consistent by only following one of these rules.

Finally, you have to remember *Its* and *It's*. When you omit the apostrophe in *its*, *it is* possessive. *It's* is a contraction of *it is*.

ACTIVITY 1 | SKILLS ▶ INNOVATION

USING APOSTROPHES

Insert the nine apostrophes required here.

'Glad youve come,' she said. 'Ive been lookin for you everywhere. I cant imagine whats the matter ere.'

'Troubles comin soon. Wed best go home.'

LEARNING OBJECTIVES

This lesson will help you to:
- understand how to use different punctuation marks.

COLONS, SEMI-COLONS, DASHES, BRACKETS, ELLIPSES

There is a range of different punctuation marks, each capable of achieving a particular effect or changing the meaning of a sentence. Being able to use them all will ensure your writing is varied and engaging.

COLONS

Colons are used to introduce evidence or examples.

> They could see what was stopping the car: a brick wedged under the tyre.

▶ **Write three sentences using a colon like this.**

SEMI-COLONS

Semi-colons are used to join closely related sentences or separate long items in a list.

> It was too late; slowly he raised his hands.

> They were all there; Billy who had broken his leg last year; Charlie who had rescued him, although he too had been wounded; and the dog.

▶ **Write two sentences following the first example and two following the second example.**

DASHES

Dashes are used to signal clearly the insertion of non-essential material into a sentence. Their purpose could be to add emphasis, to interrupt or to indicate an abrupt change of thought.

> They were all there – two men and a dog – and she realised that the police would have to be called.

▶ **Write two sentences following the pattern of this example.**

BRACKETS

Brackets are used to add additional material about a preceding item. Remember that, unlike dashes, brackets must be used in pairs.

> Kevin (lead singer) and Sharon were the band's best performers.

▶ **Insert information in brackets about the asterisked words in the following sentence.**

> 'Their guide* who had joined them at the airport helped two of them* to carry their bags.'

ELLIPSES

Ellipses are used where a word is omitted and are made up of three dots (like full stops). They are most useful in direct speech; when you speak, you are more likely to pause or break off in mid-sentence.

> He paused. 'I don't think I'm...' With that he turned away.

> 'If you don't stop that I'll, I'll...' Before she could finish they had drowned her in laughter.

▶ **Work with a partner and construct two dialogues between two or more characters. Each of you should write the first line of a dialogue, then pass it to your partner who should write the second line. Continue like this until you have written at least ten lines.**

SUBJECT VOCABULARY

dialogue the speech between two or more people involved in a conversation

KEY POINT

Remember that each of these punctuation marks has a distinctive function.

COMMON SPELLING ERRORS

It is easy to find lists of commonly misspelt words on the internet. These sites often provide reminders for some spellings and suggest that you make a list of the words that you find difficult to spell.

Correct spelling is something that depends on your visual memory so reading will help. You should also try to find ways of remembering something about the word, for example, *station*a*ry* and *station*e*ry*.

Where *a* is the final vowel the word *stationary* means *not moving* or *stopped*. Think of *stopped* as **a**rrested, a word which begins with an *a*.

Where *e* is the final vowel the word *stationery* refers to **e**nvelopes and writing paper.

Stationary/stationery; similar words, very different things

Another way to help yourself to remember difficult spellings is to look closely at the word, jotted down perhaps on a scrap of paper, and try to memorise it. Then cover up the word while you try to write it down accurately. Repeat this process if necessary. (Here's another difficult word, necessary. Remember, *shirts are ne*c*e*ss*ary* – one **c**ollar and two **s**leeves.)

Words that contain *e* and *i* together are sometimes easier to spell if you remember the following **mnemonic**:

i before e*, except after* c*, unless the sound matches weigh.*

So you have: *yield, receive, sleigh*. There are exceptions such as *seize*.

Particularly important words that you should make an effort to spell correctly include:

accompany	disguise	lightening	suspicious
agreeable	dumb	lightning	temperature
anxious	engineer	naughty	thorough
applaud	exhibition	neighbour	though
certificate	experiment	niece	thought
civilised	fulfil	occur	tremendous
compliment	government	occurred	vegetable
complement	fatigue	privilege	ventilation
conferred	height	prosperous	
deceitful	immediately	succession	
decision	language	suspicion	

LEARNING OBJECTIVES

This lesson will help you to:
- start checking your writing automatically.

IMPROVE YOUR WRITING

Like any practical activity, writing will improve with practice. Write regularly, at least ten minutes a day and always check your writing as you go. It's a good idea to check each paragraph as you proceed. That way you will also have a second look at your ideas and an opportunity to consider again how you will lead your ideas into the next paragraph.

Spelling, punctuation and grammar must all come together when you write. In practice you have been able to deal with them separately, but when you write you have to cope with all of them at once.

TIPS TO REMEMBER

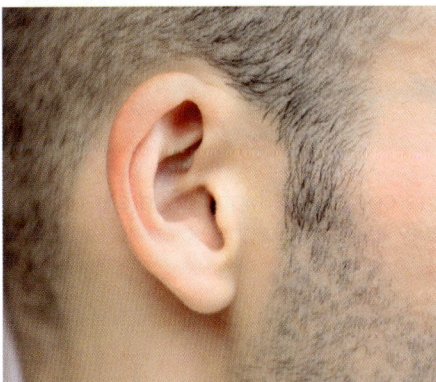

▲ Listening to how your writing reads is almost as important as reading it thoroughly when checking your work.

KEY POINT

Remember that your aim should always be to write clearly, accurately and effectively. As you write ask yourself, is this clear, is this accurate, will this be effective when someone else reads it?

- Allow your hearing (or the imagined sound of reading) to check grammar and punctuation.
- Allow your sight to check spelling. If you are typing, don't rely on spell checkers.
- When you edit a piece of writing you have to consider the way words are used and put together so that you can correct errors. At the same time, you must consider the ideas that are conveyed and whether they could have been clearer and better organised.

Remember that you must do the following:

- Begin a sentence with a capital letter. A capital letter marks clearly the start of a new sentence. Capital letters must also be used to mark proper nouns and all components of a proper noun, such as Abdul, Singapore and Hong Kong Airport.
- Stop sentences clearly with a full stop, a question mark or an exclamation mark. Use these punctuation marks in direct speech to mark the end of a spoken sentence.
- Use commas for pauses and lists, as well as for clarifying information and in direct speech. Here the commas indicate the pauses as you read, to help indicate the words that are actually spoken.

  Marie uttered the words, 'You fool!' She swallowed hard before continuing. 'What do you think you're doing?' She raised her mobile. 'The police,' she said, 'the police will like this when I send it.'

When you want to include additional information without interrupting the flow of the sentence you must choose between dashes and brackets:

- Dashes lead the eye to the next word so that the additional information can be easily taken in as you read on. For example, 'It was light – the sort of morning that calls to early risers – so staying in bed seemed sinful.'
- Brackets allow the insertion of shorter, more practical items of information. For example, 'Take out the flour (wholemeal, remember) and weigh out 200 grams.'

LEARNING OBJECTIVES

This lesson will help you to:
- detect items that require correction or that could be improved.

PROOF-READING, CHECKING AND EDITING

There are two important aspects of checking what has been written:

Proof-reading: marking errors in a draft

Editing: looking for opportunities to modify and improve the material

PROOF-READING: MECHANICAL ACCURACY

When proof-reading, ask yourself the following questions.

▶ **Are words spelt and ordered correctly?**

▶ **Are words changed where necessary so that they work together?**

▶ **Do the words flow when read out loud? If you are unable to read aloud, try imagining reading aloud instead.**

▶ **Have you double checked?**

ACTIVITY 1   SKILLS ▶ INNOVATION

▼ FINDING ERRORS

Work on your own or with a partner and correct the highlighted errors in the first sentence below. Then identify and correct the errors in the second sentence.

There is a hard frost which have been anticipating for some days. Many of the smaler animals had burrow deeply but, fortunately for them, heavy rain then caused the river to bursted it's banks and many of them was drowned.

EDITING

When editing, ask yourself the following questions:

▶ **Do the ideas flow?**

▶ **Are they easy to follow?**

▶ **Could more effective words be chosen?**

▶ **Could the presentation of ideas be more effective?**

ACTIVITY 2

SKILLS ▸ ADAPTIVE LEARNING, INNOVATION

▼ EDITING TEXT

Working on your own, read through these two sentences and edit them, choosing more effective words where you can and re-ordering them where this will improve the passage.

Across the river he could see the old railway track which had been on the sea-wall. No trains had been seen there for half a century but now a bunch of men who gathered in the Railway Arms, a well-known public house, had decided to campaign for its restoration. One of his neighbours, now in his eighties, remembered the sound of the whistle from the midday train which was his signal to stop work in the fields and go home for lunch.

KEY POINT

Language is firstly a spoken matter, something understood through hearing before reading or writing. One of the best ways of checking written material is to read it aloud.

When checking your work, you should try to imagine the sound of a voice reading it aloud. Remember that the purpose of writing accurately is to make it easy for someone to read it and understand it with little effort. This is what you should check for when proof-reading and editing a piece of writing, whether it is your own or someone else's.

▶ An old-fashioned steam engine

Proof-reading and editing are essential to any form of writing. Even the best ideas or most carefully thought-out argument can benefit from these processes, ensuring they are as engaging and effective as possible. Spelling mistakes, grammatical errors or poorly constructed sentences can greatly lessen the impact of a piece of writing, so it is important to carefully check your work and ensure it is of the best possible quality.

CALLE
DE LOS
OFICIOS

DONACIÓN DE M. METAMOROS A LA CIUDAD DE LA HABANA.- J. INS - ONDA.

OFICIOS

SECTION A: READING

Assessment Objective 1

Read and understand a variety of texts, selecting and interpreting information, ideas and perspectives

Assessment Objective 2

Understand and analyse how writers use linguistic and structural devices to achieve their effects

Assessment Objective 3

Explore links and connections between writers' ideas and perspectives, as well as how these are conveyed

In Section A, the Assessment Objectives are worth the following amounts.
AO1 – 5%
AO2 – 20%
AO3 – 15%

This chapter focuses on Section A of Paper 1 of the English Language B course. Working through these lessons and activities will help you to develop the reading skills that you will need for Section A of the Paper 1 exam.

The chapter is split into the following sections:
- Non-fiction texts
- Comparing texts
- Unseen texts.

Section A is worth 40% of the total marks for Paper 1.

In Section A of your exam, you will need to be able to meet Assessment Objectives AO1, AO2 and AO3.

TYPES OF TEXT

The types of non-fiction text that may appear in Section A of
Paper 1 include examples of:

■ biography or autobiography
■ obituaries
■ speeches
■ newspaper or magazine
articles

■ travel writing
■ diaries or letters
■ reviews
■ reference books.

The texts that you will write about in Section A of Paper 1 will be non-fiction.
Fiction describes scenes imagined (at least partly) by the writer. Non-fiction
writing does the opposite: it is about things that really happened, although you
cannot rely on all non-fiction to be accurate.

In an **autobiography**, the writer describes his or her own life. However, some
events may not have been remembered accurately, or some events may be
exaggerated for effect, perhaps to show the writer as positively as possible.
Some autobiographies may be considered more like fiction than non-fiction by
their readers because they are not very accurate.

A **biography** is the life story of a famous or interesting person, whether from
history or from the present day. Today, there are also 'authorised biographies',
in which the subject of the biography gives the writer specific legal permission
to produce the biography. The subject can decide which events are included
or omitted and how the writer describes them.

Another form of autobiographical writing is the **diary** or **journal**, or the modern
equivalent, the **blog** (short for 'web log'). For example, *The Diary of a Young
Girl* by Anne Frank contains important factual material about her daily life
during the German occupation of the Netherlands. It is therefore more than just
a personal account. However, not all diaries set out to be accurate or truthful.
Many diaries have other purposes, such as to entertain, to give personal views
and to communicate with friends.

News reports may appear in newspapers or magazines. News is expected
to be objective or unbiased and based on clear evidence. As readers, you
want to know whether a reporter is trying to present the material in a particular
way because of their own opinions on the topic. However, some newspaper
and magazine articles are undoubtedly biased. In all forms of non-fiction text,
therefore, the question of truth and accuracy really matters. This means that
part of the reader's analysis should include looking for any examples of bias or
opinion that is not supported by evidence.

Feature articles are usually about a topic of interest to a large number of
readers: they can be about almost anything, from family matters to global
politics. They are usually based on research. Opinion or comment pieces will
contain factual evidence and explanation, but aim to argue a case about a
topic of general interest.

An **obituary** is a newspaper article, found most frequently in broadsheet
newspapers, about a remarkable or well-known person who has just died. Its
length depends on the fame or significance of the subject.

ACTIVITY 1   A01   **SKILLS** CRITICAL THINKING, REASONING, DECISION MAKING

▼ IDENTIFYING TYPES OF NON-FICTION

Which of the types of non-fiction text described on page 58 do you think the following extracts come from? Give reasons for your decision. Which one do you think is more objective? Explain why you think this.

▼ FROM *THE INDEPENDENT* NEWSPAPER

Even the keenest gamers generally suffer nothing more than sore thumbs or tired eyes from their hobby. But scientists looking into the health effects of video game consoles have linked overplaying to dozens of injuries – some even life-threatening. The cases were uncovered after a team of Dutch researchers gathered all reported cases of Nintendo-related injuries, spanning 30 years.

▼ FROM *IN THE EMPIRE OF GENGHIS KHAN* BY STANLEY STEWART

On a low stool stood a mountainous plate of sheep parts, with the favoured cut, the great fatty tail, like a grey glacier on its summit. Younger sisters hustled in and out making last-minute preparations. While we were at breakfast the first lookouts were posted to watch for the return of the truck bearing the wedding party from the bride's camp.

BIOGRAPHY AND AUTOBIOGRAPHY

Read the following extract from an autobiography that tells Ellen MacArthur's account of her extraordinary life as a lone yachtswoman. While reading it, think about what MacArthur is writing about and how she has written her account.

▲ Yachtswoman Dame Ellen MacArthur

jib A small sail.

foredeck The deck near the bows of the yacht.

forestay Another sail.

knot A nautical mile per hour.

▼ FROM *TAKING ON THE WORLD* BY ELLEN MACARTHUR

The wind continued to rise during the first few days, and by the third I was changing down to the storm jib on the foredeck, and was thrown off my feet before cracking my head hard against the inner forestay rod, resulting in an instant lump and a strange nausea. Soon afterwards, the weather front passed, only to bring even stronger 55-knot gusts in a steady 45-knot wind. It was an unreal, crazy situation: just trying to hang on inside the boat took every ounce of strength. Food was hurled around the cabin along with water containers and spares, while I tried to scrape things up and put them back in the boxes. My hands stung, my eye was swollen, and my wrists were already covered in open sores…   5   10

Dawn brought some respite. My body temperature warmed after the freezing night, but if I sweated through the physical exertion of a sail change, when I stopped, I'd once again cool to a shiver. Sleep proved virtually impossible – just snatched ten-minute bursts ended by the cold.   15

Just two days later conditions began to worsen again. Doing anything was not only difficult but painful. My hands were red-raw and swollen, and my head was aching – even more so when the freezing water washed breathtakingly over it each time I went forward to change sails. Shifting the sails was hard, brutal work. Whenever it was time to change one I would pull it forward, clipping myself on and hanging on for dear life. Waves would continuously power down the side-decks, often washing me and the sail back a couple of metres, and I had to hang on and tighten my grip on the sail tie even further. I would often cry out loud as I dragged the sail along; it was one way of letting out some of that frustration and of finding the strength to do it… 20 25

After a week things finally began to calm, and with my legs red-hot and sore, and my wrists and fingers swollen, I finally enjoyed the first opportunity to remove my survival suit. Though the relief was wonderful, the smell was not! 30

KEY POINT

Read the exam questions carefully. Tailor your answer to the number of marks available and make sure you follow the key instructions.

SUBJECT VOCABULARY

first person written from the perspective of one person – that is, using 'I'; this differs from the second person, which directly addresses the reader ('you'), and the third person ('he', 'she' and 'it')

HINT

You will need to analyse the techniques used by the writer in order to meet Assessment Objective 2. Think about:

- the story or narrative and what actually happened
- use of precise detail
- frequent use of personal pronouns
- **first-person** perspective maintained throughout
- use of emotive language
- use of descriptive language.

ACTIVITY 2 | **AO1** | **AO2** | SKILLS ▷ CRITICAL THINKING, ANALYSIS, INTERPRETATION, REASONING

▼ PREPARING FOR THE EXAM QUESTIONS

Questions 1, 2, 4 and 5 in the exam require short answers, each of which is usually worth 1 or 2 marks. Questions 3, 6 and 7 require longer answers and will be worth 10 or 15 marks. The number of marks on offer will give you a good idea about how many points you should make and how much you should write.

You should answer the shorter questions in your own words. The longer questions permit you to use brief quotations to support your points, but you must keep them short. Copying long phrases and sentences straight from the text is not a good idea, unless the question specifically says that it is acceptable to do so.

Now look again at the extract from *Taking on the World* by Ellen MacArthur and answer the following questions.

1. **In lines 1–10, the writer describes the weather.**
   Identify one point the writer makes about the experience. **(1 mark)**

2. **In lines 10–19, the writer suffers injury and illness.**
   State one thing from which the writer suffers. **(1 mark)**

3. **Explain how the writer presents her account of life at sea.**
   You should support your answer with close reference to the passage, including brief quotations. **(10 marks)**

Choose two or three of the techniques in the 'Hint' box, then find an example or two of each technique in the extract and describe what you think the effects are.

GENERAL VOCABULARY

apartheid the former political and social system in South Africa, in which only white people had full political rights and people of other races, especially black people, were forced to go to separate schools, live in separate areas, and so on

An obituary is a very abbreviated biographical sketch of a remarkable person in the form of a newspaper article. These are usually published in newspapers shortly after the person's death has been announced. The length of obituaries varies, but an important world leader is likely to get a full page. Here are extracts from two examples: one for Nelson Mandela, who after years of imprisonment eventually became president of post-apartheid South Africa, and the other for David Bowie, the famous musician. Both are taken from *The Guardian* newspaper.

◀ Nelson Mandela

▼ FROM 'NELSON MANDELA OBITUARY' FROM *THE GUARDIAN*

Mandela greatly enjoyed university, particularly boxing and athletics, and, on the strength of his first-year studies in English, anthropology, politics, native administration and Roman-Dutch law, nursed an ambition to become a civil servant and interpreter – about as high a position as a black man might aspire to in those days. But his ambition seemed to be crushed when, in 1940, in his second year, as a member of the student representative council he was expelled for his part in a rebellion over poor quality food. He returned to Mqhekezweni to find another potential disaster – an arranged marriage was being planned for him.

◀ David Bowie

▼ FROM 'DAVID BOWIE OBITUARY' FROM *THE GUARDIAN*

In July 1969 Bowie released *Space Oddity*, the song that would give him his initial commercial breakthrough. Timed to coincide with the Apollo 11 moon landing, it was a top five UK hit. The accompanying album was originally called *Man of Words / Man of Music*, but was later reissued as *Space Oddity*.

The following year was a momentous one for Bowie. His brother Terry was committed to a psychiatric institution (and would kill himself in 1985), and his father died. In March, Bowie married Angela Barnett, an art student. He dumped Pitt [his manager] and recruited the driven and aggressive Tony DeFries, prompting Pitt to sue successfully for compensation. Artistically, Bowie was powering ahead. *The Man Who Sold the World* was released in the US in late 1970 and in the UK the following year under Bowie's new deal with RCA Victor, and with its daring songwriting and broody, hard-rock sound, it was the first album to do full justice to his writing and performing gifts.

ACTIVITY 3   A01   A02   SKILLS   CRITICAL THINKING, ANALYSIS, INTERPRETATION

▼ IDENTIFYING TECHNIQUES IN OBITUARIES

Obituaries are often sympathetic accounts of someone's achievements.

► How does the writer of the Mandela extract begin to influence the reader's sympathies?

► What makes these extracts more appropriate for obituaries than for biographies?

Copy and complete the following table, finding examples of the methods and techniques in the two extracts and commenting on their effect. Now identify some methods for yourself, remembering to back them up with evidence from the text and comment on their effect.

▼ METHOD OR TECHNIQUE	▼ EXAMPLE	▼ COMMENT ON EFFECT
Formal register		
Focus on factual information		
Conciseness of writing		

SPEECHES

Speeches can be given for many different reasons. Lawyers make speeches in court for the defence or the prosecution. People make speeches in debates or after formal dinners to entertain an audience. However, the most famous speeches are those made by politicians as part of campaigns. The purpose of such speeches is often to rally supporters and give listeners a sense of purpose and inspiration.

The following speech was made by the American civil rights campaigner, Martin Luther King Junior, who was later assassinated for his beliefs and his work on behalf of black Americans.

As you read the speech, think about how Martin Luther King shows his listeners that he is fighting for a better and fairer society in America, using techniques such as:

■ repetition of key words

■ repetition of the beginning of sentences

■ reference to particular individuals

■ use of geographical references (i.e. different parts of the United States)

■ describing the difficulties black people have faced over the years

■ the idea of bringing all people together

■ the use of words from a patriotic song.

▲ Martin Luther King at the March on Washington rally in August 1963

all men are created equal A quotation from the US Declaration of Independence, written just before the start of the war against Great Britain.

Georgia Southern American slave-owning state before the American Civil War.

colour of their skin but by the content of their character Note the alliteration of the sound /k/ five times.

let freedom ring Part of a patriotic American song.

New York New York State, which is very large.

Alleghenies A range of hills.

the old Negro spiritual A traditional hymn-like song of the Afro-Caribbeans, many of which originated during the era of slavery.

▼ 'I HAVE A DREAM' BY MARTIN LUTHER KING AT WASHINGTON DC, AUGUST 1963

I have a dream…

I have a dream that one day this nation will rise up and live out the true meaning of its creed: 'We hold these truths to be self-evident, that all men are created equal.'

I have a dream that one day on the red hills of Georgia, the sons of former slaves and the sons of former slave owners will be able to sit down together at the table of brotherhood.

I have a dream that my four little children will one day live in a nation where they will not be judged by the colour of their skin but by the content of their character.

I have a dream today!

And this will be the day – this will be the day when all of God's children will be able to sing with new meaning:

My country 'tis of thee, sweet land of liberty, of thee I sing.

Land where my fathers died, land of the Pilgrim's pride,

From every mountainside, let freedom ring!

And if America is to be a great nation, this must become true.

And so let freedom ring from the prodigious hilltops of New Hampshire.

Let freedom ring from the mighty mountains of New York.

Let freedom ring from the heightening Alleghenies of Pennsylvania…

Let freedom ring from every hill and molehill of Mississippi.

From every mountainside, let freedom ring.

And when this happens, when we allow freedom ring, when we let it ring from every village and every hamlet, from every state and every city, we will be able to speed up that day when all of God's children, black men and white men, Jews and Gentiles, Protestants and Catholics, will be able to join hands and sing in the words of the old Negro spiritual:

Free at last! Free at last!

Thank God Almighty, we are free at last!

The art of persuasive writing and speaking is called **rhetoric**. Rhetorical devices include many techniques used in poetry, since they can make all kinds of writing more memorable. These techniques include **alliteration**, **onomatopoeia**, figurative language (**similes**, **metaphors** and **personification**), **emotive language** and word choices.

ACTIVITY 4   **AO2**   **SKILLS** CRITICAL THINKING, ANALYSIS, INTERPRETATION

▼ IDENTIFYING TECHNIQUES USED IN SPEECHES

Look again at the bullet list of techniques on page 62. Copy and complete the following table, adding techniques and giving an example or two of each.

▼ METHOD OR TECHNIQUE	▼ EFFECT
Repetition of key words	
Geographical names	

▶ Pick out two quotations from the passage which give you the idea that Martin Luther King believes strongly in a fair society for people of all kinds. In each case, say why the language is so successful.

▶ Give three examples of rhetoric used in the extract and explain why they are effective.

ACTIVITY 5   **AO2**   **SKILLS** CRITICAL THINKING, ANALYSIS, INTERPRETATION

▼ APPEALING TO LISTENERS' FEELINGS

Effective speeches will nearly always have a strong appeal to the listeners' feelings. Copy and complete the following table to help you to analyse how Martin Luther King achieves this.

▼ APPEALS TO	▼ QUOTATION	▼ COMMENT
Love of justice and fairness	'they will not be judged by the colour of their skin'	
Patriotism		
Idealism		

▶ How does Martin Luther King build up a strong impression of the rightness of his cause in this extract?

DIARIES AND LETTERS

KEY POINT

The most famous published diaries show that the personal viewpoint can be an extremely powerful tool in non-fiction writing.

HINT

As you read the passage, think about:
- the age of the girl who is writing the diary
- signs of her ability to write in an unusually mature way about what she is experiencing
- her explanation as to why she writes the diary.

people Anne personifies the paper.

home Is it surprising to find that a diary is preoccupied with home life, family and friends?

time Notice the informal register here.

Many people express their most personal thoughts about their lives in writing that is less planned and more informal than an autobiography. This can be done either in a diary that they write regularly – often to an imaginary friend, such as Anne Frank's 'Kitty' – or in a letter to someone close: a friend, a lover or a relative. This means that the perspective of diaries and letters is personal, and many writers of diaries and letters did not originally intend them to be published. Remember that someone's thoughts and feelings can be an important part of a non-fiction text, just like in fiction.

Some of the most powerful diaries and letters that have been published give readers a remarkable understanding of the suffering of individuals in wartime. One example is Anne Frank's diary, published as *The Diary of a Young Girl*. Anne was a Dutch teenager who kept a diary over a period of two years during the Second World War. As she and her family were Jewish, they hid from the Nazis in a house in Amsterdam. The diary entries ended when the Frank family was eventually found and arrested. Anne was sent to a concentration camp, where she died. The following extract comes from the early months of Anne's period in hiding.

▼ FROM *THE DIARY OF A YOUNG GIRL* BY ANNE FRANK

'Paper has more patience than people.' I thought of this saying on one of those days when I was feeling a little depressed and was sitting at home with my chin in my hands, bored and listless, wondering whether to stay in or go out. I finally stayed where I was, brooding. Yes, paper does have more patience, and since I'm not planning to let anyone else read this stiff-backed notebook grandly referred to as a 'diary', unless I should ever find a real friend, it probably won't make a bit of difference.

Now I'm back to the point that prompted me to keep a diary in the first place: I don't have a friend.

Let me put it more clearly, since no one will believe that a thirteen-year-old girl is completely alone in the world. And I'm not. I have loving parents and a sixteen-year-old sister, and there are about thirty people I can call friends. I have a throng of admirers who can't keep their adoring eyes off me and who sometimes have to resort to using a broken pocket mirror to try and catch a glimpse of me in the classroom. I have a family, loving aunts and a good home. No, on the surface I seem to have everything, except my one true friend. All I think about when I'm with friends is having a good time. I can't bring myself to talk about anything but ordinary everyday things. We don't seem to be able to get any closer, and that's the problem. Maybe it's my fault that we don't confide in each other. In any case, that's just how things are, and unfortunately they're not liable to change. This is why I've started the diary.

ACTIVITY 6   **A01**   **SKILLS** CRITICAL THINKING, PROBLEM SOLVING, ANALYSIS, INTERPRETATION

▼ INTERPRETING WRITING

Write an answer for each of the following questions. A student answer for question 2 has been included to give you an idea of what you should be aiming to produce.

1 What reason does Anne give for keeping a diary?
2 In your own words, say how the final paragraph develops this thought.
3 Pick out two phrases which show that, at times, Anne is still quite young in her way of thinking and comment on each.

EXAMPLE STUDENT ANSWER TO QUESTION 2

The statement that Anne does not have a friend is explored in an interesting way in the final paragraph. Anne distinguishes in quite a mature way between having a loving family and many people who admire her, although this may be ironic, and having someone in whom she can really confide. She recognises that her life is going to be extremely difficult, and that she risks feeling isolated from the community. She regrets the superficial relationships that she has with her friends, and is looking for some deeper and more trusting relationships.

▶ How good do you think this answer is and why do you think this?

D. H. Lawrence was an English novelist and poet. Born in 1885, his career was focused on writing poetry and fiction; most famously *Lady Chatterley's Lover*. His letters, sent to friends and family, are useful records into his life and history, particularly his traumatic wartime experiences despite not undertaking military service during the First World War on grounds of his personal beliefs and health.

The following extract from a letter that he wrote gives an insight into his feelings at the end of the war.

▼ FROM 'D. H. LAWRENCE TO LADY CYNTHIA ASQUITH, 30 JANUARY 1915'

It seems like another life – we *were* happy – four men. Then we came to Barrow in Furness, and saw that the war was declared. And we all went mad. I can remember soldiers kissing on Barrow station, and a woman shouting defiantly to her sweetheart 'When you get at 'em, Clem, let 'em have it', as the train drew off – and in all the tram-cars 'War'. – Messrs Vickers Maxim call in their workmen and the great notices on Vickers' gateways – and the thousands of men streaming over the bridges. Then I went down the coast a few miles. And I think of the amazing sunsets over flat sands and the smoky sea – then of sailing in a fisherman's boat, running in the wind against a

▶

heavy sea – and a French onion boat in with her sails set splendidly, in the morning sunshine – and the electric suspense everywhere – and the amazing, vivid, visionary beauty of everything, heightened by the immense pain everywhere.

And since then, since I came back, things have not existed for me. I have spoken to no one, I have touched no one, I have seen no one. All the while, I swear, my soul lay in the tomb – not dead, but with the flat stone over it, a corpse, become corpse cold. And nobody existed because I did not exist myself.

KEY POINT

The strong impact of letters comes from their directness, often written soon after the author's experiences.

Read the passage again and think about:

- the locations that D. H. Lawrence describes
- how he describes his emotions
- his feelings about and attitudes towards death
- the reasons for these feelings.

ACTIVITY 7   **A01**   **A03**   **SKILLS**   CRITICAL THINKING, ANALYSIS, REASONING, DECISION MAKING

▼ PREPARING FOR EXAM QUESTIONS

Before answering the following questions, pick out (by underlining, highlighting or writing out) the key sentences or phrases you will need for your answer. Think about how you can re-word them in your own words.

1 Explain in your own words why D. H. Lawrence finds nature so striking in the first paragraph.

2 Explain in your own words how the first paragraph gives a real sense of D. H. Lawrence's feelings towards the war.

3 Both the passages by Anne Frank and D. H. Lawrence are about experiences of difficulties and hardships in a time of war. What similarities and differences do you find in the attitudes of the two writers?

4 Fill in the gaps in the following answer with the suggested words in the box. In some cases, more than one of these words may be suitable.

Anne	writing	horrible	thoughts
dreadful	awful	Lawrence	experiences
feelings	events	friend	nature
ideas	war	differences	soldiers
trapped	similarities	person	

▶

There are more _____ than _____ in the way the two writers experience _____ and its horrors. This is partly because Anne is _____ indoors, so has not actually seen the suffering of the _____. D. H. Lawrence, however, experiences _____ conditions. Both write about themselves, and both are sharing their innermost _____ with someone special, even if in _____'s case this is not a real _____. The power of _____'s descriptions gives a really vivid impression of war, whereas in this extract, Anne seems more preoccupied with the act of _____ a diary than with recording important _____.

TRAVEL WRITING

A lot of both fiction and non-fiction writing deals with travel. When it is non-fiction, travel writing is generally autobiographical in form. Travel writers usually try to record their actual experiences. When analysing travel writing, ask yourself the following questions about the writing.

- Does the writer bring the events to life, so that you can really imagine the people, and picture the place and the way of life there? How do they do this?

- What attitudes does the writer show towards the places visited? Are there feelings of amazement, delight, humour or sadness?

- Why is the writer telling you about his or her travels? Is it to make you want to visit the place? To entertain you? To enable you to experience places and people that you may never be able to visit personally?

- Does the writer bring out the ways in which customs, clothing, food or traditions differ from those you are used to?

The following two extracts are about the writers' experiences in different places: one is describing Mongolia, while the other is describing Somalia.

In *In the Empire of Genghis Khan*, Stanley Stewart sees the beauty and fun of the wedding preparations he watches and wishes to share his enjoyment with the reader, by bringing events to life as vividly as he can. As you read the passage, think about:

- whether this wedding seems like weddings that you have witnessed
- how the writer felt as someone not used to these traditions
- signs that, at times, he found the celebrations very amusing
- the way it presents a detailed picture of events.

▼ A scene from a Mongolian wedding

▼ **TEXT ONE**
**FROM *IN THE EMPIRE OF GENGHIS KHAN*
BY STANLEY STEWART**

Throughout the evening people came to warn me about themselves. They sat on the grass outside my tent, unburdening themselves with pre-emptive confessions. The following day would be difficult, they said. Weddings were boisterous occasions. People became unpredictable. They counselled me about particular individuals, then admitted that they themselves could be as bad as the next fellow. I would be wise to get away early before things got out of hand.   5

In the morning the groom and his supporters, a party of about seven or eight relations, set off to fetch the bride from her **ger**, which lay some 15 miles away. An old Russian truck, the equivalent of the wedding **Rolls**, had been specially hired for the occasion.   10

When they arrived the groom would be obliged to search for his bride who by tradition must hide from him. It would not be too difficult. The tradition is that she hides under a bed in the neighbouring ger. While we waited for their return we were given breakfast in the newlyweds' ger. Over the past weeks it had been lovingly prepared by relations. It was like a show ger from **Ideal Gers**… Biscuits, slabs of white cheese and boiled sweets had been **arrayed** on every surface in dizzy tiers like wedding cakes. On a low stool stood a mountainous plate of sheep parts, with the favoured cut, the great fatty tail, like a grey glacier on its summit.   15   20

Younger sisters hustled in and out making last-minute preparations. While we were at breakfast the first lookouts were posted to watch for the return of the truck bearing the wedding party from the bride's camp. By mid-afternoon we were still waiting. Apparently a wedding breakfast would have been given to the groom and his accompanying party at the bride's camp, and complicated calculations were now performed concerning the number of miles to the bride's ger, divided by the speed of the truck combined with the probable duration of the breakfast, and finally multiplied by the estimated consumption of **arkhi**.   25   30

At four o'clock a spiral of dust finally appeared beyond a distant ridge. When the truck drew up in front of the wedding ger, it was clear that the **lavish** hospitality of the bride's camp had been the cause of the delay. The back of the truck was crammed with wedding guests in such a state of **dishevelled** merriment that we had some difficulty persuading them to disembark. The bride's mother, apparently convinced that they were at the wrong ger, required four men to convey her to **terra firma**. The bride's elder sister, shrugging off all assistance, fell headfirst from the **tailgate**, bounced twice and came to rest, smiling, against a door post.   35   40

---

ger Mongolian home.

Rolls Rolls Royce, a luxury make of car that is often used for weddings.

Ideal Gers A play on the name of a British magazine, Ideal Home.

arrayed Arranged.

arkhi A clear spirit distilled from milk.

lavish Very generous.

dishevelled Disordered, disarranged.

terra firma [Latin] Solid ground.

tailgate The back end of the truck.

ACTIVITY 8 | A01 | A02 | SKILLS ▸ CRITICAL THINKING, ANALYSIS, REASONING, INTERPRETATION

▼ PREPARING FOR EXAM QUESTIONS

1 In paragraph 2, there is a custom involving a bride. What is it?
2 Describe the features of the preparations that take place in the newlyweds' ger.

These two questions are similar to Questions 1, 2, 4 and 5 in Paper 1 Section A. They are comprehension questions asking you to identify information in the text.

The following question is similar to Questions 3 and 6 and is worth 10 marks in the exam.

3 In what ways does the writer make this passage entertaining? When answering the question, you should support your answer with close reference to the passage, including **brief** quotations.

In your answer you could write about:

■ the writer's account of what happened
■ his handling of pace and suspense or anticipation
■ his descriptions of unusual things or customs
■ his use of language.

The following passage is an example of a very different kind of travel writing. While you are reading it, consider what makes it different from the previous extract.

▼ TEXT TWO
FROM *A PASSAGE TO AFRICA* BY GEORGE ALAGIAH

Alagiah writes about his experiences as a television reporter during the war in Somalia, Africa in the 1990s. He won a special award for his report on the incidents described in this passage.

I saw a thousand hungry, lean, scared and betrayed faces as I criss-crossed Somalia between the end of 1991 and December 1992, but there is one I will never forget.

I was in a little hamlet just outside Gufgaduud, a village in the back of beyond, a place the aid agencies had yet to reach. In my notebook   5
I had jotted down instructions on how to get there. 'Take the Badale Road for a few kilometres til the end of the tarmac, turn right on to a dirt track, stay on it for about forty-five minutes – Gufgaduud. Go another fifteen minutes approx. – like a ghost village.'…

In the ghoulish manner of journalists on the hunt for the most striking   10
pictures, my cameraman… and I tramped from one hut to another. What might have appalled us when we'd started our trip just a few days before no longer impressed us much. The search for the shocking

▶

is like the craving for a drug: you require heavier and more frequent doses the longer you're at it. Pictures that stun the editors one day are written off as the same old stuff the next. This sounds callous, but it is just a fact of life. It's how we collect and compile the images that so move people in the comfort of their sitting rooms back home.   15

There was Amina Abdirahman, who had gone out that morning in search of wild, edible roots, leaving her two young girls lying on the   20
dirt floor of their hut. They had been sick for days, and were reaching the final, enervating stages of terminal hunger. Habiba was ten years old and her sister, Ayaan, was nine. By the time Amina returned, she had only one daughter. Habiba had died. No rage, no whimpering, just a passing away – that simple, frictionless, motionless deliverance   25
from a state of half-life to death itself. It was, as I said at the time in my dispatch, a vision of 'famine away from the headlines, a famine of quiet suffering and lonely death'.

There was the old woman who lay in her hut, abandoned by relations who were too weak to carry her on their journey to find food. It was   30
the smell that drew me to her doorway: the smell of decaying flesh. Where her shinbone should have been there was a festering wound the size of my hand. She'd been shot in the leg as the retreating army of the deposed dictator took revenge on whoever it found in its way. The shattered leg had fused into the gentle V-shape of a boomerang. It was 35
rotting; she was rotting. You could see it in her sick, yellow eyes and smell it in the putrid air she recycled with every struggling breath she took.

And then there was the face I will never forget.

My reaction to everyone else I met that day was a mixture of pity   40
and revulsion. Yes, revulsion. The degeneration of the human body, sucked of its natural vitality by the twin evils of hunger and disease, is a disgusting thing. We never say so in our TV reports. It's a taboo that has yet to be breached. To be in a feeding centre is to hear and smell the excretion of fluids by people who are beyond controlling their   45
bodily functions. To be in a feeding centre is surreptitiously to wipe your hands on the back of your trousers after you've held the clammy palm of a mother who has just cleaned vomit from her child's mouth.

There's pity, too, because even in this state of utter despair they aspire to a dignity that is almost impossible to achieve. An old woman   50
will cover her shrivelled body with a soiled cloth as your gaze turns towards her. Or the old and dying man who keeps his hoe next to the mat with which, one day soon, they will shroud his corpse, as if he means to go out and till the soil once all this is over.

I saw that face for only a few seconds, a fleeting meeting of eyes   55
before the face turned away, as its owner retreated into the darkness of another hut. In those brief moments there had been a smile, not from me, but from the face. It was not a smile of greeting, it was not a smile of joy – how could it be? – but it was a smile nonetheless. It touched me in a way I could not explain. It moved me in a way that   60
went beyond pity or revulsion.

What was it about that smile? I had to find out. I urged my translator to ask the man why he had smiled. He came back with an answer.

revulsion Disgust.

surreptitiously Secretly.

inured Hardened.

▶ The civil war in Somalia began in 1991.

'It's just that he was embarrassed to be found in this condition,' the translator explained. And then it clicked. That's what the smile had been about. It was the feeble smile that goes with apology, the kind of smile you might give if you felt you had done something wrong. 65

Normally inured to stories of suffering, accustomed to the evidence of deprivation, I was unsettled by this one smile in a way I had never been before. There is an unwritten code between the journalist and his subjects in these situations. The journalist observes, the subject is observed. The journalist is active, the subject is passive. But this smile had turned the tables on that tacit agreement. Without uttering a single word, the man had posed a question that cut to the heart of the relationship between me and him, between us and them, between the rich world and the poor world. If he was embarrassed to be found weakened by hunger and ground down by conflict, how should I feel to be standing there so strong and confident? 70 75

I resolved there and then that I would write the story of Gufgaduud with all the power and purpose I could muster. It seemed at the time, and still does, the only adequate answer a reporter can give to the man's question. 80

I have one regret about that brief encounter in Gufgaduud. Having searched through my notes and studied the dispatch that the BBC broadcast, I see that I never found out what the man's name was. Yet meeting him was a seminal moment in the gradual collection of experiences we call context. Facts and figures are the easy part of journalism. Knowing where they sit in the great scheme of things is much harder. So, my nameless friend, if you are still alive, I owe you one. 85 90

▲ BBC newscaster George Alagiah

ACTIVITY 9   **AO3**   **SKILLS** CRITICAL THINKING, ANALYSIS, INTERPRETATION, DECISION MAKING

COMPARING TEXTS

This is the type of question you will have to answer when tackling Question 7 of Paper 1 Section A. It carries a large number of the marks for the section in the exam (15 marks out of 40).

1 Compare how the writers of Text One and Text Two convey their ideas and experiences. Support your answer with examples from **both** texts.   **(15 marks)**

Read the information in the box in the margin, then copy and complete the table to help you plan your answer.

▼ METHOD/ TECHNIQUE	▼ MONGOLIA	▼ SOMALIA	▼ COMPARISON
Type of detail or incident	Strange, odd or comical Example:	Distressing Example:	They are describing very different types of…
Communication of thoughts and attitudes	In describing the strange customs, his tone is… Example:	By focusing on the sad fates of individuals, he… Example:	
Language			

HINT

What particular effects do different writers use to interest the reader? For example, the use of emotive description in *A Passage to Africa* and the use of dramatic words and comic situations in *In the Empire of Genghis Khan*.

NEWSPAPER AND MAGAZINE ARTICLES

Reading newspapers or magazines regularly will not only improve your reading and writing skills; it will also steadily increase your general knowledge and understanding of current affairs. Many newspapers and magazines now exist in online versions, which makes them much easier to access.

Articles come in various types and lengths. They can be about anything of general current interest, from politics and economics to shopping and education. Articles may or may not express strong views or come to definite conclusions about the topic, but they usually inform you of developments, make you aware of things of interest and warn you of dangers. The following articles do express opinions meaning that they are known as 'opinion pieces'. In opinion pieces, it is particularly important that the views are well argued and backed up by evidence.

When you read the following extracts, or any newspaper or magazine articles, think about:

- what the writer is saying
- the aims of the writer
- how the writer achieves these aims
- how successful the writer has been.

Find some examples from the text as evidence for your points.

▲ Changing social habits are a fertile subject for writers.

> reversion Returning to something.

▼ 'SOCIAL MEDIA ADDICTION IS A BIGGER PROBLEM THAN YOU THINK' BY MIKE ELGAN FOR *COMPUTER WORLD*

Social networks are massively addictive. Most people I know check and interact on social sites constantly throughout the day. And they have no idea how much actual time they spend on social media.

If you're a social media addict, and your addiction is getting worse, there's a reason for that: Most of the major social network companies, as well as social content creators, are working hard every day to make their networks so addictive that you can't resist them.

Cornell Information Science published research earlier this month that looked at (among other things) the difficulty some people have in quitting Facebook and other social networks. They even have a label for the failure to quit: 'social media reversion.'

The study is interesting because they revealed the difficulty people have quitting Facebook because of addiction. Participants intended to quit, wanted to quit and believed they *could* quit (for 99 days), but many couldn't make more than a few days.

The addictive aspect of social networking is associated with FOMO – fear of missing out. Everyone is on Facebook. They're posting things, sharing news and content and talking to each other 24/7.

The network effect itself is addicting, according to Instagram software engineer Greg Hochmuth, 'A network effect is the idea that any network becomes more valuable as more people connect to that network. The phone system is the best example of this phenomenon – you have to have a phone because everybody else has a phone.

In the world of social networking, Facebook benefits most from network effect. Facebook happened to be the top social network when social networking busted out as a mainstream activity. Now, everybody's on Facebook because everybody's on Facebook. And even people who don't like the social network use it anyway, because that's where their family, friends and colleagues are – and because of addiction.

The contribution of network effect to the addictive quality of web sites is accidental. But social sites are also addictive by design.

HINT

When you are thinking about structure, look at the paragraphs and try to say what the main idea is for each one. For example, in paragraph 1, it is that social media are addictive; in paragraph 2, it is that social media companies deliberately make their social networks addictive. Then ask yourself why some paragraphs are longer and where the writer brings in evidence. Finally, consider why the last paragraph is so short.

ACTIVITY 10   **A01**   **A02**   SKILLS ▶ CRITICAL THINKING, INTERPRETATION

▼ UNDERSTANDING THE TEXT

Before answering the following questions, make sure that you have taken in the key points from the text. Think about:

- the use of detail (e.g. names and facts)
- the impact of the headline
- the problems that are mentioned
- the style and layout of the text.

1 How, according to Elgan, are social networks addictive?
2 How does he convey his own attitude to the problem?
3 How does he structure his ideas in this extract?

▼ 'ARE HUMANS DEFINITELY CAUSING GLOBAL WARMING?' FROM *THE GUARDIAN*

Just as the world's most respected scientific bodies have confirmed that world is getting hotter, they have also stated that there is strong evidence that humans are driving the warming. The 2005 joint statement from the national academies of Brazil, Canada, China, France, Germany, India, Italy, Japan, Russia, the UK and the US said:

"It is likely that most of the warming in recent decades can be attributed to human activities."

Countless more recent statements and reports from the world's leading scientific bodies have said the same thing. For example, a 2010 summary of climate science by the Royal Society stated that:

"There is strong evidence that the warming of the Earth over the last half-century has been caused largely by human activity, such as the burning of fossil fuels and changes in land use, including agriculture and deforestation."

The idea that humans could change the planet's climate may be counter-intuitive, but the basic science is well understood. Each year, human activity causes billions of tonnes of greenhouse gases to be released into the atmosphere. As scientists have known for decades, these gases capture heat that would otherwise escape to space – the equivalent of wrapping the planet in an invisible blanket.

Of course, the planet's climate has always been in flux thanks to "natural" factors such as changes in solar or volcanic activity, or cycles relating the Earth's orbit around the sun. According to the scientific literature, however, the warming recorded to date matches the pattern of warming we would expect from a build up of greenhouse gas in the atmosphere – not the warming we would expect from other possible causes.

Now re-read the article on page 75, thinking about:

- the way that quotations are used
- how the writer tries to make their own views impossible to argue against
- the use of scientific and other technical language
- the kinds of evidence that the writer relies on to support the argument.

ACTIVITY 11 | **AO3** | SKILLS | CRITICAL THINKING, ANALYSIS, INTERPRETATION, DECISION MAKING

▼ COMPARATIVE QUESTION

Studying the articles on pages 74–75 together, what do you learn about the writers' views on their chosen topic, the evidence that they are quoting and the seriousness of the way in which they are responding to it? Explain how each of the writers uses language to communicate their views.

Before answering the question, look back at a few of the tables that you have used in previous activities, then make one of your own to help you. It might look like this:

	▼ VIEW/OPINION	▼ EVIDENCE	▼ TONE/MOOD
Social media			
Climate change			

REVIEWS

Reviews play an important part in the relationship between an artistic product and the public. A series of good reviews can help a book, video game, television series or music album to succeed. A professional review performs several functions, such as:

- informing the reader about the product and its intended audience
- engaging the reader by the quality of the writing
- offering a series of critical judgements on aspects of the product
- making a recommendation as to whether the work is worth seeing, reading, hearing or buying.

immersive Involving.

epochal Helping to define a new era.

incandescent Filled with light from within.

▼ FROM A REVIEW OF *STAR WARS: EPISODE VII* BY MARK KERMODE IN *THE GUARDIAN*

The action takes place some years after the events of *Return of the Jedi*, and involves scavenger Rey (Daisy Ridley) teaming up with renegade 'First Order' Stormtrooper Finn (John Boyega) and globular droid BB-8. The opening scroll sets up an ongoing battle between the forces of good and evil and lays the groundwork for a quasi-mythical quest that will reunite friends old and new, and allow a grizzled Harrison Ford to deliver the line: 'Chewie, we're home…'

That sense of coming home runs throughout *The Force Awakens*, director JJ Abrams taking the series back to its roots while giving it a rocket-fuelled, 21st-century twist… The film feels very physical, scenes of dog-fighting TIE fighters and a relaunched Millennium Falcon crashing through trees possessing the kind of heft so sorely lacking from George Lucas's over-digitised prequels. The battle scenes are breathtakingly immersive…but also impressively joyous – the sight of a fleet of X-wings hurtling toward us over watery terrain brought a lump to my throat and a tear to my eye – just one of several occasions when I found myself welling up with unexpected emotion…

Having co-written the series's previous high-water mark, *The Empire Strikes Back*, Lawrence Kasdan here shares credits with Abrams and Michael Arndt on a screenplay… which subtly realigns its gender dynamics with Rey's proudly punchy, post-Hunger Games heroine. The spectre of Vader may live on in Adam Driver's Kylo Ren, but it's Rey in whom the film's true force resides, likeable newcomer Daisy Ridley carrying the heavily-mantled weight of the new series with aplomb. Plaudits, too, to John Boyega, who brings credibility and humour to the almost accidentally heroic role of Finn…

What's most striking about *Star Wars: The Force Awakens* is the fact that it has real heart and soul… Abrams breathes new life into Lucas's epochal creations in a manner that deftly looks back to the future. And it's a future that works. Watching the film in a packed auditorium with an audience almost incandescent with expectation, I found myself listening to a chorus of spontaneous gasps, cheers, laughs, whoops and even occasional cries of anguish.

What's really surprising is that many of them were coming from me.

ACTIVITY 12   **A01**   SKILLS ▶ CRITICAL THINKING, ANALYSIS, INTERPRETATION

▼ LANGUAGE USED IN REVIEWS

Copy and complete the following table, finding examples of language used in the review that correspond with the categories in the first column. Then, using your examples, answer the questions.

▼ POSITIVE COMMENTS ABOUT…	▼ EXAMPLES FROM THE TEXT
the director/screenplay	
the audience reaction	
the acting	

▶ Explain two aspects of the film that the writer finds engaging.

▶ How does the writer build up or communicate his positive feelings about the film?

REFERENCE BOOKS AND WEBSITES

Reference books and websites are designed to be consulted, not read all the way through. They usually consist of a large number of articles, sometimes on a great variety of topics. Some reference books offer an overview of all knowledge, such as the famous *Encyclopaedia Britannica*. Other reference books have a much more specialised range – there are thousands of reference books covering every academic discipline and field of knowledge.

Read the following extracts from *Encyclopaedia Britannica*, considering how the writing style differs from the other types of non-fiction writing that you have encountered so far.

▼ 'ACQUISITION AND RECORDING OF INFORMATION IN DIGITAL FORM' FROM *ENCYCLOPAEDIA BRITANNICA*

The versatility of modern information systems stems from their ability to represent information electronically as digital signals and to manipulate it automatically at exceedingly high speeds. Information is stored in binary devices, which are the basic components of digital technology. Because these devices exist only in one of two states, information is represented in them either as the absence or the presence of energy (electric pulse). The two states of binary devices are conveniently designated by the binary digits, or bits, zero (0) and one (1).

▼ 'RAP' FROM *ENCYCLOPAEDIA BRITANNICA*

Rap, a musical style in which rhythmic and/or rhyming speech is chanted ('rapped') to musical accompaniment. This backing music, which can include digital sampling (music and sounds extracted from other recordings), is also called hip-hop, the name used to refer to a broader cultural movement that includes rap, deejaying (turntable manipulation), graffiti painting, and break dancing. Rap, which originated in African American communities in New York City, came to national prominence with the Sugar Hill Gang's 'Rapper's Delight' (1979). Rap's early stars included Grandmaster Flash and the Furious Five, Run-D.M.C., LL Cool J, Public Enemy (who espoused a radical political message), and the Beastie Boys. The late 1980s saw the advent of 'gangsta rap,' with lyrics that were often misogynistic or that glamorized violence and drug dealing. Later stars include Diddy, Snoop Dogg, Jay-Z, OutKast, Eminem, Kanye West, and Lil Wayne.

ACTIVITY 13 | **AO1** | **SKILLS** CRITICAL THINKING, ANALYSIS, INTERPRETATION

▼ CHARACTERISTICS OF REFERENCE WRITING

KEY POINT

Some reference works can be consulted by those with no subject knowledge at all. Others can be pitched at a higher level.

Characteristics of this kind of reference writing include those listed in the first column of the table below. Copy and complete the table and find another feature of your own.

▼ FEATURES	▼ EXAMPLES	▼ COMMENT ON EFFECT
A large amount of factual information		
Clusters of words from a specialised branch of knowledge		
A lack of emotive vocabulary		
Most sentences are complete statements		

LEARNING OBJECTIVES

This lesson will help you to:

- identify the writer's perspective
- understand how a writer communicates their perspective to a reader.

IDENTIFYING THE WRITER'S PERSPECTIVE

A writer's perspective is their point of view, or the angle from which they see the subject matter. Even the most purely informative articles, which show no personal angle at all, can be said to have a point of view, even if that point of view is objective or unbiased.

Many articles or pieces of writing that claim to be objective are not always unbiased, because everyone brings a personal, societal or national bias to bear on what they write. An article written for an encyclopaedia in the United States of America will be written from an American perspective, which means that the article may be different to one written in China, even though it is apparently unbiased. If the subject of the writing is politics, history or culture, national perspectives will often be very different. For example, in the travel writing extract on page 69, Stanley Stewart writes from the perspective of a curious British traveller, not from that of a native Mongolian. This fact means that his account of the wedding is entirely different from that of a native Mongolian.

There are many different types of perspective. The writer's origin in a particular community or ethnic group may give them a particular perspective. Having a certain job or occupation might also influence their perspective – you could say they write from the perspective of an economist, a student, a singer, and so on. Martin Luther King's famous speech, 'I have a dream…' is written from the point of view of a black American minister who has become the voice of a whole people.

DIFFERENCES IN PERSPECTIVE

In comparison, one of the commonest reasons for difference in perspective is the fact that people interact with others whom they do not necessarily understand. This may not be because of what they do or where they come from, but simply because people cannot know exactly what is going on in another person's thoughts. This is shown by the following accounts of the same event.

▼ DEV'S ACCOUNT

It was awful. He hit me hard in the face and all his friends laughed at me when I started to cry. I was just walking past and was trying to be helpful by pointing out that the bell had gone. They always laugh at me in the corridor and I thought if I tried to help they would like me more. I don't understand what is going on.

▼ DANIL'S ACCOUNT

This has nothing to do with my friends. They didn't even realise what had happened until after I hit him. I think they were laughing at a joke Adesh had made. I did punch him, but that was because he told me I was going to be late with this smirk on his face like he was going to tell the teacher. I have never really seen him before and I thought he was trying to show me up in front of my friends.

ACTIVITY 1 **AO1** SKILLS PROBLEM SOLVING, ANALYSIS, CREATIVITY

▼ THINKING ABOUT PERSPECTIVE

Neither Dev's nor Danil's account of the same incident is false, but the writer of each version of events has a different perspective.

1 Describe what happened in the corridor.

2 What might have influenced the two boys to view the events in such different ways? Write down your ideas.

3 Dev's perspective is that he has been bullied by this group for a long time. Write a sentence explaining Danil's perspective on Dev. Why is it important to have heard Danil's perspective?

DIFFERENT ATTITUDES

KEY POINT

Attitude affects language. When you read extracts, think about how the writer uses language to communicate certain things to you and what this reveals about the writer's purpose and personality.

Another way of thinking about perspectives is to think of the writer in relation to two or more groups of people with different attitudes – one group which shares their views and another group, or other groups, which do not share these views. Ask yourself which groups would agree with a particular idea or argument and which would disagree. For example, one group might be more conservative (resistant to change), while another group might be more progressive (looking for positive change). Another common opposition is that between the authoritarian or restrictive and the liberal or tolerant. Often, the older generation is seen as being authoritarian and young people are considered to be more liberal.

ACTIVITY 2 **AO1** SKILLS PROBLEM SOLVING, INNOVATION, EMPATHY

▼ DIFFERING ATTITUDES

Think of other ways in which people can be divided into groups whose attitudes are often different from each other.

Are these issues strictly defined so a person can only be in one group or the other? Or are some of them more complicated so that there is some overlap between them and some people can be placed more in between the groups?

▲ Kickz is a youth football programme in the UK.

ACTIVITY 3 · **A01** · SKILLS ▸ CRITICAL THINKING, ANALYSIS, INTERPRETATION

▼ IDENTIFYING A WRITER'S PURPOSE

Read the following extracts. Identify the writer's purpose, making a note of the language choice and other writing techniques that allow you to identify the purpose. Then copy and complete the table, re-reading the extracts to find more examples to back up your ideas.

EXTRACT A

Kickz is a national programme, funded by the Premier League and Metropolitan Police, that uses football to work with young people at risk of offending in deprived areas. Arsenal FC delivers Kickz in Elthorne Park, getting kids off the street in the evening and playing football. The project has helped to transform the local area: there has been a reduction of 66% in youth crime within a one-mile radius of the project since it started.

… The projects are targeted at neighbourhoods with high levels of antisocial behaviour and crime… The sessions mostly involve football coaching, but they also provide coaching in other sports, such as basketball, and workshops on issues including drug awareness, healthy eating, volunteering, careers and weapons.

▶

the Premier League The highest league of English football.

Arsenal FC A Premier League football team based in London.

the Grand National A famous British horse race over large jumps.

Eagle A British children's comic.

the Mekon A character in Eagle.

EXTRACT B

... If you saw your neighbour whipping a dog, you'd be on the phone to the police immediately, right? Of course, anyone with a shred of decency condemns hurting animals. Yet, inexplicably, some still turn a blind eye to the cruelty to horses during the Grand National, in which riders are required to carry a whip. Nearly every year, racehorses sustain injuries. Many have paid with their lives.

▲ Horse racing is a popular pastime across the world, but is it cruel?

EXTRACT C

Daddy says I have to eat to get well, even if it hurts. The nurse smiles at me when she brings the jam sandwiches. She smiles differently at the other nurses, and when she smiles at sister it is different again. I wish there were bubbles coming out of her head with words, like in Eagle... Thought bubbles would be a useful invention in real life. When you wake in the night there are strange slapping and scraping noises on the marble, and sometimes screams, but I close my eyes, and pretend I'm at home, and think of my presents, and imagine the Mekon in his bubble, and I do not cry, Daddy, I do not, I do not.

	▼ A	▼ B	▼ C
What attitude does the writer express?			
What is the likely age group of the writer?			
Why do you think the writer wrote the piece?			
What other types of people might share the attitude of each writer?			
What have you noticed about the language used in each extract?			

▶ **How is the language of these extracts influenced by the writer's perspective? You could draw another table to help you answer this question, and remember to include examples.**

LEARNING OBJECTIVES

This lesson will help you to:
- identify the text's audience and understand the purpose.

AUDIENCE AND PURPOSE

It is not always easy to appreciate a text unless you understand its purpose and who it was written for. Sometimes this is not difficult, such as when the reader is a member of the writer's intended audience. If you were a child born in Ghana or Jamaica, then the stories of Anansi the spider would be intended for you and there would be no additional context to learn about. However, in other cases, you may need some background knowledge: for example, Martin Luther King's speech, 'I have a dream...', does not mean all that it should if its reader is ignorant of the history and culture of the USA.

HINT

Writers do not only write **from** a particular perspective. They also write with a particular '**view**' in front of them, which includes their purpose and audience, meaning that these three aspects are closely connected.

When you are reading, you should try to bear in mind the audience known as 'the general reader' or 'the general public'. These phrases are used to indicate that all kinds of people may want to read a book about an expedition to the Himalayas or up the River Amazon, and that you do not need to have any particular interests to find the book interesting. However, it would also be reasonable to suggest that such books will appeal to readers interested in adventurous travel. This group will cross boundaries of age, gender, race, and so on, as it is defined by interest only, although it may include more of one section of the population than another.

▶ Do a survey of people you know and find out if, for example, outdoor sports books such as Ellen MacArthur's autobiography might appeal more to male readers than female, or more to younger readers than older ones. You could try this on other texts and genres.

ACTIVITY 1   A01   SKILLS ▷ CRITICAL THINKING, ANALYSIS, REASONING

▼ IDENTIFYING AUDIENCE AND PURPOSE

As you work through this book, you will read a wide range of texts written for different audiences and for very different reasons. The following table will help you to compare some of the passages that you have already encountered between pages 58 and 79. Copy and complete it as best you can.

▼ TEXT	▼ AUDIENCE	▼ PURPOSE
The Diary of a Young Girl	Herself; perhaps also for others.	To confide her thoughts with an imaginary friend.
Ellen MacArthur's autobiography	People interested in ocean yachting and racing or in tough sporting exploits.	
In the Empire of Genghis Khan		
Martin Luther King's 'I have a dream...' speech		

Now do a similar exercise on some of the passages in the Unseen Texts section of this chapter.

▼ TEXT	▼ AUDIENCE	▼ PURPOSE
The Great Railway Bazaar	Those interested in travel writing; those interested in Asia; those interested in railways and trains.	To communicate the author's experiences in Myanmar (Burma).
'Why all this selfie obsession?'	Readers of *The Guardian*; teenagers; those interested in technology and social trends.	
'My family moved from Pakistan...'		

AUDIENCE, PURPOSE AND LANGUAGE

KEY POINT

Audience is always relevant to a text. The language is affected by the audience and vice versa.

Get into the habit of thinking about audience, purpose and language use whenever you read a text. Think about the relationship between these three aspects of the text. This skill will help you in the exam as well as in everyday life.

A writer's purpose has a good deal to do with their audience: a writer will never write for everyone. A writer's choice of language is also affected by both. Suppose that you were writing a story about a crime for a seven-year-old child. You would choose appropriate language for the reader, considering their age or level of understanding and the subject matter. Your choices would be very different if you had to write a script for a stand-up comedian.

ACTIVITY 2 | **A01** | **A02** | **SKILLS** CRITICAL THINKING, ANALYSIS, REASONING

▼ CHOOSING LANGUAGE FOR AN AUDIENCE AND A PURPOSE

Copy and complete the following table with some of the ways in which language is affected by audience and purpose. Add more entries of your own to the table. The more you think about these aspects of a text, the better you will understand them.

▼ TEXT	▼ AUDIENCE	▼ PURPOSE	▼ LANGUAGE
Martin Luther King's 'I have a dream...' speech (see page 63)	The people at the rally for black civil rights.		
Review of *Gravity* (see page 134)	Film fans; readers interested in space or space travel.		
A Passage to Africa (see pages 70–72)			
The School Food Plan (see page 133)			
The Men Who Stare at Goats (see page 135)			

Re-read the extract from *The Diary of a Young Girl* (page 65) and answer the following question:

▶ **In what ways is the language of this passage affected by its audience and purpose?**

LEARNING OBJECTIVES

This lesson will help you to:

- understand how writers use their expertise with language to create a range of varied effects.

LANGUAGE FOR DIFFERENT EFFECTS

Many writers think about their potential readers when they are writing. You have already looked at **purpose** and **perspective**, and now you are going to build on this by considering more of the effects that writers can achieve with their choice of words, phrases and sentences. Some of the examples in this section will be taken from the passages you have already looked at.

GETTING CLOSE TO THE READER

Some writers want to create a close relationship with their readers, while others do not. In autobiographies, writers may share very private thoughts and deal with difficult emotions. They can use chatty or colloquial speech if they feel that that is the best way to engage with their readers. Diaries can be good examples of this, whether their authors are writing only for themselves or for others.

EMOTIVE LANGUAGE

In *A Passage to Africa*, George Alagiah wants to shock the reader and to communicate the suffering that he sees in the villages that he visits. He wants you to see in your mind's eye the things he writes about.

Of the writers that you have read so far, which other writers have used emotive language?

ACTIVITY 1   A02   SKILLS   CRITICAL THINKING, ANALYSIS, REASONING

▼ THINKING ABOUT PURPOSE AND EFFECT

Read the following quotations, taken from passages in this book, then copy and complete the table.

▼ QUOTATION	▼ LANGUAGE	▼ PURPOSE	▼ EFFECT
'As a little boy in the 70s, mine was an insular existence, enclosed within the Pakistani bubble of Bury Park and largely unaware that any other world existed. I was a teenager in the 80s, a decade of frustration as I realised I was different from my white friends who were allowed to have girlfriends and parties and free will.'	Narrative, with some emotive adjectives.	To show how cultures and experiences differ.	You learn from this anecdote how the author had a different childhood and teenage years to his peers.
'I would like to claim an immediate fury which was followed by the noble determination to break the restricting tradition. But the truth is, my first reaction was one of disappointment. I'd pictured myself, dressed in a neat blue serge suit, my money changer swinging jauntily at my waist.'	Emotive, focused on feelings.		
'Kickz is a national initiative that uses football to engage 12- to 18-year-olds in deprived areas. The projects are targeted at neighbourhoods with high levels of antisocial behaviour and crime. Kickz is delivered on three or more evenings a week.'	Explanatory (or expository).		

▶

▼ QUOTATION	▼ LANGUAGE	▼ PURPOSE	▼ EFFECT
'He looks past his awards to the wall itself. There is something he feels he needs to do even though the thought of it frightens him. He thinks about the choice he has to make. He can stay in his office or he can go into the next office. That is his choice. And he has made it.'	Narrative.		
'All these unhappy manifestations of teenagehood can happen at a school disco, too, but at least your parents haven't blown their wages for it to happen, you don't consider it the most significant night of your life to date, and it doesn't have the power to ruin your summer.'	Thoughts and opinions.		
'Because we are all together, united for the cause of education. And if we want to achieve our goal, then let us empower ourselves with the weapon of knowledge and let us shield ourselves with unity and togetherness.'	Emotive, using sensational language and personal pronouns 'we' and 'us'.		
'As my raft glides through the smooth mocha current, I'm enveloped in the surreal mist of a jungle paradise. I work the paddle silently, steering past hanging vines.'	Vividly descriptive.		

ACTIVITY 2 · A02 · SKILLS · CRITICAL THINKING, ANALYSIS, INTERPRETATION

▼ THINKING ABOUT EFFECT AND LANGUAGE

Now think about this the other way around. What effect does the writer want to achieve with their choice of language? Copy and complete the following table, looking through passages in this book for examples of each purpose.

▼ PURPOSE	▼ LANGUAGE	▼ EXAMPLE	▼ EFFECT
To make the reader imagine something.	Vividly descriptive.	*A Passage to Africa*, lines…	You imagine the scene or person described.
To direct the reader's emotions.	Emotive, using the language of the emotions.		
To be friendly to the reader.	Chatty.		
To impress the reader with the writer's style.			
To amuse.	Humourous, jokey, playful.		
To inform.			
To argue.			
To create suspense.	Short sentences with mini-cliffhangers.	'And then the trouble began.'	

KEY POINT

The skilled writer can create a wide range of effects on the reader because they have an excellent command of the language.

LANGUAGE FOR PATTERN AND EFFECT

A lot of writing is concerned at least partly with creating patterns and certain effects within those patterns.

ACTIVITY 3 **AO2** **SKILLS** CRITICAL THINKING, ANALYSIS, INTERPRETATION

▼ SIMPLE DESCRIPTIONS DESCRIBING THE AUTHOR'S CHOICE OF LANGUAGE

It is important that you can use the correct terminology when commenting on and describing language use.

1 Copy and complete this table.

▼ WRITER	▼ SUBJECT	▼ PHRASE	▼ TYPE OF LANGUAGE	▼ EFFECT
Paul Rosolie	The Amazon	'The once-untouched wilderness is hemorrhaging timber, gold, and wildlife…'	Metaphor and personification.	The description is more vivid, suggesting that the place has life of its own.

2 Copy and complete the following table by finding examples of each technique and commenting on their effects.

	▼ TECHNIQUE	▼ EXAMPLE	▼ EFFECT
H	Hyperbole or exaggeration		
E	Emotive language		
R	Register		
C	Contrast		
R	Repetition		
A	Alliteration and assonance		
S	Structure		
H	Humour		
F	Figurative language (e.g. similes)		
A	Antithesis		
C	Contrast		
T	Tripling		
O	Onomatopoeia		
R	Rhetorical questions (and other rhetorical devices)		
S	Short sentences or paragraphs		
L	Lists		

DESCRIPTORS FOR LANGUAGE

Many students find it difficult to think of ways to describe the effects of language and tend to overuse words like 'descriptive' when it is not strictly accurate, or rely on vague phrases such as 'draws the reader in'. Try using some of the following alternatives.

KEY POINT

Learning the technical terms for descriptive effects will allow you to express yourself more precisely in your analysis of writing.

Alliteration and assonance	Makes language more emphatic/more rhythmic/more memorable.
Onomatopoeia	Makes phrases more vivid and powerful.
Descriptive phrasing	Makes the reader imagine the scene.
Verbs of motion and action	Make the language more dynamic and energetic.
Wordplay, exaggeration	Makes writing light-hearted, amusing.
Abstract nouns	Make writing more intellectual or more to do with ideas.
Repetition	Emphasises a particular point or word.
A mixture of techniques	Makes language varied or lively.

Other techniques include:

- anaphora
- balanced phrases
- allusions
- juxtaposition.

Look these technical terms up in a dictionary and see if you can find examples in the texts in this book.

USING SENTENCE TYPES FOR EFFECT

There are two obvious ways of classifying sentence types: by their function and by their grammatical complexity.

SENTENCE FUNCTION

Statements	Dominate informative writing and narrative in stories.
Questions	Common in dialogue and in explorative articles. They can be used in speeches to engage the audience, particularly in the form of rhetorical questions.
Exclamations	Mainly found in dialogue, but also in first-person accounts of adventures, real-life experiences and so on.
Commands	Usually found in dialogue and instructions. They use the imperative form of the verb (for example, 'Come on, let's move').
Wishes	Expressions of thoughts and feelings often found in diaries, letters and dialogue (for example, 'If only I hadn't done that').

HINT

Help yourself to learn these different types of sentence by thinking of and writing an example of each one.

SENTENCE COMPLEXITY

Simple sentences	Consist of only one main clause.
Compound sentences	Two or more main clauses joined by 'and', 'but', 'so' or 'or'.
Complex sentences	Contain at least one subordinate clause.
Incomplete sentences	Do not have a complete main clause; used frequently in conversation and in writing for effect or emphasis or in one-word sentences such as, 'He stopped. Silence.'

LEARNING OBJECTIVES

This lesson will help you to:

- distinguish between these three types of writing
- distinguish facts from opinions.

FACT, OPINION AND EXPERT ADVICE

Often, the purpose of a text is to inform its audience about something. You have come across several texts with the purpose of informing readers about something, using a mixture of three main types of writing: description, reporting or narrative, and explanation. All of these are types of factual writing.

ACTIVITY 1 **A01** SKILLS CRITICAL THINKING, ANALYSIS

▼ TYPES OF FACTUAL WRITING

Look through this book to find examples of these different types of writing, then copy and complete the following table.

▼ TYPE	▼ QUOTATION FROM TEXT	▼ PAGE
Description		
Reporting or narrative		
Explanation		

FACTS AND OPINION

▲ 'The best sport in the world' Is this a fact or an opinion?

As you have already seen, non-fiction texts often include people's opinions and beliefs, even if they may not be factually true. This includes:

- opinions as statements of belief, such as, 'I think football is the best sport in the world'
- opinions stated as fact such as 'Football is the best sport in the world'.

Be careful when someone states an opinion or belief as though it is a fact. For example, the second statement about football has the form of a factual statement, but it is still really just a statement of belief about football. People often make statements of belief as though they are facts, so you should always ask questions of what you read and analyse what people write as facts when they may in fact be statements of belief.

For example, advertisers may state opinion as fact. Washing products may be advertised as making clothes whiter than other brands of washing detergent, but it is unlikely that these statements can be said to be 'facts'.

In comparison, an argument is an opinion or set of opinions backed up by reasons and evidence. It would be easy to express an opinion that you are the President of the United States, but hard to construct an argument that proves that you are the President of the United States.

▶ Over a day or two, write down a collection of opinions stated as facts that you hear or see in the media, among your friends and family or in advertisements.

ACTIVITY 2 | A01 | SKILLS PROBLEM SOLVING

▼ FACT, OPINION OR ARGUMENT?

Read the following extracts, then decide whether they are fact, opinion, argument, or opinion presented as fact.

'It's a fact that boys are stronger than girls.'

'Everyone knows that Britain will be better off outside the European Union. I don't know anyone who thinks otherwise.'

'We should encourage immigration into this country for three reasons: it supplies us with more skills, it helps us to understand other cultures and it is morally a good thing to do.'

'The USA is more powerful in military terms than Russia.'

'I think that all religions are equally valid: I don't know about all of them, but they all have their good points and their less good points.'

KEY POINT

You need to know how to recognise writing that states facts and then question whether the use of the factual form is justified.

ADVICE

Non-fiction texts can contain examples of advice. For example, a book review may advise you to read or not to read a particular book. An online article may advise you how to save money, how to prepare for a hot summer, or recommend places to visit. An 'agony aunt' in a magazine could suggest ways of coping with problems in a personal relationship.

Generally speaking, people appreciate advice more if it comes from someone who knows what they are talking about: an expert. Advice is linked to persuasive writing, since it tries to influence the person being advised.

coolest The expert makes the advice seem more attractive by associating the recommended course of action with 'the coolest' people.

you can do it The tone is encouraging.

set... stick... try... keep These are imperatives: they are all commands. What effect does this have?

get some support Advice often suggests how to get more support and advice.

avoid the shops Advice is often both positive and negative ('dos and don'ts'); for example, 'avoid the shops' is a 'don't'.

Dear Billy,

Your letter shows you really want to give up smoking and that is the first step to making it happen. You won't be alone; all the coolest people are giving it up now.

Make no mistake, it is difficult to stop – but you can do it. Lots of people have managed to kick the habit.

Here's how you start.

Make a plan.

1. Set a date for your last cigarette and stick to it!

2. Try to get some support from a friend or relative. It always helps to talk to someone about problems – a problem shared is a problem halved!

3. Keep busy to help take your mind off ciggies. Perhaps take up a new hobby or sport, like cycling.

4. Try to change your routine, and avoid the shops where you usually buy cigarettes.

5. Save up the money that you normally spend on cigarettes and buy something special for yourself with it.

Good luck – I hope it all goes well. Quitting smoking will make you feel a lot better and, with the exercise from your cycling, you should be able to wave stress goodbye!

All the best,

Nadiya

LEARNING OBJECTIVES

This lesson will help you to:
- understand what structure in writing is and how you can write about it.

THE STRUCTURE OF A TEXT

What do you understand is meant by the word 'structure'? Try writing down a short definition of 'structure' in relation to a piece of writing. You could use one of the extracts in this book or another text that you know.

Most people respond to a skilfully structured piece of writing without understanding exactly why. When analysing structure, then, you have to understand the purpose of a passage, which can only be done by careful reading. The next task is to see the structure within it that helps put the purpose into effect. You can then write about:

- the writer's intention in the text
- the structure that the writer has used to achieve that intention
- the effects of each part of the structure.

Many students find it difficult to analyse structure in writing, but the following techniques should help you.

- Think in terms of the beginning, middle and end of the text or extract. How are they different from each other?
- Look at the paragraphs and identify the content of each one. Then consider what the writer is doing with that content and why he or she chose to put the content in that order.
- Look at the way in which the writer uses the basic types of writing that you find in non-fiction:
  - description (of the setting or the appearance of people and objects)
  - narrative (what happened or is happening)
  - dialogue or speech (including talking to one self)
  - thoughts and feelings (when not in direct speech)
  - background information, facts, or explanation.

HINT

Look also at the relative sizes of the paragraphs. If they vary quite noticeably then there is probably a good reason for it (a short paragraph might be an effective opening or conclusion, or used for emphasis elsewhere)

SUBJECT VOCABULARY

setting the place where something is or where something happens, and the general environment

---

ACTIVITY 1 **AO1** **AO2** **SKILLS** CRITICAL THINKING, ANALYSIS, INTERPRETATION, CREATIVITY

▼ IDENTIFYING A PASSAGE'S STRUCTURE

Read the following passage, using the techniques you have just learned to help you think about the structure of the passage.

▼ FROM *CIDER WITH ROSIE* BY LAURIE LEE

I was set down from the carrier's cart at the age of three; and there with a sense of bewilderment and terror my life in the village began.

The June grass, amongst which I stood, was taller than I was, and I wept. I had never been so close to grass before. It towered above me and all around me, each blade tattooed with tiger-skins of sunlight. It was knife-edged, dark, and a wicked green, thick as a forest and alive with grasshoppers that chirped and chattered and leapt through the air like monkeys.

▶

I was lost and didn't know where to move. A tropic heat oozed up from the ground, rank with sharp odours of roots and nettles. Snow-clouds of elder-blossom banked in the sky, showering upon me the fumes and flakes of their sweet and giddy suffocation. High overhead ran frenzied larks, screaming, as though the sky were tearing apart.

For the first time in my life I was out of the sight of humans. For the first time in my life I was alone in a world whose behaviour I could neither predict nor fathom: a world of birds that squealed, of plants that stank, of insects that sprang about without warning. I was lost and I did not expect to be found again. I put back my head and howled, and the sun hit me smartly on the face, like a bully.

► **Sum up, in three sentences, the beginning, middle and end of the extract. Use the third person ('he') in your summary. How is the first paragraph different from the others? Can you see a reason for this?**

► **Look again at the four paragraphs from _Cider with Rosie_ and write a line about the purpose or effect of each paragraph. Then explain why you think Lee chose to put the content in that order.**

► **Can you identify more structural features? Use the correct terminology.**

► **What do you think is the effect of structuring the passage in these four paragraphs? Choose the comment from the following list that you think is most useful and accurate, and fill in the blanks.**

   ■ The structure enables the writer to develop and _____ the narrator's feelings of _____ and _____ in slightly different ways _____.

   ■ The structure arranges the description of the setting and the narrator's _____ in a way that _____ the feeling to _____.

   ■ The structure gives the description a sense of _____ and _____.

It can also be useful to consider the types of writing that the writer is using, such as description, narrative and so on. For example, a passage with some description of the setting, or a character, followed by some narrative in which something happens. As soon as you notice these different types of writing, you should be able to say something about why they are there in the passage. Many students do not consciously register when a writer is using dialogue or telling them a character's thoughts, so if you do notice these things, you will give yourself an immediate advantage.

ACTIVITY 2   **A02**   **SKILLS** ▷ CRITICAL THINKING, INTERPRETATION

▼ IDENTIFYING DIFFERENT TYPES OF WRITING

Copy and complete the following table, using the analysis you have just made, to list four examples of different types of writing used by Lee in the passage that you have just read.

▼ TYPE OR FUNCTION	▼ QUOTATION	▼ EFFECT (OR PURPOSE)
Description		
Narrative		

LEARNING OBJECTIVES

This lesson will help you to:

- understand how to tackle Questions 1–6 on a pair of unseen texts.

UNSEEN TEXTS

The questions in Paper 1 Section A will be based on two non-fiction passages that you will not have seen before. Understanding and analysing these unseen texts is critical to your success in this part of the exam.

READING UNSEEN TEXTS

The first thing to do when faced with an unseen text is to read it and start thinking about what it is saying. Try not to be scared by the fact that you have never seen it before. By using the skills that you have learned by studying other texts, you should have all the tools you need to understand it and analyse it effectively.

When you have read the text, use the following questions to help you think about what you have read.

- What sort of text is it?
- What is the text about?
- Who is the intended audience for the text?
- Is the writer trying to make a particular point?
- What and linguistic techniques does the writer use?
- What effects do these techniques have?
- How does the text make you feel personally?

KEY POINT

These pages will help you to utilise what you have learned in analysing texts to answer questions 1–6 in the exam. Question 7 is a comparative question on the unseen texts and information on comparing texts can be found in the section on pages 100–123.

Simply by answering these questions, you will find that you are able to say a lot about the unseen text. You should spend a short time reading the text and getting a good understanding of it. This will then allow you to focus on answering the specifics in the exam questions.

For this section, you will use the passages from Malala Yousafzai's speech to the UN General Assembly on page 128 and *I Know Why the Caged Bird Sings* on page 129 as the unseen text.

| ACTIVITY 1 | A01 | A02 | SKILLS ▸ | CRITICAL THINKING, ANALYSIS, INTERPRETATION |

▼ UNDERSTANDING THE UNSEEN TEXTS

Read the passages from Malala Yousafzai's speech and *I Know Why the Caged Bird Sings*. Spend ten minutes quickly answering the questions from the list above. Discuss your answers with a partner.

QUESTIONS 1 AND 2

Questions 1 and 2 are comprehension questions to check your understanding of the first unseen text. They will ask you to find information from the text and to give an example of this. You only need to provide one example for each question; there are no extra marks for providing more.

EXAM-STYLE QUESTIONS

A01   **SKILLS ▸ INTERPRETATION**

Read Text One, from Malala Yousafzai's speech to the UN General Assembly, which focuses on the well-known campaigner's hopes for the future of education.

1 In lines 1–3 the writer explains the attack by the Taliban.
   State **one** thing that happened to the writer.   **(1 mark)**

2 In lines 8–34 the writer describes her wishes for the future.
   Identify **one** thing the writer hopes for.   **(1 mark)**

QUESTION 3

HINT

When answering, it is always better to explain a few techniques in detail rather than to list points without explaining them properly.

Question 3 is a longer question on the first unseen text. It focuses on the whole text and is worth 10 marks. It may ask you to consider the writer's impressions of the subject or to concentrate on the writer's thoughts and feelings.

You need to have an understanding of what the text is about and what the writer is saying. You should support your answer with short quotations from the text as evidence to back up your point. Point-Evidence-Explain (P-E-E) is a good model to use when answering this question.

You may need to think about how you know what the writer is feeling – is this information given explicitly or is it implicit? You should also think about how you know this and the language that the writer uses in order to convey what they are thinking and how they feel.

ACTIVITY 2   **A01**   **SKILLS** ADAPTIVE LEARNING, INNOVATION

▼ THOUGHTS AND FEELINGS

SUBJECT VOCABULARY

synonyms words that share the same meaning as other words; for example, 'quick' might be a synonym for 'fast'

Thinking about the passage from Malala Yousafzai's speech, list all of the things that the writer says about how she feels. In the exam you will be asked to use your own words to explain this, so write a list of **synonyms** for the words the writer uses.

EXAM-STYLE QUESTION

A02   **SKILLS** CRITICAL THINKING, ANALYSIS, REASONING, INTERPRETATION

3 How does the writer describe her thoughts and feelings about her experiences and beliefs?
   You should support your answer with close reference to the passage, including brief quotations.   **(10 marks)**

QUESTIONS 4, 5 AND 6

HINT

For Questions 3 and 6, rather than simply repeating the question, it might be better to find a way straight into the answer, such as 'At first the writer is not at all impressed with what he finds…'

Questions 4 and 5 are comprehension questions about the second unseen text. Question 4 is worth one mark but Question 5 is worth two marks so you need to provide two examples.

Question 6 is a 10-mark question like Question 3 but is about the second unseen text.

EXAM-STYLE QUESTIONS

A01   **SKILLS** INTERPRETATION

Read Text Two, from _I Know Why the Caged Bird Sings_, which is about a young woman's experience of finding a job.

4 In lines 16–18 the writer explains that she was unable to work on the streetcars.
   Identify **one** thing the writer feels about this rejection.   **(1 mark)**

5 In lines 1–6 the writer describes different jobs she has considered.
   Name **two** places the writer is unable to work.   **(2 marks)**

A02   **SKILLS** CRITICAL THINKING, ANALYSIS, REASONING, INTERPRETATION

6 Explain how the writer presents her impressions of work.
   You should support your answer with close reference to the passage, including brief quotations.   **(10 marks)**

LEARNING OBJECTIVES

This lesson will help you to:
- prepare for answering non-fiction exam questions.

PUTTING IT INTO PRACTICE

The passages you will be given for Paper 1 are likely to be between 750 and 1000 words long, or about 60 lines in length. Use the following texts to practise your reading, planning and writing skills in preparation for the exam. Read the unseen passages and answer the questions that follow. Aim to complete all seven questions from Section A in one hour.

KEY POINT

To ensure the most efficient use of time, a direct approach to answering the question is usually best, rather than spending a long time getting to your main points.

humitas A sweet, steamed fresh corn cake, traditional in the Ande, similar to the Mexican tamale. What is the effect of using these South American words?

red Why are they 'disturbingly red'? What is the effect?

usual suspects What is the tone here? Where does this phrase come from?

gizzards Stomach parts.

maize Crop from which sweetcorn grows.

like freshly run over roadkill An unusual simile – what is the effect?

▲ A street scene in Quito, Ecuador

▼ TEXT ONE
FROM *THE HUNGRY CYCLIST* BY TOM KEVILL-DAVIES

Sheltering from torrential rain in a dirty roadside hamlet just north of Quito, I surveyed my options for dinner. A few limp limbed chickens did another turn in their mechanical rotisserie; a plate of worn-out humitas, a sweet tamale, waited for that unlucky customer to save them from another night under the heat lamp; a bored teenager with   5
too much hair-gel prodded and probed a row of disturbingly red hotdog sausages. Not at all tempted by the usual suspects that made up the options in these small Ecuadorian towns, I began to wonder if my hunger could hold out until breakfast.

But hello! What's this?   10

At the end of the street, sheltering from the rain under a tatty umbrella, an old lady was fanning frantically at the coals of her small grill. I took a seat on the cold steps of the grocery store from which she served, and watched her work while a steady stream of customers pulled in from the rain.   15

I ordered a bowl of grilled chicken gizzards, served on a heap of sweet corn and fried kernels of salted maize and it was immediately clear that she knew what she was doing. As the evening passed by the buses, trucks and pick-ups splashed through the rain filled potholes of the main street. We didn't talk much, but that seemed normal here   20
in Ecuador, but from what little was said, and my persistent interest in the secret of her giblets, it was obvious we enjoyed a common love of food, and it wasn't long before our conversation turned to Cuy. I expressed my dismay at having only found this traditional dish strung up like freshly run over roadkill in front of the tourist restaurants   25
en route from Otavalo to Quito, and my keenness to see how these rodents were prepared at home. I was invited for lunch the next day.

Cuy, conejillo de Indias – Indian rabbits, or guinea pigs as we know them in the pet shop – have been an important food source in Peru and Ecuador since pre-Inca times. Fifteen centuries later, they still   30
remain an Andean delicacy, and on average Peruvians and Ecuadorians gobble down twenty-two million of these tasty rodents every year. Most Andean households keep cuy at home in the same way that we might keep chickens. Considered a speciality, they are mostly saved for special occasions. Rather like a bottle of champagne or perhaps   35

conejillo de Indias What is the effect of using this Spanish phrase?

delicacy A much-prized dish.

Ferrero Rocher Italian chocolates wrapped in gold foil.

pods Small groups of whales.

fjord A long, narrow strip of the sea, between steep mountains.

mattak or blubber The fat of the whale.

scurvy A painful, weakening disease caused by lack of vitamin C.

tupilaks Charms or figures with magical powers.

predilection Liking.

a box of Ferrero Rocher, a mating pair of guinea pigs are a typical house warming gift for a newlywed couple. Playing an integral role in Andean religious and ceremonial practices, as well as providing dinner, cuy are also used in the traditional medicine of the region. A live cuy is rubbed over the body of someone sick. The cuy's squeaking indicates the diseased area of the human patient.   40

▼ TEXT TWO
FROM *THE EXPLORER'S DAUGHTER* BY KARI HERBERT

Two hours after the last of the hunters had returned and eaten, narwhal were spotted again, this time very close. Within an hour even those of us on shore could with the naked eye see the plumes of spray from the narwhal catching the light in a spectral play of colour. Two large pods of narwhal circled in the fjord, often looking as if   5
they were going to merge, but always slowly, methodically passing each other by. Scrambling back up to the lookout I looked across the glittering kingdom in front of me and took a sharp intake of breath. The hunters were dotted all around the fjord. The evening light was turning butter-gold, glinting off man and whale and catching the   10
soft billows of smoke from a lone hunter's pipe. From where we sat at the lookout it looked as though the hunters were close enough to touch the narwhal with their bare hands and yet they never moved. Distances are always deceptive in the Arctic, and I fell to wondering if the narwhal existed at all or were instead mischievous tricks of the   15
shifting light…

The narwhal rarely stray from High Arctic waters, escaping only to the slightly more temperate waters towards the Arctic Circle in the dead of winter, but never entering the warmer southern seas. In summer the hunters of Thule are fortunate to witness the annual return of the   20
narwhal to the Inglefield Fjord, on the side of which we now sat.

The narwhal… is an essential contributor to the survival of the hunters in the High Arctic. The mattak or blubber of the whale is rich in necessary minerals and vitamins, and in a place where the climate prohibits the growth of vegetables or fruit, this rich source of   25
vitamin C was the one reason that the Eskimos have never suffered from scurvy… For centuries the blubber of the whales was also the only source of light and heat, and the dark rich meat is still a valuable part of the diet for both man and dogs (a single narwhal can feed a team of dogs for an entire month). Its single ivory tusk, which can   30
grow up to six feet in length, was used for harpoon tips and handles for other hunting implements (although the ivory was found to be brittle and not hugely satisfactory as a weapon), for carving protective tupilaks, and even as a central beam for their small ancient dwellings. Strangely, the tusk seems to have little use for the narwhal itself; they   35
do not use the tusk to break through ice as a breathing hole, nor will they use it to catch or attack prey, but rather the primary use seems to be to disturb the top of the sea bed in order to catch Arctic halibut for which they have a particular predilection. Often the ends of their tusks are worn down or even broken from such usage.   40

The women clustered on the knoll of the lookout, binoculars pointing in every direction, each woman focusing on her husband or family

▶

member, occasionally spinning round at a small gasp or jump as one of the women saw a hunter near a narwhal… Each wife knew her husband instinctively and watched their progress intently; it was crucial to her that her husband catch a narwhal – it was part of their staple diet, and some of the mattak and meat could be sold to other hunters who hadn't been so lucky, bringing in some much-needed extra income. Every hunter was on the water. It was like watching a vast, waterborne game with the hunters spread like a net around the sound. 45

50

The narwhal… are intelligent creatures, their senses are keen and they talk to one another under the water. Their hearing is particularly developed and they can hear the sound of a paddling kayak from a great distance. That was why the hunters had to sit so very still in the water.

One hunter was almost on top of a pair of narwhal, and they were huge. He gently picked up his harpoon and aimed – in that split second my heart leapt for both hunter and narwhal. I urged the man on in my head; he was so close, and so brave to attempt what he was about to do – he was miles from land in a flimsy kayak, and could easily be capsized and drowned. The hunter had no rifle, only one harpoon with two heads and one bladder. It was a foolhardy exercise and one that could only inspire respect. And yet at the same time my heart also urged the narwhal to dive, to leave, to survive. 55

60

This dilemma stayed with me the whole time that I was in Greenland. I understand the harshness of life in the Arctic and the needs of the hunters and their families to hunt and live on animals and sea mammals that we demand to be protected because of their beauty. And I know that one cannot afford to be sentimental in the Arctic. 'How can you possibly eat seal?' I have been asked over and over again. True, the images that bombarded us several years ago of men battering seals for their fur hasn't helped the issue of polar hunting, but the Inughuit do not kill seals using this method, nor do they kill for sport. They use every part of the animals they kill, and most of the food in Thule is still brought in by the hunter-gatherers and fishermen. Imported goods can only ever account for part of the food supply; there is still only one annual supply ship that makes it through the ice to Qaanaaq, and the small twice-weekly plane from West Greenland can only carry a certain amount of goods. Hunting is still an absolute necessity in Thule. 65 70 75

▼ Traditional ways of life in the Arctic are under threat.

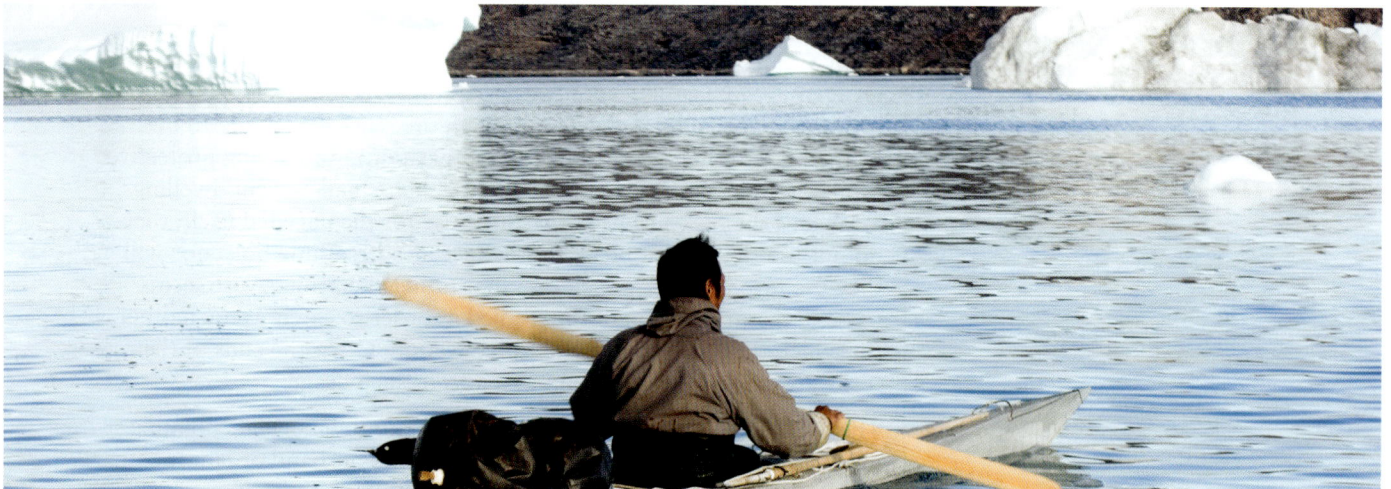

EXAM-STYLE QUESTIONS

| A01 | SKILLS | INTERPRETATION |

| A01 | SKILLS | INTERPRETATION |

| A02 | SKILLS | CRITICAL THINKING, ANALYSIS, REASONING, INTERPRETATION |

| A01 | SKILLS | INTERPRETATION |

| A01 | SKILLS | INTERPRETATION |

| A02 | SKILLS | CRITICAL THINKING, ANALYSIS, REASONING, INTERPRETATION |

| A03 | SKILLS | CRITICAL THINKING, ANALYSIS, INTERPRETATION, DECISION MAKING |

HINT

Use connectives that help you make comparisons. For example, 'Both travellers are exploring places, but whereas Herbert..., Kevill-Davies...'

Read Text One, from *The Hungry Cyclist*, which is about a man's experience of Ecuador.

1 In lines 1–9 the writer arrives in the village feeling very hungry.
   State **one** thing the writer sees. **(1 mark)**

2 In lines 28–41 the writer describes cuy.
   Identify **one** use of cuy by the people of Ecuador. **(1 mark)**

3 Explain how the writer presents his impressions of the food.
   You should support your answer with close reference to the passage, including **brief** quotations. **(10 marks)**

Read Text Two, from *The Explorer's Daughter*, which is about a woman's return to the Arctic.

4 In lines 51–54 the writer describes the narwhal.
   Name **one** thing the writer mentions about the creatures. **(1 mark)**

5 In lines 55–91 the writer explains her feelings on the Arctic way of life.
   Name **two** things the writer finds difficult about hunting. **(2 marks)**

6 How does the writer describe her thoughts and feelings about her return to the Arctic?
   You should support your answer with close reference to the passage, including **brief** quotations. **(10 marks)**

7 Compare how the writers of Text One and Text Two convey their ideas and experiences.
   Support your answer with examples from **both** texts. **(15 marks)**

AN EXTRACT FROM A SAMPLE STUDENT ANSWER

One of the key differences between the texts is their tone. Text One uses humour, such as in the description of the 'disturbingly red hotdog sausages', the personification of the 'worn-out' humitas waiting to be 'save[d]' by someone and the unexpected simile comparing guinea pigs with 'a bottle of champagne'. This tone amuses the reader, which helps to engage their interest in what the writer wants to tell them about Ecuador. However, the tone becomes a little more serious towards the end of the text, as the writer explains the uses of cuy. In comparison, Text Two uses a more serious tone throughout. Its style, especially in the third paragraph, is similar to that of an encyclopaedia, using technical terms such as 'pods', 'mattak' and 'tupilaks' and giving the reader a great deal of factual information without much use of simile or personification. This helps to convey the seriousness of the writer's ethical dilemma and the 'absolute necessity' of hunting in the Arctic.

LEARNING OBJECTIVES

This lesson will help you to:
- read and interpret non-fiction texts.

IDENTIFYING KEY INFORMATION

In Paper 1 Section A, the passages will be non-fiction and both of the passages will be 'unseen texts' which will be unfamiliar to you. When dealing with unseen texts, you must give yourself plenty of time to read them carefully. However, you won't have time to read and re-read each passage lots of times so try to apply some of the following active reading strategies.
- Before you read the passage, read the title carefully and think about what it suggests. Based on the title, what do you think the passage may be about?
- If there are a few lines of introduction, read and consider these carefully.
- Read the passage to get a sense of the tone and content.
- Read the passage again. While you read, use your pen or highlighter to circle different things of interest. This is to highlight key words and phrases to help you answer the questions.

TAP IT!

When you read an unseen text for the first time you should **TAP** it!
- **T**ype: What type of text is it?
- **A**udience: Who is the intended audience? How do you know this?
- **P**urpose: What is the purpose of this passage? Is it informing you, explaining to you or persuading you?

TYPE OF TEXT

You should be able to establish the type of text that you are reading very quickly. There are three things that will help you here: the subject, the narrative perspective and the tense.
- **Subject**: What is the subject of the text? Is the subject matter aimed at a particular age group? Where does the text come from?
- **Narrative perspective**: If it is a first-person autobiographical narrative, for example, it is likely to be a personal account. Does it seem to be an autobiography?
- **Tense**: Is it written in the present tense or is it retrospective?

SUBJECT VOCABULARY

retrospective written in the past tense; looking back at events that have already occurred

ACTIVITY 1 | A01 | SKILLS CRITICAL THINKING

▼ TYPES OF NON-FICTION TEXT

Cover the list below with your hand or a piece of paper, then see how many different types of non-fiction text can you name

newspaper article	autobiography	interview	advertorial feature
magazine article	biography	report	newspaper column
travel writing	text book	journal	

▶ **Select one of the types of non-fiction above. What does it look like? Add any conventions of this text type that you think are important.**

GENERAL VOCABULARY

conventions features normally associated with something

AUDIENCE

KEY POINT

Clues as to the writer's intended audience include the level of difficulty of the language and the assumed knowledge contained in the text.

A writer will usually have a particular audience in mind when they write. Look for any clues that might tell you about the intended reader for example.

- **Age**: Is the subject matter aimed at a particular age group? Does the difficulty of the language suggest a certain readership?
- **Knowledge**: What do you need to know to make sense of the passage?
- **Tone**: What kind of tone is the piece written in? Is the language used formal or informal?

PURPOSE

The main difference between fiction and non-fiction is that non-fiction is usually written for a precise practical purpose, whereas fiction is usually written to entertain. You will need to identify the writer's intention in order to establish the purpose of a non-fiction text. It may help you to think of these 'writing triplets' in order to give you a system for thinking about purpose.

- **Inform, explain, describe**: Is the writer writing to make something clear or to give information?
- **Argue, persuade, advise**: Is the writer writing to discuss an issue or persuade someone to share their views?
- **Explore, imagine, entertain**: Is the writer writing with no other purpose than to entertain the reader?

ACTIVITY 2 | **A01** | **SKILLS** CRITICAL THINKING, PROBLEM SOLVING, INTERPRETATION

▼ TEXT TYPE, AUDIENCE AND PURPOSE

1 Read the extract from *Touching The Void* on pages 113–114 and TAP it. What is the type, audience and purpose of the text? Remember that texts usually have a combination of several purposes. Use highlighters to colour code any evidence of different purposes.

EXAMPLE STUDENT ANSWER

Type: First-person account.

Audience: Anyone who is interested in the story. Joe does not use any technical language associated with mountaineering and in this way he does not seek to exclude the general reader.

Purpose: To engage and inform.

2 Summarise briefly in your own words:
- what happened to Joe
- what choices face Simon.

EXAMPLE STUDENT ANSWER

Touching the Void is a book by Joe Simpson. It is a true story of how he and his climbing partner, Simon Yates, set out to become the first people to climb Siula Grande in Peru. They were nearing the end of their climb in the Peruvian Andes when a disastrous accident occurred in which Joe broke his leg. Simon, who was tied to Joe with a rope, felt that if he did not break free, they would both die. As a result, he cut the rope supporting Joe and returned down the mountain, believing Joe to be dead. Although his leg was broken, Joe crawled his way back down the mountain and was eventually rescued.

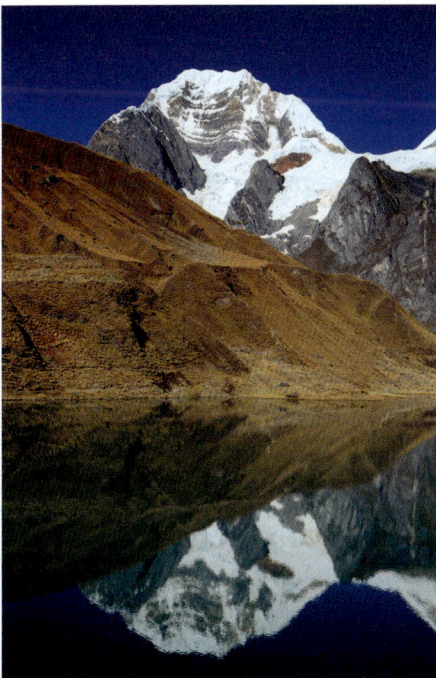

▲ Siula Grande, Peru

LEARNING OBJECTIVES

This lesson will help you to:

■ look at unseen texts in detail, considering language and structure.

ANALYSING THE TEXTS

Once you have read an unseen extract and used the TAP technique to begin analysing it, you need to consider the writer's technique. How has the writer used language and sentence structure to influence the reader?

COPING WITH UNSEEN TEXTS

■ Before you read an unseen passage, read the title carefully. What does it suggest the passage may be about? What might you infer, predict or expect from the passage after reading the title?

■ Consider the beginning and ending of the passage carefully.

■ Read the text in full to get a sense of the passage's tone and content. Underline:

  ■ words you don't understand

  ■ words or phrases that you feel are important – you may choose to come back and comment on these.

■ What type of text is it? A first-person autobiographical narrative, for example? What about the tense – is it written in the present tense or is it retrospective?

■ Who is the intended audience? How do you know this?

■ What is the purpose of the passage? Is it informing you, explaining to you or persuading you?

■ How has the writer used language and sentence structure to create effect?

■ Also consider what effect is created by the narrative perspective and the tone.

WRITER'S TECHNIQUE

Once you are clear about what the piece is about and what the writer is trying to achieve, you will be able to consider technique. A good writer will have a range of techniques that they use in order to create effect. You should look for a variety of techniques but always relate them back to **audience** and **purpose**. A useful way to identify and understand writers' techniques is to consider the different levels at which devices are used:

■ word level

■ sentence level

■ text level.

ACTIVITY 1 | A02 | SKILLS ANALYSIS

▼ FEATURES AT WORD LEVEL

Read the following short lines of text. What do you notice about the language used? Can you identify which of the techniques in the Hint box are being used in each?

> Nine out of ten dogs would recommend Doggibix.

> Best Ever Mega Monday Amazing Discount Sale!

> Work, work, work? Get the laughs back in your life this Thursday at the Comedy Club.

> Sunshine Spas: simply the best!

> This film was fast, funny and full of surprises! ★★★★★

> Is your girlfriend afraid of your mother?

HINT

It may help you if you think about these specific devices:

- rhetorical questions
- hyperbole
- facts and statistics
- rule of three
- superlative
- repetition.

SUBJECT VOCABULARY

superlative a word that expresses the highest or a very high degree of a quality, e.g. 'cleverest' or 'most practical'

ACTIVITY 2 | A01 | SKILLS CRITICAL THINKING, ANALYSIS, INTERPRETATION

▼ *TOUCHING THE VOID*

Imagine that the extract from *Touching the Void* on pages 113–114 is the unseen passage. What words or phrases in Joe's account most vividly shows:

- the pain he suffers as a result of his injuries
- his thoughts and feelings?

STRUCTURING YOUR RESPONSE

Copy and complete the following table, adding your own examples of word level features to comment on. Review the section, 'Use of Language' (pages 16–23), if you need help thinking about language features in more detail.

▼ WORD LEVEL FEATURE	▼ EXAMPLE	▼ EFFECT
Simple language	'He would leave me. He had no choice.'	Joe's simple language portrays the starkness of the choices available to Simon and how life-threatening Joe's injury really is.
Use of direct speech	'"You're dead" "I'm dead." Everyone said it… if there's just two of you a broken ankle could turn into a death sentence.'	Direct speech helps to convey the immediacy of thought and to bring other perspectives into the first-person narrative.

ACTIVITY 3   A02 **SKILLS** CRITICAL THINKING, ANALYSIS, INTERPRETATION

▼ FEATURES AT SENTENCE LEVEL

The way in which a writer combines words and phrases into sentences is important. Look again at the extract from *Touching the Void*, considering it as a typical unseen passage. Look at the example in the table below, then find two more examples of sentence level features that you could comment on. Go back to the section, 'Use of Language' (pages 16–23), if you need a reminder of sentence structure features.

▼ SENTENCE LEVEL FEATURE	▼ EXAMPLE	▼ EFFECT
Simple sentences	'My leg!... My leg!'	Joe's account uses a number of short, simple exclamatory sentences that show the sudden horror of the situation. Here, the two exclamation marks and ellipsis convey the panic he is feeling while the repeated simple sentence is sharp, mirroring the sudden pain he feels.

ACTIVITY 4   A02 **SKILLS** CRITICAL THINKING, ANALYSIS, INTERPRETATION

▼ FEATURES AT TEXT LEVEL

The appearance of the text on the page can also be used to create meaning, such as the use of subheadings and paragraphing. There will be less to say about this when analysing some texts; however, always be aware of text level features how the writer creates an effect at the level of the whole text. Copy and complete the following table, adding examples and explaining their effects.

▼ TEXT LEVEL FEATURE	▼ EXAMPLE	▼ EFFECT
First-person narrative		
Two different perspectives	'I hit the slope...' 'Joe had disappeared...'	By using two different perspectives, *Touching the Void* allows the reader to appreciate the horror from the perspective of the victim and the friend. As such, the suspense and discomfort is even more acute as the reader is forced to engage with Joe's physical pain but also Simon's grief as he believes his friend is dead.

HINT

The grammatical construction of a sentence is called its syntax. This includes both punctuation and sentence type. For example: 'Robbed!' The syntax of this exclamatory, one-word simple sentence evokes a sense of emotion and drama. The message is conveyed quickly to the reader and in an emotive manner.

HINT

Your aim is not simply to identify techniques, but to explain the *effects* of the writer's craft. A weak answer simply re-tells the events of the passage; a strong answer comments on the way in which language is used to create meaning and prompt reader response.

ACTIVITY 5   A02   SKILLS   CRITICAL THINKING, ANALYSIS, INTERPRETATION

▼ CONSIDERING LANGUAGE

Refer back to the extract from Ellen MacArthur's autobiography on pages 59–60. It deals with an emergency she faced on the 44th day of the Vendée Globe yacht race when she had to replace an essential sail. How does this passage bring out the thoughts and feelings of Ellen MacArthur as she sails alone in a race around the world?

INDICATIVE CONTENT

KEY POINT

In analysing texts, try to cultivate the skill of registering effects at different levels, including the syntax and the text. This is like zooming in and panning out.

MacArthur's style is unaffected and frank, and seems very powerful because it is a very personal narrative. The passage highlights the enormous physical and psychological challenges in sailing alone in heavy seas. Because the narrative focuses on the physical effects of the bad weather, it makes the fact that MacArthur finds the strength to continue seem even more extraordinary. The challenge seems almost superhuman, but MacArthur's narrative shows that she is very human and subject to the same feelings as other people. This leads the reader to marvel at her strength and motivation. There is much use of the first-person pronoun. Other features include:

- use of technical details ('the storm jib', 'the inner forestay rod') gives the reader a sense of the reality of the situation, although this is not overdone
- plenty of active verbs ('continued', 'snatched', 'dragged', 'enjoyed') give the reader a sense of immediacy and action
- straightforward, direct language; the limited use of adjectives and adverbs means that they have an impact when used ('unreal, crazy situation')
- use of words, phrases and clauses that suggest struggle, effort or challenge ('not only difficult but painful', 'hang on')
- conversational features, such as contractions ('I'd') and repetition of the same words for emphasis ('freezing night', 'freezing water'), all of which add immediacy to the writing

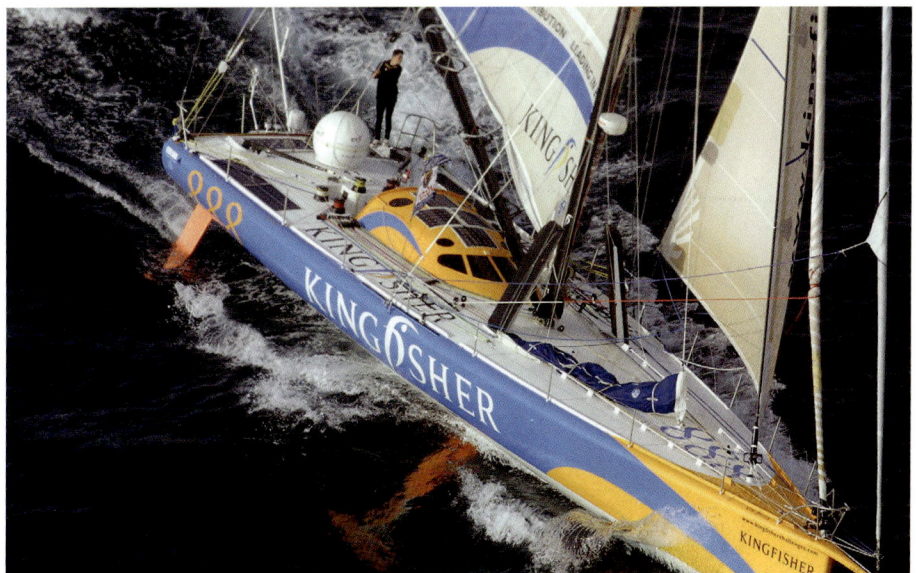

▲ Ellen MacArthur's yacht *Kingfisher* competing in the Vendeé Globe race

- varying lengths of sentence keeps the reader's attention; they often alternate between short, punchy sentences and more complex descriptive sentences ('Dawn brought some respite. My body temperature warmed after the freezing night, but if I sweated through the physical exertion of a sail change, when I stopped, I'd once again cool to a shiver.')
- little figurative language gives the impression of unrelenting action
- simple, clear descriptions of her sensations ('My hands were red-raw', 'my head was aching', 'the freezing water washed breathtakingly over [me]') make the reader imagine how she must have felt
- the use of familiar phrases or **clichés** ('ounce of strength', 'hanging on for dear life') ensure that the reader can understand what MacArthur is explaining immediately, without having to devote time to considering a new or innovative use of language
- personification of the weather as someone throwing MacArthur's possessions around the yacht ('Food was hurled') gives the impression that the weather is fighting with MacArthur
- the lack of speech emphasises the fact that MacArthur is all alone; the only sound described ('I would often cry out loud') is just a wordless noise that is relayed to the reader indirectly, rather than as direct speech
- humorous lightening of tone at the end, juxtaposing the 'wonderful' relief of being out of her survival suit with the smell from her body and survival suit. The comedy of the moment is emphasised by MacArthur's use of **litotes**, to describe the smell as 'not… wonderful', which is funnier than if the smell had been described directly.

> **KEY POINT**
>
> Even though Ellen MacArthur is a yachtswoman, not a writer, and her style is not 'literary', it is still complex.

> **SUBJECT VOCABULARY**
>
> **clichés** phrases that are used so often that they start to lose their impact
> **litotes** ironic understatement used to mean something by saying its opposite

▼ FROM *HOW THE POOR DIE* BY GEORGE ORWELL

After some days I grew well enough to sit up and study the surrounding patients. The stuffy room, with its narrow beds so close together that you could easily touch your neighbour's hand, had every sort of disease in it except, I suppose, acutely infectious cases. My right-hand neighbour was a little red-haired **cobbler** with one leg   5
shorter than the other, who used to announce the death of any other patient (this happened a number of times, and my neighbour was always the first to hear of it) by whistling to me, exclaiming 'Numéro 43!' (or whatever it was) and flinging his arms above his head. This man had not much wrong with him, but in most of the other beds   10
within my angle of vision some squalid tragedy or some plain horror was being enacted. In the bed that was foot to foot with mine there lay, until he died (I didn't see him die — they moved him to another bed), a little **weazened** man who was suffering from I do not know what disease, but something that made his whole body so intensely   15
sensitive that any movement from side to side, sometimes even the weight of the bedclothes, would make him shout out with pain. His worst suffering was when he urinated, which he did with the greatest difficulty. A nurse would bring him the bedbottle and then for a long time stand beside his bed, whistling, as grooms are said to do with   20
horses, until at last with an agonized shriek of 'Je fisse!' he would get started. In the bed next to him the sandy-haired man whom I had seen being **cupped** used to cough up blood-streaked mucus at all hours. My left-hand neighbour was a tall, flaccid-looking young man who used periodically to have a tube inserted into his back and   25
astonishing quantities of frothy liquid drawn off from some part of his

cobbler Someone who mends shoes.

weazened Shrivelled or wrinkled (alternative spelling for wizened).

cupped Bled by a doctor for medical reasons.

▶

imperial A small pointed beard.

legacy Something left to someone in a will, usually an amount of money.

bedbottle A bottle into which an invalid can urinate while in bed.

cirrhosis A severe disease of the liver.

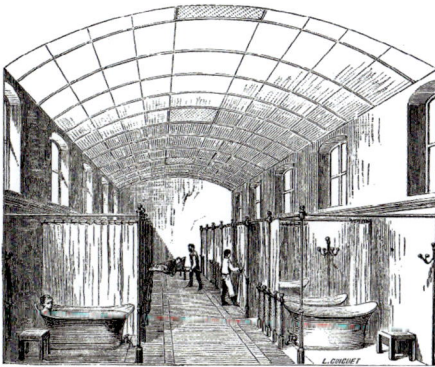
▲ Orwell wrote *How the Poor Die* in 1929 after being in hospital in Paris.

vellum Parchment made from the skin of a calf.

sabots Simple shoes made from a block of wood.

body. In the bed beyond that a veteran of the war of 1870 was dying, a handsome old man with a white imperial, round whose bed, at all hours when visiting was allowed, four elderly female relatives dressed all in black sat exactly like crows, obviously scheming for some pitiful legacy. In the bed opposite me in the farther row was an old bald-headed man with drooping moustaches and greatly swollen face and body, who was suffering from some disease that made him urinate almost incessantly. A huge glass receptacle stood always beside his bed. One day his wife and daughter came to visit him. At sight of them the old man's bloated face lit up with a smile of surprising sweetness, and as his daughter, a pretty girl of about twenty, approached the bed I saw that his hand was slowly working its way from under the bedclothes. I seemed to see in advance the gesture that was coming — the girl kneeling beside the bed, the old man's hand laid on her head in his dying blessing. But no, he merely handed her the bedbottle, which she promptly took from him and emptied into the receptacle.

About a dozen beds away from me was Numéro 57 — I think that was his number — a cirrhosis-of-the-liver case. Everyone in the ward knew him by sight because he was sometimes the subject of a medical lecture. On two afternoons a week the tall, grave doctor would lecture in the ward to a party of students, and on more than one occasion old Numéro 57 was wheeled in on a sort of trolley into the middle of the ward, where the doctor would roll back his nightshirt, dilate with his fingers a huge flabby protruberance on the man's belly — the diseased liver, I suppose — and explain solemnly that this was a disease attributable to alcoholism, commoner in the wine-drinking countries. As usual he neither spoke to his patient nor gave him a smile, a nod or any kind of recognition. While he talked, very grave and upright, he would hold the wasted body beneath his two hands, sometimes giving it a gentle roll to and fro, in just the attitude of a woman handling a rolling-pin. Not that Numéro 57 minded this kind of thing. Obviously he was an old hospital inmate, a regular exhibit at lectures, his liver long since marked down for a bottle in some pathological museum. Utterly uninterested in what was said about him, he would lie with his colourless eyes gazing at nothing, while the doctor showed him off like a piece of antique china. He was a man of about sixty, astonishingly shrunken. His face, pale as vellum, had shrunken away till it seemed no bigger than a doll's.

One morning my cobbler neighbour woke me up plucking at my pillow before the nurses arrived. 'Numéro 57!' — he flung his arms above his head. There was a light in the ward, enough to see by. I could see old Numéro 57 lying crumpled up on his side, his face sticking out over the side of the bed, and towards me. He had died some time during the night, nobody knew when. When the nurses came they received the news of his death indifferently and went about their work. After a long time, an hour or more, two other nurses marched in abreast like soldiers, with a great clumping of sabots, and knotted the corpse up in the sheets, but it was not removed till some time later. Meanwhile, in the better light, I had had time for a good look at Numéro 57. Indeed I lay on my side to look at him. Curiously enough he was the first dead European I had seen. I had seen dead men before, but always Asiatics and usually people who had died violent deaths. Numéro 57's eyes were still open, his mouth also

the Litany Petitions or prayers included in the Book of Common Prayer.

open, his small face contorted into an expression of agony. What most impressed me, however, was the whiteness of his face. It had been pale before, but now it was little darker than die sheets. As I gazed at the tiny, screwed-up face it struck me that this disgusting piece of refuse, waiting to be carted away and dumped on a slab in the dissecting room, was an example of 'natural' death, one of the things you pray for in the Litany. There you are, then, I thought, that's what is waiting for you, twenty, thirty, forty years hence: that is how the lucky ones die, the ones who live to be old. One wants to live, of course, indeed one only stays alive by virtue of the fear of death, but I think now, as I thought then, that it's better to die violently and not too old. People talk about the horrors of war, but what weapon has man invented that even approaches in cruelty some of the commoner diseases? 'Natural' death, almost by definition, means something slow, smelly and painful. Even at that, it makes a difference if you can achieve it in your own home and not in a public institution. This poor old wretch who had just flickered out like a candle-end was not even important enough to have anyone watching by his deathbed. He was merely a number, then a 'subject' for the students' scalpels.

80

85

90

95

EXAM-STYLE QUESTIONS

Re-read the passage from *How the Poor Die*, then answer these questions.

| A01 | SKILLS | INTERPRETATION |

| A01 | SKILLS | INTERPRETATION |

| A02 | SKILLS | CRITICAL THINKING, ANALYSIS, REASONING, INTERPRETATION |

1 In lines 22–27, the writer describes some of the patients.
State one illness the writer sees.   **(1 mark)**

2 In lines 75–87, the writer reacts to the death of one of the patients.
Identify one point the writer makes about the experience.   **(1 mark)**

3 Explain how the writer presents his impressions of the patients and the hospital.
You should support your answer with close reference to the passage, including **brief** quotations.   **(10 marks)**

INTERPRETING TEXT

The text below is an extract from a review of a car, the Capybara, when it first went on sale. Read the extract and answer the questions below.

| ACTIVITY 1 | A01 | SKILLS | CRITICAL THINKING, ANALYSIS, INTERPRETATION |

▼ FROM REVIEW OF THE 'CAPYBARA'

First impressions count for a lot, and unfortunately, the first impression of the Capybara isn't great. The styling can at best be described as 'challenging' and at worst 'capable of frightening small children'. Things do get better on climbing through the oddly proportioned door, but the shocked look of passers-by acts as a constant reminder of the styling.

So it's safe to say the exterior is an acquired taste and relocating to the driver's seat is recommended. The interior quality is incredibly strong and suggests the manufacturer's money has been directed here whilst the designers were left to play outside. Beautifully finished equipment and

▶

finishes suggest that this is a much more expensive car than it actually is. Anyone sat in the sculpted seats is likely to feel reassured that they are experiencing a quality product and have invested their funds wisely.

Inserting the futuristic key into the central console, you are greeted with a gentle murmur, rather than the expected rasping shout of other cars in this class. This lack of soundtrack continues as you smoothly drive away. Road noise is often an issue for small cars, but there is none here.

The longer you spend in the Capybara, the more you can appreciate its character. This is a happy car, unhampered by its looks and far more focused on transporting you in comfort and luxury. State of the art safety features including laser-guided cruise control, ABS+ and a GPS controlled gearbox cocoon the driver in a relaxed environment that you would expect in luxury cars.

But this isn't a luxury car, this is a relatively cheap, well-engineered small car that does its best to defy the first impressions the exterior styling inspires. If you can look beyond these, you have one of the best small cars on the road.

Remember, first impressions can also be misleading – it's what's on the inside that counts.

▶ How does the writer use language to convey information and ideas to the reader? How does this language try to influence the reader's response? Use these questions to help you to identify relevant points.

▶ How does this text address the reader? Why does it do this?

▶ This is a car review, but does it remind you of any other kind of speech or writing? Why might it be trying not to seem too obviously like an advert?

▶ Does the review use many technical terms? Why? Why not?

▶ Identify some of the adjectives and adverbs which are used. What is their purpose here?

▶ Can you identify any nouns which are extensively premodified? Why might adverts tend to use a lot of premodification of nouns?

▶ Can you identify any rhetorical devices which are used to persuade the reader?

▶ Can you identify and comment on any dynamic verbs that are used? Look also at the use of modal auxiliary verbs.

▶ Where does the advert use personification? Why does it use this metaphorical device?

▶ What phonological feature is employed and why?

SUBJECT VOCABULARY

premodified a noun with a description before it, e.g. 'the big blue car'
dynamic verb: a verb that describes actions or events that are happening, e.g. 'I go'
modal auxiliary verb a verb that helps another verb to express a meaning, e.g. 'can', 'would', 'should'
personification when something which is not human is made to seem human by attributing human qualities to it
phonological relating to the sound structure of words

LEARNING OBJECTIVES

This lesson will help you to:

■ practise and perfect skills to respond effectively to unseen non-fiction in the exam.

SELECTING EVIDENCE

You will need to locate quotations in order to support your points quickly, under exam conditions. It is important that the quotations that you use are short and directly relevant to your point.

ACTIVITY 1 | **A01** | **SKILLS** ANALYSIS

▼ SELECTING EVIDENCE FROM *TOUCHING THE VOID*

Read the passage from *Touching the Void* on pages 113–114. Copy and complete the following tables, finding evidence of each technique or stylistic choice in the passage.

▼ JOE'S ACCOUNT	▼ EVIDENCE
Short sentences	
Description of how physically painful the accident is	
Descriptions of feeling lonely	
Use of modal verbs (*must, could, should, would, shall, will*) to speculate about the future	
Punctuation for effect	

▼ SIMON'S ACCOUNT	▼ EVIDENCE
Careful and considered tone	
Realist is understanding of the situation	
Unsympathetic descriptions	
Use of modal verbs (*must, could, should, would, shall, will*) to speculate about the future	
Punctuation for effect	

HINT

Remember to always use quotation marks to indicate direct quotation. Wherever possible, quotations should be integrated into the main body of your own sentences. Longer quotations should be used sparingly and set off from the main paragraph.

HINT

The exam involves a mixture of short and longer answer questions. You will need to locate the relevant part of the passage for each question, but you do not need to offer direct quotation for the shorter questions. Read the question carefully and look at the number of marks available to help you to determine how much information to include and whether you need to quote.

ACTIVITY 2 **A02** SKILLS ANALYSIS

▼ BEAT THE CLOCK!

You have three minutes to find an example of each of the following techniques in the *Touching the Void* extract:

- ellipsis
- exclamation mark
- direct speech
- emotive language
- rhetorical question
- use of first-person narrative
- colloquial language.

ACTIVITY 3 **A02** SKILLS CRITICAL THINKING, ANALYSIS, INTERPRETATION

▼ POINT-EVIDENCE-EXPLAIN

For each of the techniques listed in Activity 2, construct a P-E-E paragraph exploring the effect that the technique has on the context of the story and its effect on the reader. Start by completing the following example.

Point: Both Simon and Joe use ellipses in their accounts. Joe's passage even ends with it.

Evidence: 'I kept staring at him, expecting him to fall…'

Explanation: Ellipsis is used as a structural device to create suspense and anticipation.

EXAM-STYLE QUESTION

A02

SKILLS CRITICAL THINKING, ANALYSIS, REASONING, INTERPRETATION

Explain how the writer presents two different impressions of the accident. You should support your answer with close reference to the passage, including **brief** quotations. **(10 marks)**

▶ *Touching the Void* is a true story of overcoming incredible hardship.

LEARNING OBJECTIVES

This lesson will help you to:

■ explore links and connections between writers' ideas and perspectives and how these are conveyed.

COMPARISONS

Before you start, read or re-read the 12 pieces of contemporary non-fiction on pages 124–137. These pieces have been chosen so you can practise reading and responding to passages in preparation for your exam. They include a range of the types of text that you need to be familiar with. The pieces are paired together with each pair sharing a theme that can be used as the basis for comparison.

QUESTION 7

HINT

The final question is worth approximately one third of the marks for the whole section. You should divide your time accordingly.

SUBJECT VOCABULARY

implicit suggested or understood without being stated directly
explicit expressed in a way that is very clear and direct

HINT

Make sure you select information that is relevant to the question.

Question 7 is the final question of Section A, and it will ask you to compare the two unseen texts that you have been given. This question is the longest and most complex and represents about a third of the marks available in Section A.

5 STEPS TO SUCCESS

STEP 1: Remember that the essay that you write in response to the question will be comparative, based on both Text One and Text Two. You will not have seen either of the texts before. The question is likely to focus on:

■ what the texts are about, key themes and the authors' conclusions
■ the authors' use of language, character and other effects.

STEP 2: Make sure that you focus on the question. Begin by stating what the texts are about, both obviously and at a deeper level, considering **implicit** and **explicit** meaning.

STEP 3: Make sure you refer to interesting or relevant points of detail, as a very general answer will not be as successful. It is not enough to point things out and 'translate' the text; avoid retelling the story and make sure you explain how the devices and features work, what their effect is on the reader, and so on. Ask yourself why the author might have used that kind of language, imagery and so on. Remember: Point-Evidence-Explain.

STEP 4: Draw clear links and contrasts between the texts. Depending on which texts you are given, you may also be able to draw contrasts and links within the texts as well. Make sure that you compare and contrast the texts by using words and phrases such as 'similarly', 'in comparison' or 'on the other hand'.

STEP 5: Quote briefly, using a single word or phrase, to support your comments. You may refer to a whole paragraph or long section, but do not copy it out in full. Show that you are quoting by using inverted commas. Because you should only use short quotations, you should integrate them into your sentences and introduce them with a comma or colon. Whenever you quote, always explain in your own words what the quotation means and comment on its effect, with particular focus on language and structure.

TEXT ONE

Touching the Void is an autobiography by Joe Simpson. Unusually for an autobiography, it is presented from both the perspective of Joe, and of his climbing partner, Simon Yates, in the first person.

Published in 2003, it is a true story of how he and Simon set out to become the first people to climb Siula Grande in Peru. However, the pair are involved in a terrible accident which results in Joe breaking his leg and becoming separated from his partner. Simon is forced to cut the rope connecting the pair as he believes Joe to be dead and his only chance of survival.

Read the following extract that details the accident from both perspectives.

▼ FROM *TOUCHING THE VOID* BY JOE SIMPSON

Joe's account

I hit the slope at the base of the cliff before I saw it coming. I was facing into the slope and both knees locked as I struck it. I felt a shattering blow in my knee, felt bones splitting, and screamed. The impact catapulted me over backwards and down the slope of the East Face. I slid, head-first, on my back. The rushing speed of it confused   5
me. I thought of the drop below but felt nothing. Simon would be ripped off the mountain. He couldn't hold this. I screamed again as I jerked to a sudden violent stop.

Everything was still, silent. My thoughts raced madly. Then pain flooded down my thigh – a fierce burning fire coming down the inside of my   10
thigh, seeming to ball in my groin, building and building until I cried out at it, and my breathing came in ragged gasps. My leg!… My leg!

I hung, head down, on my back, left leg tangled in the rope above me and my right leg hanging slackly to one side. I lifted my head from the snow and stared, up across my chest, at a grotesque distortion in the   15
right knee, twisting the leg into a strange zigzag. I didn't connect it with the pain which burnt my groin. That had nothing to do with my knee. I kicked my left leg free of the rope and swung round until I was hanging against the snow on my chest, feet down. The pain eased. I kicked my left foot into the slope and stood up.   20

A wave of nausea surged over me. I pressed my face into the snow, and the sharp cold seemed to calm me. Something terrible, something dark with dread occurred to me, and as I thought about it I felt the dark thought break into panic: 'I've broken my leg, that's it. I'm dead. Everyone said it… if there's just two of you a broken ankle could turn   25
into a death sentence… if it's broken… if… It doesn't hurt so much, maybe I've just ripped something.'

I kicked my right leg against the slope, feeling sure it wasn't broken. My knee exploded. Bone grated, and the fireball rushed from groin to knee. I screamed. I looked down at the knee and could see it was   30
broken, yet I tried not to believe what I was seeing. It wasn't just broken, it was ruptured, twisted, crushed, and I could see the kink in the joint and knew what had happened. The impact had driven my lower leg up through the knee joint. …

I dug my axes into the snow, and pounded my good leg deeply into the   35
soft slope until I felt sure it wouldn't slip. The effort brought back the nausea and I felt my head spin giddily to the point of fainting. I moved

---

Face Side of a mountain.

nausea Sensation of physical sickness.

kink A sharp bend or twist in something.

axes Ice axes, used by mountaineers and climbers to cut footholds in ice.

and a searing spasm of pain cleared away the faintness. I could see the summit of Seria Norte away to the west. I was not far below it. The sight drove home how desperately things had changed. We were above 19,000 feet, still on the ridge, and very much alone. I looked south at the small rise I had hoped to scale quickly and it seemed to grow with every second that I stared. I would never get over it. Simon would not be able to get me up it. He would leave me. He had no choice. I held my breath, thinking about it. Left here? Alone?... For an age I felt overwhelmed at the notion of being left; I felt like screaming, and I felt like swearing, but stayed silent. If I said a word, I would panic. I could feel myself teetering on the edge of it.

Simon's account

Joe had disappeared behind a rise in the ridge and began moving faster than I could go. I was glad we had put the steep section behind us at last. ... I felt tired and was grateful to be able to follow Joe's tracks instead of breaking trail.

I rested a while when I saw that Joe had stopped moving. Obviously he had found an obstacle and I thought I would wait until he started moving again. When the rope moved again I trudged forward after it, slowly.

Suddenly there was a sharp tug as the rope lashed out taut across the slope. I was pulled forward several feet as I pushed my axes into the snow and braced myself for another jerk. Nothing happened. I knew that Joe had fallen, but I couldn't see him, so I stayed put. I waited for about ten minutes until the tautened rope went slack on the snow and I felt sure that Joe had got his weight off me. I began to move along his footsteps cautiously, half expecting something else to happen. I kept tensed up and ready to dig my axes in at the first sign of trouble.

As I crested the rise, I could see down a slope to where the rope disappeared over the edge of a drop. I approached slowly, wondering what had happened. When I reached the top of the drop I saw Joe below me. He had one foot dug in and was leaning against the slope with his face buried in the snow. I asked him what had happened and he looked at me in surprise. I knew he was injured, but the significance didn't hit me at first.

He told me very calmly that he had broken his leg. He looked pathetic, and my immediate thought came without any emotion. ... You're dead... no two ways about it! I think he knew it too. I could see it in his face. It was all totally rational. I knew where we were, I took in everything around me instantly, and knew he was dead. It never occurred to me that I might also die. I accepted without question that I could get off the mountain alone. I had no doubt about that.

... Below him I could see thousands of feet of open face falling into the eastern glacier bay. I watched him quite dispassionately. I couldn't help him, and it occurred to me that in all likelihood he would fall to his death. I wasn't disturbed by the thought. In a way I hoped he would fall. I knew I couldn't leave him while he was still fighting for it, but I had no idea how I might help him. I could get down. If I tried to get him down I might die with him. It didn't frighten me. It just seemed a waste. It would be pointless. I kept staring at him, expecting him to fall...

breaking trail The process of making a trail through deep snow.

40

45

50

55

60

65

70

75

80

85

ACTIVITY 1   **A03**   SKILLS ▷ ANALYSIS, INTERPRETATION

▼ COMPARING JOE AND SIMON'S ACCOUNTS

To help you to develop comparative skills, look back at the *Touching the Void* extract again in order to make comparisons within the text. Work with a partner to copy and complete the following table, considering Simon's account.

▼ WHAT WORDS OR PHRASES IN JOE'S ACCOUNT MOST VIVIDLY SHOW HIS PAIN AND HIS THOUGHTS AND FEELINGS?	▼ WHAT WORDS OR PHRASES IN SIMON'S ACCOUNT SHOW MOST CLEARLY THE DIFFICULT DECISION HE FACES? EXPLAIN THE REASONS FOR YOUR CHOICES.
Joe's account focuses on pain and shock: agony, panic and fear. He is obsessed with pain and the extremity of the damage, using powerful and emotive verbs: 'it was ruptured, twisted, crushed'. This uses the rule of three and emotive language to make the reader feel his pain.	
Sharp, onomatopoeic sounds, such as 'bones splitting' and 'shattering blow', using emotive verbs.	
Sometimes uncompromisingly direct to intensify sense of reality: 'the impact had driven my lower leg up through the knee joint'; 'we were above 19,000 feet… and very much alone'. Sometimes detailed descriptions involve the reader and put them in his shoes.	
Words and images that convey thoughts and feelings vividly and frankly, sometimes in a sequence that conveys dramatic changes of mood and thought (paragraph 4: 'A wave of nausea… I'm dead.'); phrasing becomes abstract and almost vague at times, suggesting trauma: 'something terrible, something dark with dread'; 'teetering on the edge of (panic)'.	
Uses rhetorical questions, such as 'Left here? Alone?'. This creates an atmosphere of uncertainty, putting the reader in his shoes and creating a sense of drama and suspense.	

SUBJECT VOCABULARY

atmosphere the feeling that an event or place gives you

ACTIVITY 2   **A03**   SKILLS ▷ CRITICAL THINKING, ANALYSIS, INTERPRETATION, DECISION MAKING

▼ DIFFERENT ATTITUDES

Compare and contrast Joe and Simon's attitudes towards the accident described in the passage from *Touching the Void*. Support your answer with examples from both accounts.

You might like to consider some of the following points: biographical and autobiographical writing, style, structure, viewpoint, selection of detail, presentation of fact/opinion.

Note that in the exam you will be comparing two different text extracts. Here you are comparing two different perspectives from the same text, so this is for illustrative purposes only and is not indicative of the exam.

KEY POINT

The individuality of your answer will lie in your choices of which details to highlight and the effect you think they have on the reader. Focus your energy on these aspects rather than making very general comments.

▼ MEETING ASSESSMENT OBJECTIVES

Read the following student responses to the question in Activity 2. How well do you think they meet the following assessment objective?

■ AO3: Explore links and connections between writers' ideas and perspectives, as well as how these are conveyed

EXAMPLE STUDENT ANSWER A

Joe's account of the climb is very matter of fact and doesn't spare us the grim details of the injury that he sustained earlier in the climb: 'I felt a shattering blow in my knee, felt bones splitting, and screamed'. This indicates that he isn't really too badly affected currently by the psychological trauma of his ordeal. In Simon's account he is also very matter of fact about the experiences of Siula Grande, but the way in which he presents it isn't so horrific, more clinical. As if he isn't really there and is just doing a commentary on someone else climbing the mountain.

Joe's account of the climb uses a lot more exciting language and a richer vocabulary to keep the reader interested: 'Everything was still, silent. My thoughts raced madly'. Whereas Simon's account only uses very simple language and is more factual rather than exciting: 'I rested a while when I saw that Joe had stopped moving'. I think this suggests that Joe is perhaps more experienced at writing or was more affected by the incident on the Siula Grande. This helps us to understand that Joe and Simon aren't professional writers; I feel that this does take some of the possible atmosphere away from the story. In conclusion I think that there really aren't that many differences between the two accounts, other than the ones that I have stated. I think this is because they are both about the same incident and are both written from the same aspect of climbers.

EXAMPLE STUDENT ANSWER B

Both Simon and Joe use ellipses in their accounts: 'I kept staring at him expecting him to fall…'. The ellipses help to add tension and makes the reader wonder what will happen next. It keeps you on the edge of your seat and introduces the idea of an unfortunate event, which can help to build up to a climax point. Simon's account ends with an ellipsis, leaving it up to your imagination and making you want to find out more.

▶

HINT

You must COMPARE and CONTRAST. To do this, use phrases that show you are comparing, such as, 'in comparison', 'in contrast', 'similarly', 'however'.

SUBJECT VOCABULARY

juxtaposition putting two very different things close together in order to encourage comparison between them

This extract consists of two pieces of autobiographical prose narrative (or monologues) giving different perspectives on the same event. Relatively short paragraphs follow a sequence of time, but the real demarcations are provided by crucial developments in thought. The key to understanding the piece is to appreciate the different ways Joe and Simon respond to the accident. Though both accounts are very similar in style, there are significant differences to be explored.

Simon and Joe both use exclamatory sentences in their accounts. 'My leg!... my leg!' Joe uses this in particular to emphasise a thought and to bring a greater level of attention to the phrase. In this example it highlights how painful this experience is for him and forces an emotional response from the reader.

In keeping with this idea, emotive language is used more frequently by Joe: 'something dark with dread occurred to me, as I thought about it I felt the dark thought break into a panic'. The use of words like 'dread', 'dark' and 'break' create a semantic field of horror and sadness.

In comparison with Joe's account, Simon is less emotional and more objective in considering the situation in hand: 'I could see it in his face. It was all totally rational'. The use of short simple sentences helps keep his point of view very black and white and provokes a less emotional response from the reader. It seems fitting that Simon, as the observer, is more pragmatic in his analysis of the situation – the reader is aware that he feels a responsibility to act and is weighing up his decisions in as calm and factual a way as he is able to.

In conclusion, the juxtaposition between Simon and Joe's narratives illuminates the pathos in the two accounts. The starkly different tones force the reader to take sides. The reader is more likely to side with Joe's emotive and deeply personal account.

▲ Joe Simpson's is a great story of mountaineering survival.

TEXT TWO

▲ Blue John Canyon, Utah, USA

drop-off A sheer downward slope.

chockstone A stone that has become stuck between rocks.

overhang A part of something (in this case, the rock) that extends over something else.

traverse Cross.

teeters Balance unsteadily.

torque Rotating force.

Between a Rock and a Hard Place is an autobiography written by Aron Ralston, an engineer turned outdoorsman and motivational speaker. It relates his experience in 2003 of being trapped for five days and seven hours in Blue John Canyon, in the Utah desert in the southern United States.

His right arm was trapped by a boulder and, unable to free himself, he amputated his arm using a blunt pocketknife. He then had to return through the canyon and climb down a 20-metre slope before he could reach safety and receive medical care.

▼ FROM *BETWEEN A ROCK AND A HARD PLACE* BY ARON RALSTON

I come to another drop-off. This one is maybe eleven or twelve feet high, a foot higher and of a different geometry than the overhang I descended ten minutes ago. Another refrigerator chockstone is wedged between the walls, ten feet downstream from and at the same height as the ledge. It gives the space below the drop-off the claustrophobic feel of a short tunnel. Instead of the walls widening after the drop-off, or opening into a bowl at the bottom of the canyon, here the slot narrows to a consistent three feet across at the lip of the drop-off and continues at that width for fifty feet down the canyon. 5

Sometimes in narrow passages like this one, it's possible for me to stem my body across the slot, with my feet and back pushing out in opposite directions against the walls. Controlling this counterpressure by switching my hands and feet on the opposing walls, I can move up or down the shoulder width crevice fairly easily as long as the friction contact stays solid between the walls and my hands, feet, and back. This technique is known as stemming or chimneying; you can imagine using it to climb up the inside of a chimney. 10 15

Just below the ledge where I'm standing is a chockstone the size of a large bus tire, stuck fast in the channel between the walls, a few feet out from the lip. If I can step onto it, then I'll have a nine-foot height to descend, less than that of the first overhang. I'll dangle off the chockstone, then take a short fall onto the rounded rocks piled on the canyon floor. 20

Stemming across the canyon at the lip of the drop-off, with one foot and one hand on each of the walls, I traverse out to the chockstone. I press my back against the south wall and lock my left knee, which pushes my foot tight against the north wall. With my right foot, I kick at the boulder to test how stuck it is. It's jammed tightly enough to hold my weight. I lower myself from the chimneying position and step onto the chockstone. It supports me but teeters slightly. After confirming that I don't want to chimney down from the chockstone's height, I squat and grip the rear of the lodged boulder, turning to face back upcanyon. Sliding my belly over the front edge, I can lower myself and hang from my fully extended arms, akin to climbing down from the roof of a house. 25 30 35

As I dangle, I feel the stone respond to my adjusting grip with a scraping quake as my body's weight applies enough torque to disturb it from its position. Instantly, I know this is trouble, and instinctively, I let go of the rotating boulder to land on the round rocks below. When

▶

ricochets Bounces off.

apocryphal Doubtful, untrue.

I look up, the backlit chockstone falling toward my head consumes the sky. Fear shoots my hands over my head. I can't move backward or I'll fall over a small ledge. My only hope is to push off the falling rock and get my head out of its way.   40

The next three seconds play out at a tenth of their normal speed. Time dilates, as if I'm dreaming, and my reactions decelerate. In slow motion: the rock smashes my left hand against the south wall; my eyes register the collision, and I yank my left arm back as the rock ricochets; the boulder then crushes my right hand and ensnares my right arm at the wrist, palm in, thumb up, fingers extended; the rock slides another foot down the wall with my arm in tow, tearing the skin off the lateral side of my forearm. Then silence.   45   50

My disbelief paralyzes me temporarily as I stare at the sight of my arm vanishing into an implausibly small gap between the fallen boulder and the canyon wall. Within moments, my nervous system's pain response overcomes the initial shock. Good God, my hand. The flaring agony throws me into a panic. I grimace and growl... My mind commands my body, 'Get your hand out of there!' I yank my arm three times in a naive attempt to pull it out. But I'm stuck.   55

Anxiety has my brain tweaking; searing-hot pain shoots from my wrist up my arm. I'm frantic, and I cry out... My desperate brain conjures up a probably apocryphal story in which an adrenaline-stoked mom lifts an overturned car to free her baby. I'd give it even odds that it's made up, but I do know for certain that *right now*, while my body's chemicals are raging at full flood, is the best chance I'll have to free myself with brute force. I shove against the large boulder, heaving against it, pushing with my left hand, lifting with my knees pressed under the rock. I get good leverage with the aid of a twelve-inch shelf in front of my feet. Standing on that, I brace my thighs under the boulder and thrust upward repeatedly, grunting, 'Come on... move!' Nothing.   60   65   70

EXAM-STYLE QUESTION

A03   **SKILLS**   CRITICAL THINKING, ANALYSIS, INTERPRETATION, DECISION MAKING

Refer to BOTH Text One AND Text Two to answer the following question.

Compare how the writers of Text One and Text Two convey their ideas and experiences.

Support your answer with examples from **both** texts.   **(15 marks)**

▲ 'Another chockstone is wedged between the walls...'

LEARNING OBJECTIVES

This lesson will help you to:
■ prepare for Section A of the Paper 1 exam.

PUTTING IT INTO PRACTICE

You should prepare for Section A of the Paper 1 exam by answering questions on unprepared non-fiction reading passages. The texts could be drawn from a range of contemporary non-fiction, including autobiography, travel writing, reportage, media articles, letters, diary entries and opinion pieces.

PREPARING FOR THE EXAM: NEED TO KNOW

■ All questions are compulsory.
■ Questions will test reading skills: factual comprehension; inference and an understanding of how writers use language; evaluation of how writers use linguistic and structural devices to achieve effect and comparative skills.
■ The pattern of questioning consists of short, specific questions on Text One and Text Two (separately targeted) followed by a more sustained comparative question drawing on the two passages as a whole.
■ Questions will be phrased so that they are understandable and clear. The shorter questions (1, 2, 4 and 5) will be more factually-based and phrased more directly, for example, Identify one point... or Name two things... Questions 3, 6 and 7 are longer and will require more overall interpretation, for example, How does the writer describe... or, in Question 7, Compare how the writers convey...
■ Section A is worth 40% of the total marks for the exam.
■ Further examples can be found in the Pearson Edexcel exemplar assessment materials.

HINT

Timing is crucial for exam success. You should spend one hour on Section A. As the texts will be unfamiliar to you, make sure you read them carefully. It is recommended that you spend 10 minutes reading the extracts, leaving 50 minutes to write your responses.

EXAM-STYLE QUESTIONS

A01	SKILLS ▶ INTERPRETATION
A01	SKILLS ▶ INTERPRETATION
A02	SKILLS ▶ CRITICAL THINKING, ANALYSIS, REASONING, INTERPRETATION

Read the extract from *How the Poor Die* (pages 106–108), which is about the writer's time in a hospital in Paris.

1 In lines 1–4 the writer describes his hospital ward.
   State **one** thing the writer observes about the room.   **(1 mark)**

2 In lines 88–95 the writer shares his thoughts on life and death.
   Identify **one** point the writer makes.   **(1 mark)**

3 How does the writer describe his thoughts and feelings about the hospital?
   You should support your answer with close reference to the passage, including **brief** quotations.   **(10 marks)**

Read the extract from *A Passage to Africa* (pages 70–72), which is about the writer's experiences reporting on the civil war in Somalia

A01	SKILLS ▶ INTERPRETATION
A01	SKILLS ▶ INTERPRETATION
A02	SKILLS ▶ CRITICAL THINKING, ANALYSIS, REASONING, INTERPRETATION
A03	SKILLS ▶ CRITICAL THINKING, ANALYSIS, INTERPRETATION, DECISION MAKING

4 In lines 4–9 the writer travels to a village.
   Identify **one** thing the writer says about the village. one thing the writer observes about the room.   **(1 mark)**

5 In lines 29–38 the writer describes seeing an old woman.
   State **two** things the writer observes about the woman.   **(2 marks)**

6 How does the writer present his views about his experiences as a television reporter?
   You should support your answer with close reference to the passage, including **brief** quotations.   **(10 marks)**

7 **Refer to BOTH Text One AND Text Two to answer the following question.**
   Compare how the writers of *How the Poor Die* and *A Passage to Africa* convey their ideas and experiences.
   Support your answer with examples from **both** texts.   **(15 marks)**

ANSWERS

1 One mark for any one of the following:
   - stuffy room
   - narrow beds
   - beds close enough together to touch your neighbour's hand
   - every sort of disease except infectious ones were present.

2 One mark for any one of the following:
   - people want to live
   - fear of death is what keeps people alive
   - better to die violently and not too old
   - disease is crueller than war
   - 'natural' death means something slow, smelly and painful.

3 Reward responses that demonstrate how the writer describes his thoughts and feelings about the hospital. Responses may include:
   - the writer's use of adjectives to make judgements about the hospital environment – 'stuffy room' and 'narrow beds'
   - use of numbers rather than names suggests the impersonality of treatment at the public hospital
   - the analogy between the nurse and a groom at a stableyard suggests a lack of empathy among the hospital staff
   - the lack of patient privacy – 'Everyone in the ward knew him by sight' and '[the corpse] was not removed till some time later'
   - jarring use of the phrase 'as usual' to describe the doctor's lack of interaction with Numéro 57, meaning 'as he always did' but suggesting somehow that this lack of empathy is 'usual' or normal
   - use of metaphor and simile to show how the medical staff dehumanise the patients – Numéro 57 is handled 'like a rolling pin' and 'showed [...] off like a piece of antique china'
   - ungrammatical sentence structure (line XX) emphasises the fact that 'nobody knew when' he had died; this fact is revisited at the end of the extract
   - juxtaposition of nurses and soldiers
   - onomatopoeia of 'clumping' to suggest the nurses' indelicacy and lack of feeling
   - shocking conclusion – Orwell decides that it is 'better to die violently' than in a public hospital like the one he has described to the reader.

4 One mark for any one of the following:
   - just outside Gufgaduud
   - it is in the back of beyond
   - no aid agencies had yet reached it
   - wrote instructions on how to reach it
   - like a ghost village.

5 One mark each for any two of the following:
   - abandoned by relations
   - smell of decaying flesh
   - festering wound where her shinbone should be
   - shot in the leg
   - leg had fused itself into the shape of a boomerang
   - leg was rotting
   - sick yellow eyes.

6 Reward responses that demonstrate how the writer presents his views about his experiences as a television reporter. Responses may include:

- language choices, describing his and his cameraman's actions as 'ghoulish' and as a 'hunt', which has connotations of predation
- use of analogy, such as that between news agencies' need for shocking stories or pictures with the 'craving for a drug', which seems exploitative
- surprisingly casual language used to describe the way in which editors consider once-shocking pictures to be 'the same old stuff'
- the writer's focus on the 'people in the comfort of their sitting rooms back home', which suggests that they are complicit in the ghoulishness of news reporters and news agencies
- contrast – the description of Habiba's death as 'famine away from the headlines' contrasts the two aspects of Alagiah's story (the horror of individual suffering and headlines about the famine in general)
- the image of the apologetic smile, which is more moving and memorable than 'stories' and 'evidence' of terrible events
- contrast between journalism that is focused on 'facts and figures', which he describes as 'easy' journalism,
- the reporter's helplessness – he describes his response as 'adequate', rather than more positive language choices such as 'good' or 'worthwhile', suggesting that he feels that it was 'the only' thing he could do
- extrapolation from the smile to make a comparison between Alagiah and the man, and therefore 'between the rich world and the poor world'
- the extract concludes with a sense of disappointment, focusing on Alagiah's regret that he never found out the man's name.

Read the following sample student answer to question 6 and then consider the examiner's comments.

the way he focuses on particular individuals and their tragedies. This shows an understanding of structure, and the different possibilities of writing about this subject.

He describes the death of the ten year-old Habiba... Here, the student begins to analyse language. Is there anything else you could say about this quotation to show a deeper analysis?

He is also skilled at creating not only images of the terrible sights he saw... This is an excellent point; sensory description is a key feature of this text.

drawing attention to a particular moment or sight. The student shows insight into structure again here.

George Alagiah has clearly been struck in a powerful way by what he encountered in Somalia. He wants to make his readers see what terrible conditions existed there and how fortunate we are to live in such a different world. He also shows that journalists often just start out by looking for the best stories they can find. But in this case, the stories affected him on a deeply emotional level.

The most powerful effect of Alagiah's writing is the way he focuses on particular individuals and their tragedies. He describes the death of the ten year-old Habiba in a graphic way: 'No rage, no whimpering, just a passing away'. He is also skilled at creating not only images of the terrible sights he saw but also uses the other senses to convey the horror, as when he writes: 'the smell of decaying flesh'.

One of the striking ways he presents his experiences is by drawing attention to a particular moment or sight. He does this especially when writing about the smile of the unknown man. His translator's explanation that he was 'embarrassed to be found in this condition' disturbed him and he could not get it out of his mind. He also realises that he never even found the man's name, and feels guilty about that, too. He almost seems ashamed of his life as a journalist and the way in which he was normally able to report on such events in a detached way.

Overall, Alagiah communicates to the reader the way in which people in that situation lack basic necessities and human respect. However, he also reflects on how he felt to be witnessing and reporting on these events.

7   Reward responses that compare how the writers present their ideas about their experiences. Responses may include the following elements or points.

■ Both texts describe a memorable experience from a retrospective first-person perspective.

■ Both texts describe events seen from an adult's perspective.

■ *How the Poor Die* begins with a short narrative sentence about how the writer comes to see the things that he goes on to report to the reader ('After some days…'). The second sentence then focuses on immediate descriptive details ('stuffy room'; 'narrow beds') rather than looking ahead to the deeper reflections that Orwell will discuss later. In comparison, *A Passage to Africa* begins with a list ('hungry, lean, scared and betrayed'), a rhetorical device that emphasises the overwhelmingly difficult conditions of Somalia.

■ *How the Poor Die* has a shocking, abrupt title that leads the reader to expect a description of a death and makes the text sound like a matter-of-fact report into the lives of the poor. On the other hand, the title of *A Passage to Africa* makes the reader expect to read a travelogue about a journey to or within Africa, but does not alert the reader to the horror of the writer's journey.

■ Orwell uses metaphorical and figurative language in his descriptions to emphasise the points he is making ('as grooms are said to do with horses'; 'in just the attitude of a woman handling a rolling-pin'; 'flickered out like a candle-end'). In comparison, *A Passage to Africa* is written like a piece of journalism and uses careful, predominantly objective descriptions.

■ The structure of both texts is quite similar, working slowly through descriptions of a number of characters but creating suspense: in *A Passage to Africa*, as the reader waits for the unforgettable face; in *How the Poor Die*, as the reader waits for a description of the deaths suggested by the title. Similarly, both texts end with searching reflections on humanity and life.

■ Neither of the texts uses much direct speech. The only direct speech in *How the Poor Die* is that of the patient who announces the deaths of others ('Numéro 43!' and 'Numéro 57!'), which focuses the reader's attention on seeing and hearing everything through Orwell's eyes and ears, rather than hearing for themselves. Similarly, *A Passage to Africa* only uses direct speech to give directions to the hamlet, which makes it feel immediate, as though the reader could also navigate there using these directions.

LEARNING OBJECTIVES

This lesson will help you to:

- practice reading and analysing unseen texts
- increase your familiarity with a variety of text types.

UNSEEN TEXTS

In Section A of your exam, you will be given two unseen text extracts and have to answer questions about them. The texts could be drawn from a range of contemporary non-fiction and may include different types of text. The two texts will be linked thematically. You will answer questions about each of them individually and you will also have to compare them.

This section contains 12 unseen texts for you to practice analysing and answering questions about them. The texts have been paired together with similar themes.

THE UNSEEN TEXTS

The twelve unseen texts and their themes are:

Theme	Text One	Text Two
New places	*The Great Railway Bazaar* by Paul Theroux	'Notes from an Author' by Paul Rosolie
Equal opportunities	'Speech to the UN General Assembly' by Malala Yousafzai	*I Know why the Caged Bird Sings* by Maya Angelou
Teenage life	'Lovely Prom Dress, Angel. Your Carriage to Absurdity Awaits' by India Knight	'Why all this Selfie Obsession?' by Grace Dent
Better living	*Teenage Kicks* by the Laureus Sport for Good Foundation	*The School Food Plan* by Henry Dimbleby and John Vincent
Out of this world	'Review of *Gravity*' by Robbie Collin	*The Men who Stare at Goats* by Jon Ronson
Fresh starts	'My Family Moved from Pakistan to the UK 40 Years ago – how far we've come' by Sarfraz Manzoor	A letter by W.E.B. Du Bois

You should prepare for Section A of the Paper 1 exam by answering questions on unprepared non-fiction reading passages. The texts could be drawn from a range of contemporary nonfiction, including autobiography, travel writing, reportage, media articles, letters, diary entries and opinion pieces.

▼ FROM *THE GREAT RAILWAY BAZAAR* BY PAUL THEROUX

The writer, Paul Theroux, spent four months travelling through Asia by train, publishing an account of his travels in 1975 as *The Great Railway Bazaar: By Train Through Asia*. In this extract, he is travelling through Burma, now generally known as Myanmar.

At the early sloping stations, women with trays were selling breakfast to the passengers: oranges, sliced pawpaws, fried cakes, peanuts and bananas. One had a dark shining assortment of beady objects on her tray. I beckoned her over and had a look. They were fat insects skewered on sticks—fried locusts. I asked the old man next to me if he'd like some. He said politely that he had had breakfast already, and anyway he never ate insects. "But the local people are quite fond of them."

pawpaws Tropical fruit.

5

Lashio A large town in Myanmar.

kyats Currency of Myanmar, approximately 0.001 pence

reproached Disapproved of or told off.

The sight of the locusts took away my appetite, but an hour later, in a thunderstorm, my hunger came back. I was standing near the door and struck up a conversation with a Burmese man on his way to Lashio to see his family. He was hungry too. He said we would be arriving at a station soon where we could buy food.   10

"I'd like some tea," I said.

"It is a short stop—a few minutes, not more."   15

"Look, why don't you get the food and I'll get something to drink? It'll save time."

He agreed, accepted my three kyats, and when the train stopped we leaped out—he to the food stall, I to an enclosure where there were bottles on display. The hawker explained with apologetic smiles that   20
I couldn't remove his teacups, so I had a cup of tea there and bought two bottles of soda water. Back on the train I couldn't find the Burmese man, and it was not until after the train pulled away that he appeared, out of breath, with two palm-leaf parcels, bound with a knotted vine. We uncapped the bottles on the door hinge, and, elbow   25
to elbow at the end of the coach, opened the palm leaves. There was something familiar in the contents, a wooden skewer with three blackened things on it—lumps of burned meat. It wasn't that they were irregularly shaped, but rather that they were irregular in exactly the same way. The skewers lay half-buried in beds of rice.   30

"In Burmese we call them–" He said the word.

I peered at them. "Are those wings?"

"Yes, they are birds."

Then I saw the little heads, the beaks and burned-out eyes, and dark singed claws on feeble feet.   35

"Maybe you call them sparrows," he said.

Maybe we do, I thought, but they looked so tiny without their feathers. He slipped one off the skewer, put the whole thing into his mouth, and crunched it, head, feet, wings, the whole bird; he chewed it, smiling. I pinched a little meat from one of mine and ate it. It did   40
not taste bad, but it is hard to eat a sparrow in Burma and not feel reproached by flights of darting birds. I risked the rice. I went back to my seat, so that the man would not see me throw the rest of the birds away.

▲ A woman selling food to passengers on a train in Burma (now generally known now as Myanmar)

basin An area of land that is drained by a river.

Heart of Darkness A short novel by Joseph Conrad, partly about a man's journey along a river in Africa.

watershed A river draining into a larger river.

sanctuary A refuge or safe haven.

superlative The best, or of the highest quality.

diversity Variety of plant and animal life.

Avatar An award-winning film partly set against a luxuriant rainforest backdrop.

boom A period of rapid growth in a particular market, such as rubber or timber.

mahogany An expensive type of wood.

anachronism Something that seems to belong to another time, especially a previous period of time.

pharmacy place where medicines are dispensed and sold.

mocha Coffee-coloured.

surreal Seemingly unreal.

tapir A South American mammal similar in shape to a pig.

spectacled caiman A type of alligator.

capybara A species of rodent, and the largest rodent in the world.

pristine Pure or unspoilt.

lacerated Wounded by deep cuts or tears.

hemorrhaging (American spelling of haemorrhaging) Literally, bleeding; metaphorically, losing.

geopolitical Relating to international politics affected by geography.

Goliath A giant in the Bible.

asphyxiating Depriving of oxygen or strangling.

grassroots Run by local or ordinary people.

eco-tourism Tourism to natural environments with the aim of seeing wildlife and supporting conservation work.

▼ FROM 'NOTES FROM AN AUTHOR' BY PAUL ROSOLIE

Paul Rosolie is a naturalist, author and award-winning wildlife film-maker. In this article, written for *National Geographic* in 2014, the author describes a journey into the Madre de Dios region of the Amazon basin.

In the blue pre-dawn light I'm standing in what feels like a deleted scene from *Heart of Darkness*. The river's unyielding power marches infinitely past, framed in the towering walls of misty moss-bearded jungle.

Winding like a golden snake through the heart of Peru's Madre de   5
Dios, Las Piedras is the longest watershed in the region. The vast
primary forest cover makes this river a sanctuary for the superlative
biodiversity contained in the surrounding national parks of the
Madre de Dios. There are more birds here than anywhere else,
more trees, more reptiles and amphibians, and over 70 species of   10
mammals. The river is also home to a substantial amount of isolated
tribes. In short, this place is a real-life *Avatar* of colour, diversity, and
mysterious culture.

In the pale light of dawn, I inflate my packraft and ready my paddle.
This will be day six of my travels. It's been as many days since I've   15
seen another human, and I like it that way. On Piedras it's important
to avoid accidentally encountering nomadic (uncontacted) tribes.
These are people who've been resisting contact for centuries, first
during the Spanish invasion of Peru, then during the more recent
rubber boom in the 1900s, and then again in the 1990s, when the   20
lesser-known mahogany boom swept through the region. They're a
living anachronism. While we surf the web and fly on planes, they
live naked in the jungle, surviving on what they can hunt with bows
and arrows, and staying healthy with a jungle pharmacy that Western
medicine could only dream of having access to.   25

As my raft glides through the smooth mocha current, I'm enveloped
in the surreal mist of a jungle paradise. I work the paddle silently,
steering past hanging vines. This is the best way to see wildlife,
silently moving through the morning. Earlier in the week, I paddled
beside a tapir crossing the river. Today, on an approaching beach, I   30
watch a flame red brocket deer sip water beneath a floral tapestry 10
metres tall. Lying on the beach is a spectacled caiman waiting for the
sun. Families of capybara are huddled in the river cane. The jungle
here is wildlife paradise: primary, old-growth forest packed with life.
But it may not be for much longer.   35

Just three years ago, this corner of the Earth was guarded by
hundreds of miles of deep jungle. So inaccessible and pristine, it was
a place few would ever see. Now things are different. A new road,
an offshoot of the Trans-Amazonian Highway, has lacerated deep
into the formerly pristine wilderness. The once-untouched wilderness   40
is hemorrhaging timber, gold, and wildlife as fortune seekers enter
to reap the wealth of the land. Now a very sinister race has started
in this hitherto unheard-of corner of the globe. The road is like a
tentacle of a geopolitical Goliath, steadily asphyxiating trees, wildlife,
and tribes that call the river home. The two grassroots eco-tourism   45

dike A wall or barrier designed to prevent flooding from the sea.

vortex Whirlwind.

operations that are battling to protect the river are currently stretched, with one finger in the dike and the other hand brandishing the knife they brought to this gunfight. So it is in the Amazon's Wild West.

Yet these stark realities don't seem real as I float past the ghostly visions of towering trees above. The sun is breaking up the mist and rays of gold are lighting up the landscape bit by bit. [50]

I lay my paddle over my lap and glide. The birds don't know I'm here until the last second. When they spot me the scene explodes. Brilliant red, blue and yellow birds burst from the clay and the green forest above, striking into the sun's rays with a collective shriek that shakes the water. For a breathless few moments I'm enveloped beneath a hurricane vortex of colour. [55]

The birds lift and swing south, as my raft departs the scene. They then circle around over the canopy to return to their clay-munching. As their colour and chatter fades behind, I'm left in a state of awe. Las Piedras is still the most incredible place I've ever seen. [60]

▲ The Amazon River

▼ FROM 'SPEECH TO THE UN GENERAL ASSEMBLY' BY MALALA YOUSAFZAI

the Taliban a fundamentalist Muslim movement.

Malala Yousafzai campaigns for children's right to an education. In the area of Pakistan in which she was born, the Taliban declared that girls should not be educated after the age of eight. In 2012, aged 15, she was shot in the head by the Taliban, but recovered fully and continued her campaign. In July 2013, she delivered a speech to the United Nations.

Dear friends, on the ninth of October 2012, the Taliban shot me on the left side of my forehead. They shot my friends too. They thought that the bullets would silence us. But they failed. And out of that silence came thousands of voices. The terrorists thought that they would change my aims and stop my ambitions, but nothing changed   5
in my life except this: weakness, fear and hopelessness died. Strength, power and courage were born.

I am the same Malala. My ambitions are the same. My hopes are the same. My dreams are the same.

Dear sisters and brothers, I am not against anyone. Neither am I   10
here to speak in terms of personal revenge against the Taliban or any other terrorist group. I am here to speak up for the right of education of every child. I want education for the sons and daughters of the Taliban, and all the terrorists and extremists.

Dear brothers and sisters, we want schools and education for every   15
child's bright future. We will continue our journey to our destination of peace and education. No one can stop us. We will speak up for our rights and we will bring change through our voice. We believe in the power and the strength of our words. Our words can change the whole world.   20

Because we are all together, united for the cause of education. And if we want to achieve our goal, then let us empower ourselves with the weapon of knowledge and let us shield ourselves with unity and togetherness.

Dear brothers and sisters, we must not forget that millions of people   25
are suffering from poverty, injustice and ignorance. We must not forget that millions of children are out of their schools. We must not forget that our sisters and brothers are waiting for a bright, peaceful future.

illiteracy The inability to read or write.

So let us wage a global struggle against illiteracy, poverty and   30
terrorism. Let us pick up our books and pens. They are our most powerful weapons.

One child, one teacher, one book and one pen can change the world.

Education is the only solution. Education First.

Thank you.   35

▲ Malala Yousafzai

▼ FROM *I KNOW WHY THE CAGED BIRD SINGS* BY MAYA ANGELOU

autobiography A person's account of their own life.

shorthand A technique used to enable people to take notes or minutes at high speed, most often used by journalists and secretaries.

ineligible Not allowed to take a particular position or role, often for legal reasons.

streetcars Trams.

motormen Sram drivers.

Guam An island in the Pacific Ocean, important during the Second World War.

colored (American spelling) A term previously used to refer to people of non white descent, especially black people; in modern use it is considered offensive.

serge A thick woollen fabric, from which uniforms are often made.

jauntily Cheerfully or confidently.

haughty Superior or disdainful.

terse To the point or abrupt.

▲ A traditional streetcar (tram)

Maya Angelou (1928–2014) was an African American author, poet, singer and actor. This is an extract from the first volume of her autobiography. In 1943, while still at school, she decided to get a job.

Once I had settled on getting a job, all that remained was to decide which kind of job I was most fitted for. My intellectual pride had kept me from selecting typing, shorthand or filing as subjects at school, so office work was ruled out. War plants and Shipyards demanded birth certificates, and mine would reveal me to be fifteen, and ineligible for work. So the well-paying defence jobs were also ruled out. Women had replaced men on the streetcars as conductors and motormen, and the thought of sailing up and down the streets of San Francisco in a dark blue uniform, with a money changer at my belt, caught my fancy.   5   10

Mother was as easy as I had anticipated. The world was moving so fast, so much money was being made, so many people were dying in Guam, and Germany, that hordes of strangers became good friends overnight. Life was cheap and death entirely free. How could she have the time to think about my academic career?   15

To her question of what I planned to do, I replied that I would get a job on the streetcars. She rejected the proposal with: "They don't accept colored people on the streetcars."

I would like to claim an immediate fury which was followed by the noble determination to break the restricting tradition. But the truth is, my first reaction was one of disappointment. I'd pictured myself, dressed in a neat blue serge suit, my money changer swinging jauntily at my waist, and a cheery smile for the passengers which would make their own work day brighter.   20

From disappointment I gradually ascended the emotional ladder to haughty indignation, and finally to that state of stubbornness where the mind is locked like the jaws of an enraged bulldog.   25

I would go to work on the streetcars and wear a blue serge suit. Mother gave me her support with one of her usual terse asides, "That's what you want to do? Then nothing beats a trial but a failure. Give it everything you've got. I've told you many times, "Can't do is like Don't Care." Neither of them have a home."   30

Translated, that meant there was nothing a person can't do, and there should be nothing a human being didn't care about. It was the most positive encouragement I could have hoped for.   35

prom A formal dance for students at high school or secondary school, held at the end of the school year.

rite of passage An event that marks an important moment in a person's life.

corsage A small bunch of flowers pinned to a prom dress.

demarcations Boundary lines.

nerdy Considered unfashionable or too studious.

manifestations Objects or events that clearly show an idea or concept.

over-egged Exaggerated or overdone.

mani-pedis Nail treatments: manicures for fingernails and pedicures for toenails.

Towie An acronym referring to The Only Way Is Essex, a television programme.

glitzier More glamourous or well-dressed.

vulgar Unsophisticated or in poor taste.

▲ A prom-style dress

▼ **FROM 'LOVELY PROM DRESS, ANGEL. YOUR CARRIAGE TO ABSURDITY AWAITS' BY INDIA KNIGHT**

This extract is from an article which appeared in *The Sunday Times* on 14 July 2013. In it, the writer India Knight considers the rise of the American-style school prom and argues her critical viewpoint about this rite of passage in modern teenagers' lives.

As a teenager I used to be obsessed with American proms, for which I blame the film *Grease*. I yearned for proms.

Now they're over here and I yearn for them to go back to where they came from. I've forgotten about the corsages and the pretty dresses of movie memory: what I remember now are the vivid descriptions 5
of pre-prom stress, the having no one to go to the prom with, the brutally enacted demarcations between the popular and the not so much, the nerdy girls sitting about, ignored.

All these unhappy manifestations of teenagehood can happen at a school disco, too, but at least your parents haven't blown their wages 10
for it to happen, you don't consider it the most significant night of your life to date, and it doesn't have the power to ruin your summer.

Everything that seemed appealing about proms now seems over-egged, starting with the startling levels of grooming that are expected of lovely, fresh-faced 16-year-olds: the fake tans and the extensions 15
and the mani-pedis and the giant eyelashes.

The dresses, which are, as I say, a sort of rehearsal for a wedding, cost an arm and a leg. And the whole thing looks so odd in pictures, given that girls mature much earlier than boys: a bunch of Towie'd-up women hanging out with what appear to be their little brothers. 20

Last week, a single mother, Hayley Harker, a hairdresser from Telford, Shropshire, spent £1,000 on her daughter Paige's prom night. Paige had had "five years of hell" at school and been bullied horribly. "The night was a chance for her to say goodbye to her school for good," Harker said. "I just wanted Paige to have what she 25
wanted, she deserved it and I had promised her she could have an amazing prom — no expense spared."

The story illustrates everything that's wrong with proms: the idea that they are the defining moment of your school career and that the glitzier you show yourself to be, the better you've done. Both are untrue. 30

The defining memory of Paige's school career will be having endured years of bullying. A horse-drawn carriage may have drawn gasps on the night, but if I know anything about mean teenage girls, it'll also have drawn sniggers.

Teachers spend children's school careers trying to reinforce the fact 35
that difference is valuable, that being yourself is the best you can be. And then it's prom night and all those lessons go out of the window: all that matters is how you look and how much your dress cost.

It's the opposite of what school ought to be about, and a weird note on which to end years of education. Nobody loves a party more 40
than me, but context is everything. Proms are yet another vulgar US import we could do without.

▼ FROM 'WHY ALL THIS SELFIE OBSESSION?' BY GRACE DENT

selfie A photograph that a person takes of themselves, usually using a smartphone.

buzzword A word or phrase that is very popular, often only for a short period of time.

accosted Approached boldly or aggressively.

#goodfriends #soblessed Examples of hashtags used on social media.

Woolworths A British high street retailer that went out of business in 2008.

irony Expressing a meaning in a way that appears to express the opposite, often for comic effect.

sans Without.

murky Dark and gloomy, or morally questionable.

Every year, the editors of the Oxford English Dictionary choose their 'Word of the Year': a word which they feel has been particularly important or relevant in the previous 12 months. In 2013, their chosen word was 'selfie'. On the day that their choice was announced, this article by Grace Dent appeared in *The Independent* newspaper.

Selfie – snapping a picture of yourself, largely for egotistical purposes – is the Word of the Year for Oxford Dictionaries editors. The frequency of its usage has increased by 17,000 per cent over the past 12 months.

Historians will look back at 2013 and note that in the UK, during a time of financial woe, youth unemployment and mass disenchantment, the buzzword of the year described the cheap, pocket-friendly pastime of staging a picture to look like a fantasy version of oneself. Cheeks sucked inwards. Biceps flexed. Maybe with one arm round a minor celeb whom you just accosted and who couldn't swat you away #goodfriends #soblessed. 5

10

In 1993, if you went to Woolworths three times a week to sit in the Foto-Me booth snapping pictures of yourself pulling poses, your ego would have been the stuff of local legend. Now, a selfie-a-day is unremarkable. We take selfies without irony, sans shame, posting the results online as bait in the great murky cyber-sea. We fish never-endingly for compliments, comments… indeed any feedback at all. Maybe just a Facebook like? A little Instagram regram and a new surge of followers. Anything – please God, anything – which indicates we were bathing, remotely, momentarily in another human being's gaze. 15

20

We're living through an age where a crucial aspect of public socialising is a little private party with oneself – staring at one's phone – editing, colour-filtering, posting.

By and large, though, the snapping and posting of selfies is a way to avoid our own thoughts. One reason that we sit with smartphones glued to our hands is so that, each time a difficult thought enters our brains, the distraction is literally at our fingertips. Thoughts like, "I need to load the dishwasher" or "How will I feel when my mother dies?" or "Why am I alone at Christmas?" or "Can I afford to replace the grubby stair carpet?". With a new selfie to post, and feedback to monitor, the pain is averted. Selfies are a mindless act available every time we need to be mindful. 25

30

Being mindful of difficult emotions, sitting with them, letting them torment you for a bit, and then working out solutions, 10 minutes a day of just thinking, eyes shut, without laptop, without phone, is doable. Just a short time without thinking: "Guys! How do I look? Do I look better today than yesterday? When you notice me what do you think? I'll take any feedback, stay tuned for another selfie." 35

In 2023, I can't help thinking, the happiest people will live several days a week away from their phones. And they won't need selfies to prove that they are happy. 40

▲ A woman taking a selfie

Premier League The first division of professional football in England and Wales.

Metropolitan Police The police force responsible for London and Greater London.

Arsenal FC A London football club that plays in the Premier League.

radius A specified distance from a specified centre, extending in all directions.

initiative A strategy or plan, usually designed to solve a problem or improve a situation.

antisocial behaviour Behaviour that breaks the law or social customs and causes distress or annoyance.

preventative Designed to stop a problem from occurring, rather than dealing with it once it has happened.

mentors Advisors or coaches.

▲ Football is used to work with young people at risk of offending.

▼ FROM *TEENAGE KICKS* BY THE LAUREUS SPORT FOR GOOD FOUNDATION

This extract is taken from the report *Teenage Kicks – The Value of Sport in Tackling Youth Crime*, commissioned by the Laureus Sport for Good Foundation and published in 2011. Kickz is a national project that aims to reduce youth crime by involving young people from under-privileged areas in sport, particularly football.

Kickz is a national programme, funded by the Premier League and Metropolitan Police, that uses football to work with young people at risk of offending in deprived areas. Arsenal FC delivers Kickz in Elthorne Park, getting kids off the street in the evening and playing football. The project has helped to transform the local area: there has been a reduction of 66% in youth crime within a one-mile radius of the project since it started.   5

THE PROJECT

Kickz is a national initiative that uses football to engage 12- to 18-year-olds in deprived areas. The projects are targeted at   10 neighbourhoods with high levels of antisocial behaviour and crime. Kickz is delivered on three or more evenings a week by professional football clubs. The sessions mostly involve football coaching, but they also provide coaching in other sports, such as basketball, and workshops on issues including drug awareness, healthy eating,   15 volunteering, careers and weapons. Although Kickz is open to everyone, many of the young people who attend are at risk of offending, and some are known offenders.

Football is used in two ways to stop crime:

Preventing young people from starting to offend: 20

Football keeps young people busy in the evenings when they might otherwise be on the streets getting into trouble. Youth workers and the police develop positive relationships with young people so that the authorities can better understand and react to the issues facing young people in the area. The programme is also an influential way   25 of delivering important preventative messages, for example, on the dangers of drugs and weapons.

Supporting young people who are already offending to stop, football is used to engage hard-to-reach young people, encourage positive relationships with adult mentors, and develop the confidence,   30 aspirations and skills to help young people move away from crime. Kickz also provides opportunities for young people including sports qualifications, volunteering and even employment.

Kickz is coordinated by Active Communities Network. Having started in 2006 with four clubs, there are now 39 professional   35 football clubs delivering Kickz projects to 30,000 young people in disadvantaged neighbourhoods around the UK.

▼ FROM *THE SCHOOL FOOD PLAN* BY HENRY DIMBLEBY AND JOHN VINCENT

The School Food Plan is a plan published in 2013 and agreed by the UK's Department for Education to improve the food available in schools. This is an extract from the summary of the plan.

This plan is about good food and happiness. It is about the pleasures of growing, cooking and eating proper food. It is also about improving the academic performance of our children and the health of our nation.

What we found

5

The quality of food in England's schools has improved enormously since 2005. There has been a clear, measurable improvement in the nutritional quality of most school food, and a reduction in junk foods.

The best schools do a brilliant job of weaving food education – cooking, growing vegetables, even modest efforts at animal husbandry – into school life and the curriculum. We have been hugely impressed by the energy and enthusiasm we have witnessed among school cooks, caterers, teachers, nutritionists, parents, volunteers, charity workers and many others working to make school food great.

10

15

But there is still work to be done. Some schools are lagging behind, serving food that is much too bland, boring and beige. Across the country, take-up of school food remains stubbornly low, at 43%. That means that 57% of children are not eating school lunches at all. Some graze instead on snack foods served at mid-morning break (when the standard offerings in our experience are panini, pizza and cake). Others go off-site to buy their lunch – usually junk food – or bring in a packed lunch.

20

Many parents mistakenly imagine that a packed lunch is the healthiest option. In fact, it is far easier to get the necessary nutrients into a cooked meal – even one of mediocre quality. Only 1% of packed lunches meet the nutritional standards that currently apply to school food.

25

What needs to be done

What you have in your hands (or on your screen) is not a traditional 'report', or a set of recommendations to the government. It is a plan. It contains a series of actions, each of which is the responsibility of a named person or organisation. These are the things that need to happen to transform what children eat at school, and how they learn about food.

30

35

junk foods Convenience foods that have low nutritional content.

animal husbandry The management and care of animals; in this instance, the care of farm animals.

nutritionists Experts in nutrition who advise people on food and healthy eating.

lagging behind Failing to catch up or keep up with others.

bland Dull and tasteless.

beige Pale sandy colour, often used as a way of suggesting that something is boring.

panini A sandwich made in an Italian-style roll.

mediocre Middling or average.

▲ Healthy food

toddlers Young children who are just learning to walk.

amniotic Refers to amniotic fluid, which surrounds unborn babies in the womb.

umbilical Refers to the umbilical cord, which attaches an unborn baby to its mother in the womb.

resonant A deep sound that continues to reverberate.

score The music composed for a film.

NASA The National Aeronautics and Space Administration, which is the government agency in charge of the U.S. space programme.

Hubble Telescope A observatory that is located in space and orbits the Earth.

veteran Someone with long experience of a particular subject.

zero-G Zero gravity.

country and western ballads Songs in a style that originated in rural southern areas of the U.S.

Houston A city in the U.S. state of Texas, home to NASA.

detonated Explode.

shrapnel Fragments, usually of a bomb.

ricochet Bounce.

muscovado A type of dark brown sugar.

Old Fashioneds A type of cocktail.

cosmos The universe.

▲ The Hubble Space Telescope

▼ FROM 'REVIEW OF *GRAVITY*' BY ROBBIE COLLIN

This extract is from a review of the award-winning film, *Gravity*, released in 2013 and starring George Clooney and Sandra Bullock. This review appeared in *The Telegraph* newspaper on 7 November 2013.

Watch an astronaut drifting through space for long enough and eventually you notice how much they look like a newborn baby. The oxygen helmet makes their head bigger, rounder and cuter; their hands grasp eagerly at whatever happens to be passing; their limbs are made fat and their movements simple by the spacesuit's cuddly bulk. They tumble head-over-heels like tripping toddlers or simply bob there in amniotic suspension. Even the lifeline that keeps them tethered to their ship has a pulsing, umbilical aspect. Gravity, the new Alfonso Cuarón picture, is a heart-achingly tender film about the miracle of motherhood, and the billion-to-one odds against any of us being here, astronauts or not. It's also a totally absorbing, often overpowering spectacle – a $100 million 3D action movie in which Sandra Bullock and George Clooney play two Hollywood-handsome spacefarers, fighting for their lives 375 miles above the Earth's crust. A series of captions over the opening titles reminds us that this is a dead zone: no oxygen or air pressure, and nothing to carry sound. "Life in space is impossible," the final message tells us, as the cinema shakes with Steven Price's resonant score, and then suddenly falls quiet. For Dr Ryan Stone (Bullock), a mission specialist in orbit for the first time, the lack of noise is welcome. She's a medical engineer called up by NASA to install new software on to the Hubble Telescope, but also a mother in mourning for her four-year-old daughter, whom she lost in a senseless accident, and the silence enfolds her like a comfort blanket. The shuttle pilot is Matt Kowalski (Clooney), a divorcee and veteran of zero-G. While Stone works on Hubble, he boosts around her playfully, piping country and western ballads over the team's intercom and telling stories about his unfortunate love-life.

"Houston, I have a bad feeling about this mission," Kowalski jokes, although by the end of the opening shot, which runs unbroken for a progressively astonishing 17 minutes, his fears have proven well-founded. On the other side of the planet, Russia has detonated an old spy satellite, and the shrapnel is hurtling towards our heroes at bullet-speed. Cuarón understands the power of the shot. He doesn't just show us the impact and its aftermath, his camera explains it to us; tracking objects as they crash into and ricochet off one another with terrifying solidity, then holding on Stone and Kowalski as they plummet away from the wreckage and into nothingness. Cuarón holds a close-up on Stone's face as she gulps at her falling air supply, and then moves closer still – and suddenly we become Stone, gasping at oxygen that's barely there and watching Earth spin into the distance through the glass bubble of her helmet. Cuarón and his son Jonás, who co-wrote the script, have given Bullock the role of her career, and she returns the favour with the performance of a lifetime. Clooney, meanwhile, is exactly as you'd hope Clooney in space would be: cool-headed but still flirtatious, with a muscovado drawl that suggests he's a couple of Old Fashioneds to the good. A cast like that could overwhelm a film with less in its head, veins and soul, but Gravity swings perfectly in the balance between stars and cosmos. This is one of the films of the year.

5

10

15

20

25

30

35

40

unit A subdivision of soldiers in an army.

covert Secret or undercover

Lee Marvin An American film and television actor.

terrain The ground and its physical features.

mystique An air of mystery or secrecy.

▲ A goat

▼ FROM *THE MEN WHO STARE AT GOATS* BY JON RONSON

Written by journalist Jon Ronson and published in 2004, *The Men Who Stare at Goats* is a book about the First Earth Battalion, a secret unit created by the U.S. Army in 1979 to explore the powers of the human mind. They believed that, using only their minds, soldiers could make themselves invisible, walk through walls and kill goats just by staring at them.

This is a true story. It is the summer of 1983. Major General Albert Stubblebine III is sitting behind his desk in Arlington, Virginia, and he is staring at his wall, upon which hang his numerous military awards. They detail a long and distinguished career. He is the United States army's chief of intelligence, with 16,000 soldiers under his command. 5
He controls the army's signals intelligence, their photographic and technical intelligence, their numerous covert counter-intelligence units, and their secret military spying units, which are scattered throughout the world. He would be in charge of the prisoner-of-war interrogations too, except this is 1983, and the war is cold, not hot. 10

He looks past his awards to the wall itself. There is something he feels he needs to do even though the thought of it frightens him. He thinks about the choice he has to make. He can stay in his office or he can go into the next office. That is his choice. And he has made it.

He is going into the next office. 15

General Stubblebine looks a lot like Lee Marvin. In fact, it is widely rumored throughout Military Intelligence that he is Lee Marvin's identical twin. His face is craggy and unusually still, like an aerial photograph of some mountainous terrain taken from one of his spy planes. His eyes, forever darting around and full of kindness, seem to 20
do the work for his whole face.

In fact he is not related to Lee Marvin at all. He likes the rumor because mystique can be beneficial to a career in intelligence. His job is to assess the intelligence gathered by his soldiers and pass his evaluations on to the deputy director of the CIA and the Chief of 25
Staff for the Army, who in turn pass it up to the White House. He commands soldiers in Panama, Japan, Hawaii, and across Europe. His responsibilities being what they are, he knows he ought to have his own man at his side in case anything goes wrong during his journey into the next office. 30

Even so, he doesn't call for his assistant, Command Sergeant George Howell. This is something he feels he must do alone.

Am I ready? he thinks. *Yes, I am ready.*

He stands up, moves out from behind his desk, and begins to walk.

I mean, he thinks, what is the atom mostly made up of anyway? Space! 35

He quickens his pace.

What am I mostly made up of? he thinks. *Atoms!*

He is almost at a jog now.

What is the wall mostly made up of? he thinks. *Atoms! All I have to do is* merge the spaces. *The wall is an* illusion. *What is destiny? Am I* 40
destined to stay in this room? Ha, no!

Then General Stubblebine bangs his nose hard on the wall of his office.

Damn, he thinks.

▼ FROM 'MY FAMILY MOVED FROM PAKISTAN TO THE UK 40 YEARS AGO – HOW FAR WE'VE COME' BY SARFRAZ MANZOOR

In 1974, Sarfraz Manzoor arrived in the UK from Pakistan. In this extract from his article, published in *The Guardian* newspaper in 2014, he reflects on his past, present and future.

How far we have come. Forty years ago this very week – 16 May 1974 – a plane that had set off from Lahore landed in London. Among the passengers was Rasool Bibi, a 41-year-old Pakistani woman, with her daughter, 12, and sons, aged 11 and two. It was their first plane journey and the first time any of them had left Pakistan. 5

I was the youngest of the children– I was almost three – and at the airport we waited nervously for our father to meet us and take us to our new home and our uncertain fate.

My father, Mohammed Manzoor, had been in Britain for 11 years, visiting Pakistan only twice during that time. He had left my mother 10 and his children in the hope of finding work in Britain that would enable him to send for us. When we joined him he was working on the production line at the Vauxhall car factory and that was how we came to live in Luton, in the Bury Park area.

As a little boy in the 70s, mine was an insular existence, enclosed 15 within the Pakistani bubble of Bury Park and largely unaware that any other world existed. I was a teenager in the 80s, a decade of frustration as I realised I was different from my white friends who were allowed to have girlfriends and parties and free will. In the 90s, I left Luton and my family to study and live in Manchester only to be 20 forced to return in the spring of 1995 for my father's death. I spent the next 10 years fearing an arranged marriage before finding the courage to reject it, and the fortune to find love.

My father is buried in Luton and my mother lives less than a 10-minute drive from the very first house she lived in. When I was 25 young I didn't want to spend time with my parents or their friends. It is one of the more surprising aspects about the passing of time to learn that not only do I love the things I once resented – I need them too. I need them because as the previous generation slips into the arms of history, my generation finds itself the keeper of memories, the 30 teller of stories. It will be my job to tell my daughter, Laila, about her Pakistani grandad and grandma and what life was like way back then.

I look at Laila and I see distant echoes of my father and of me but I also see how different her world will be. Her history includes the history of myself and my parents but it is not dominated by it. There 35 are fewer rigid certainties to constrain her future, she can believe that no road is closed to her.

This story began with my mother arriving at Heathrow airport and it ends, or perhaps begins again, with my daughter's birth in an east London hospital. She could only exist now. She is the past, the 40 present and the future – a joyous hope-filled reminder of how far we have come.

Luton An industrial town north-west of London.

arranged marriage A marriage planned and arranged for the couple by their families.

▲ Sarfraz Manzoor

▼ A LETTER BY W.E.B. DU BOIS

W.E.B. Du Bois was a writer and civil-rights activist. He was the first African-American to achieve a PhD from Harvard University and, in 1909, he co-founded the National Association for the Advancement of Colored People. In 1914, he sent his 13-year-old daughter, Yolanda, to a boarding school in England. She received this letter from him soon after she arrived.

New York, October 29, 1914

Dear Little Daughter,

I have waited for you to get well settled before writing. By this time I hope some of the strangeness has worn off and that my little girl is working hard and regularly.   5

Of course, everything is new and unusual. You miss the newness and smartness of America. Gradually, however, you are going to sense the beauty of the old world: its calm and eternity and you will grow to love it.

Above all remember, dear, that you have a great opportunity. You   10
are in one of the world's best schools, in one of the world's greatest modern empires. Millions of boys and girls all over this world would give almost anything they possess to be where you are. You are there by no desert or merit of yours, but only by lucky chance.

Deserve it, then. Study, do your work. Be honest, frank and fearless   15
and get some grasp of the real values of life. You will meet, of course, curious little annoyances. People will wonder at your dear brown and the sweet crinkley hair. But that simply is of no importance and will soon be forgotten. Remember that most folk laugh at anything unusual, whether it is beautiful, fine or not. You, however, must not   20
laugh at yourself. You must know that brown is as pretty as white or prettier and crinkley hair as straight even though it is harder to comb. The main thing is the YOU beneath the clothes and skin—the ability to do, the will to conquer, the determination to understand and know this great, wonderful, curious world. Don't shrink from   25
new experiences and custom. Take the cold bath bravely. Enter into the spirit of your big bed-room. Enjoy what is and not pine for what is not. Read some good, heavy, serious books just for discipline: Take yourself in hand and master yourself. Make yourself do unpleasant things, so as to gain the upper hand of your soul.   30

Above all remember: your father loves you and believes in you and expects you to be a wonderful woman.

I shall write each week and expect a weekly letter from you.

Lovingly yours,

Papa   35

colored A term previously used to refer to people of non-white descent, especially black people; in modern use it is considered offensive.

frank Open and sincere.

▲ W.E.B. Du Bois

SECTION B: READING AND WRITING

Assessment Objective 1

Read and understand a variety of texts, selecting and interpreting information, ideas and perspectives

Assessment Objective 4

Communicate effectively and imaginatively, adapting form, tone and register of writing for specific purposes and audiences

Assessment Objective 5

Write clearly, using a range of vocabulary and sentence structures, with appropriate paragraphing and accurate spelling, grammar and punctuation

In Section B, the Assessment Objectives are worth the following amounts.
AO1 – 10%
AO4 – 12%
AO5 – 8%

This chapter focuses on Section B of Papper 1 of the English Language B course. Working through these lessons and activities will help you to develop the reading and writing skills that you will need for Section B of the Paper 1 exam.

The chapter consists of the following section:
■ Transactional writing.

Section B is worth 30% of the total marks for Paper 1.

In Section B, you will need to be able to meet Assessment Objectives AO1, AO4 and AO5.

AN INTRODUCTION TO TRANSACTIONAL WRITING

Transactional writing is non-fiction writing for a purpose: to inform, explain, review, argue, persuade or advise. Each task will be aimed at dealing with one or two of these purposes (for example, 'to explain' will involve some informing).

Section B of Paper 1 will give you a task of this kind. Typically, it will present you with a debatable statement in inverted commas and ask you to write an article, a speech or a letter in which you express your views. You will have about an hour to plan and write it and it is worth 30% of the total marks for the whole paper. The topic will not require any specialised knowledge. Topics might include aspects of school life, transport and travel, common leisure activities such as sports and the internet, and aspects of the media.

TYPES OF TRANSACTIONAL WRITING

▲ Gamers need informative texts.

The six types of transactional writing covered in Section B of the paper can be defined as follows.

- To **inform**: to pass on information (this includes descriptive writing).
- To **explain**: to make clear how or why something is as it is.
- To **review**: to outline a piece of work, or an event, and comment on it.
- To **argue**: to produce an organised sequence of reasons to support a point of view.
- To **persuade**: to convince an audience or reader to think or act in a certain way.
- To **advise**: to give useful suggestions and ideas to help someone or some people.

ACTIVITY 1 **AO1** **AO2** **SKILLS** CRITICAL THINKING, PROBLEM SOLVING, ANALYSIS, ADAPTIVE WRITING

▼ TEXTS WITH DIFFERENT PURPOSES

1 Read the following extracts from texts with different purposes. Identify the language techniques that are used in each text to help it achieve its purpose.

- **Inform**: A videogame console is an interactive entertainment computer or electronic device that produces a video display signal which can be used with a display device (a television, computer monitor, etc.) to display a videogame.
- **Persuade**: Nintendo changes the way you play by maximising the fun and minimising the fuss. The Wii console makes you feel less like a player and more like you're in the game.
- **Explain**: Why do we play videogames? The need for play is a primary component of human development and has been with us since the dawn of intelligence. Even in the brains of animals can be seen the impetus that leads to play. So, before we tackle videogaming, we should assess why we, as a species, need playtime so strongly.

2 Choose a computer game, television programme or book that you particularly like. Write three short paragraphs like the paragraphs above. One should inform your reader, one should persuade your reader, and one should explain to your reader.

▼ TYPES OF TRANSACTIONAL WRITING

Look back over the following texts, then copy and complete the table. Which types of transactional writing can you find in each text?

	▼ INFORM	▼ EXPLAIN	▼ REVIEW	▼ ARGUE	▼ PERSUADE	▼ ADVISE
Malala Yousafzai's speech (page 128)	✓	✓		✓	✓	
'Why all this selfie obsession?' (page 131)						
From *A Passage to Africa* by George Alagiah (pages 70–72)						
From *Teenage Kicks – The Value of Sport in Tackling Youth Crime* (page 132)						
Review of *Gravity* (page 134)						
'Are Humans Definitely Causing Global Warming?' (page 75)						
'I have a dream' speech by Martin Luther King (page 63)						

HINT

When reading more widely, try to identify different types of transactional writing. This will help prepare you for the exam.

▼ IDENTIFY TRANSACTIONAL WRITING

Identify types of transactional writing in other passages that you have read in this book to add more examples to the table in Activity 2.

LEARNING OBJECTIVES

This lesson will help you to:

- understand in more detail the features of writing to inform, explain and review, and how you should tackle these writing tasks.

WRITING FOR A PURPOSE: INFORM, EXPLAIN, REVIEW

In many ways, writing to inform is the most straightforward writing task. Its main requirements are that it should be accurate, clear and well organised. Explanation also involves giving information, of course, but there is a greater need to select the information required and organise it so that you explain the topic clearly. A review informs you about a product or event and gives you a reasoned opinion on it.

WRITING TO INFORM

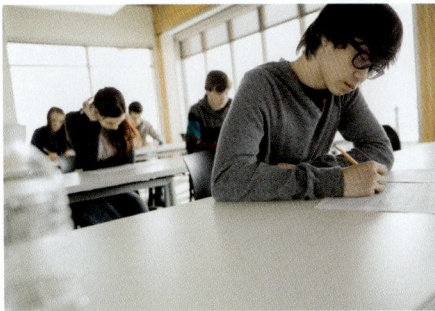

In informative text, it is important to think about your readers and make sure that they will be able to understand what you write.

▲ Informative writing is in some ways the most straightforward writing task, but does have its own challenges.

ACTIVITY 1   **A02**   SKILLS ▶ ADAPTIVE LEARNING, CREATIVITY

▼ FOCUSING ON THE READER

Read the following question and sample student response.

▶ **A young person from another country is coming to spend a term at your school or college. Write to inform them about your school or college and what happens in an ordinary day there.**

Dear Emilja,

Our school is called New City High School. The school has been built on the outskirts of our town and it is quite a new building. The school has 1200 young people from the age of 11 up to 18. The school site has been landscaped and there are lawns and trees on it. There are playgrounds and sports facilities which are very popular.

The day starts at 8.30 am. Most students get there by bus and walk up from the bus turning point outside the school gates. Registration is from 8.30 until 8.45 with your form teacher. All sorts of things go on in registration time. You can hand in notes if you have been off sick, or money if you are paying to go on a school trip. Some days you can go out to the library and return your books. On Tuesday and Friday there is assembly in the hall. This is where we have a speech from the Headteacher and sometimes she gives out prizes and cups to the sports teams that have won. We might have some music if the choir or the school bands have practised something to play to the school. Following that lesson 1 starts at 8.45 and what you have will depend upon your timetable and what day it is.

▶

Students are supposed to line up outside classrooms if the teacher is not there. When the teacher arrives you are supposed to: go in quietly; stand behind your chair; wait until the teacher has said 'good morning'; and then you can sit down. Outdoor coats should not be worn in class. Students are supposed to take them off and put them on the back of the chair. There is a cloakroom where they can be left but most students don't because it is not very convenient.

Yours sincerely,

Takuma

Annotate the sample answer, labelling all the positive things you can find in it (such as good sentences, clear writing, good vocabulary and punctuation). Now read the mark scheme (page 172) carefully and decide what mark you think this answer deserves.

ACTIVITY 2   A02   SKILLS ▶ CRITICAL THINKING, ANALYSIS, INTERPRETATION

▼ TECHNIQUES FOR INFORMATIVE WRITING

Look again at the letter in Activity 1. Identify an example of each of the techniques listed in the following table and explain the effect of each technique.

▼ ELEMENTS/TECHNIQUES	▼ EXAMPLE	▼ EFFECT
Headings		
Facts		
Statistics		
Language choices		
Structure		
Tone		
Description*		

* Remember that **description** is a type of informative writing (since it tells you what something looks like), which means that your understanding of this skill acquired from creative writing and from analysing other texts will be useful.

WRITING TO EXPLAIN

Any question that contains the word 'how' or 'why' expects you to do some sort of explanation. Use clear paragraphs to organise your response. In the 45 minutes that you will have in the exam, you will probably have time to include four to six paragraphs. Try to link your paragraphs using signposting words such as 'firstly', 'therefore' and 'in addition'.

ACTIVITY 3 **A02** SKILLS CRITICAL THINKING, ANALYSIS, INTERPRETATION

▼ FEATURES OF EXPLANATORY WRITING

A number of features will be found in explanatory writing. Copy and complete the following table using examples of your own or examples that you have found in the texts in this book.

▼ 'EXPLAIN' FEATURES	▼ EXAMPLES	▼ INTENDED EFFECT
Texts have a title that asks 'how' or 'why'.		
Texts use features such as clear paragraphs, bullet points, bold font and subheadings.		
Texts use connectives to show a series of points or events (for example, 'firstly').		
Texts use connectives to explain cause and effect (for example, 'because').		
Texts may contain diagrams.		
Texts may use technical or specialist vocabulary.		
Texts use formal or impersonal style in which neither the writer nor reader is directly involved.		
Texts are clearly structured and reach a conclusion that reminds the reader of the question.		

ACTIVITY 4 **A01** **A04** **A05** SKILLS PROBLEM SOLVING, CRITICAL THINKING, ANALYSIS, CREATIVITY, INNOVATION

▼ WRITING A PRACTICE ANSWER

The topic you may be asked to explain will be something general like this.

▶ **Write an article for your school magazine explaining how you make your decisions with regard to either your GCSE or your A level subjects.**

Plan and write an answer to this question in no more than one hour. Complete a table based on the one in Activity 2 to help you use some of the techniques listed in the table.

HINT

The strategies in Activity 5 can be applied to any writing task.

ACTIVITY 5 **A04** **A05** SKILLS ADAPTIVE LEARNING, CREATIVITY

▼ ADAPTING YOUR LANGUAGE FOR CHILDREN

Try writing the same piece that you wrote in response to Activity 4 for a group of 11-year-olds. How would you adapt your language for them?

WRITING TO REVIEW

Since reviews are written for commercial publications such as newspapers, reviews need to be well written in order to engage the reader. This also means that the register can change depending on the readership: if the readers are teenagers, the language will probably be more colloquial and 'teenager-friendly'.

If you are asked to write a review in Section B, it is likely that it will be about a book, a film, an event or a computer game of your own choice. As part of the review, you should describe the overall qualities and effects of the subject that you have chosen.

▶ **Look back at the review of *Star Wars* on page 77 and write down a list of the points that the reviewer makes about the film.**

The key to writing successfully is to make a plan in manageable sections so that you have less thinking to do while you are writing. In the hour that you have to complete Section B, you are expected to write 400–600 words (2–3 sides).

KEY POINT

Although a review is inevitably personal, readers need to trust your opinion, so assertions need to be evidenced in some way, without bias.

ACTIVITY 6   **AO4**   **SKILLS**   CRITICAL THINKING, PROBLEM SOLVING

▼ STRUCTURING A REVIEW

Think of a film that you have enjoyed recently and use the table below to plan a review of it in no more than six paragraphs. Look at your list of points made in the review of *Star Wars* for guidance. Things to write about will include the story, the characters, the dialogue or screenplay, the acting, the visual elements (settings, cinematography, effects), the pace, the music and so on.

Paragraph 1	
Paragraph 2	
Paragraph 3	
Paragraph 4	
Paragraph 5	
Paragraph 6	

Once you have created an outline, it should be quite easy to fill it in. See if you can do this now. Copy and complete the table below to structure your ideas and key points.

▼ STORY-LINE	▼ SCRIPT/ DIALOGUE	▼ CINEMATO-GRAPHY	▼ ACTING	▼ VISUAL ELEMENTS
Take care! No spoilers!		Including CGI		

LEARNING OBJECTIVES

This lesson will help you to:

■ understand how to distinguish between writing to argue, writing to persuade and writing to advise, and how to approach these writing tasks.

WRITING FOR A PURPOSE: ARGUE, PERSUADE, ADVISE

In each of these types of writing, the aim is to persuade the reader using various techniques. There are many kinds of 'argue' question, but they will generally ask you to do one or both of the following:

■ present reasons, with evidence, in support of (or against) a viewpoint

■ develop a point of view.

WRITING TO ARGUE

A typical 'argue' exam question might be:

'Some experts believe that a school uniform creates more problems than it solves and should be abolished in all schools.'

Give your views on this topic, arguing either in favour of school uniform or against it. Your argument may include:

■ the advantages and disadvantages of uniforms

■ the potential problems caused by uniforms

■ any other points you wish to make.   **(30 marks)**

Look at the following students' attempts to begin an answer to this question.

EXAMPLE STUDENT ANSWER A

Some experts say school uniform creates more problems than it solves, i am going to tell u my views. My first opinion about school uniform is very clear and I am against the school uniform, School uniforms are horrible,
i hate ours. Teachers say that it is smart but i couldn't disagree more. It makes me look fat. And the colour is soo bad it makes u feel ill. There are lots of other reasons why it is rubbish e.g. it is not cheap and it is not good kwality, they say that school uniform makes us look the same so nobody can tell the difference between rich kidz and poor kidz, but u can becos the rich ones still make there uniform look like designer wear always.
School uniform makes us look like zombies.

EXAMPLE STUDENT ANSWER B

In my opinion, school uniform should not be abolished. This is because it makes our school look neat and tidy. The ties keep our collars in check, while the shoes make us look like young businessmen and women. This is important as it helps to build a healthy relationship for our college which is what we should be striving to do.
In my view, the uniform defines us as a school; it distinguishes from others. I appreciate that we are not seen as individuals, but it is important that we are seen as easily recognised out of school and in school. This gives us a sense of pride and belonging. I think it also makes us behave better; nobody gains if our school has a reputation for bad behaviour. Moreover, uniform also has

▲ Does school uniform create more problems than it solves?

> very practical advantages. For instance, we have different ties in our school for prefects and for other students. This is useful when prefects do their duties because they are easily identifiable.

Even if you don't agree with the point of view expressed, it is easy to see that one of these answers is much better than the other.

■ **What makes Answer B better than Answer A?**

ACTIVITY 1 | **AO3** | **SKILLS** CRITICAL THINKING, DECISION MAKING

▼ **WHAT MAKES A GOOD ANSWER?**

Read the 10 statements given in the following table. Five apply to Answer A and five to Answer B. After reading each statement, put a tick in the correct column depending on whether you think the statement applies to Answer A or Answer B.

▼ STATEMENT	▼ ANSWER A	▼ ANSWER B
Sentences are badly punctuated and there are several spelling mistakes.		
A wide range of words and sentence structures is used to engage the reader.		
Text speak, abbreviations and slang are inappropriately used.		
The first sentence repeats the question and there is a limited range of words and sentence structures.		
It is firmly structured in paragraphs and ideas are carefully linked by words and phrases.		
The tone is serious and the argument is very logical.		
The tone is too informal and ideas are not linked clearly.		
The structure is weak and there are no paragraphs.		
The spelling, punctuation and grammar are correct.		
Points are made clearly, and reasons and evidence are given for them.		

WRITING TO PERSUADE

To persuade means trying to influence someone to:
■ accept a point of view
■ behave in a certain way.

The first type of question might ask you to argue persuasively in favour of a statement in a class debate (for example, 'Smoking should be banned in all public places'). The second type of question might ask you to write a letter to persuade one or more people to do something (for example, take part in a charity event).

If you want to persuade someone successfully, you will need to use a strong argument, but you will be even more successful if you use language to make them agree with you.

KEY POINT

You can persuade with the ideas in your argument, but you can also persuade with intelligent use of language itself.

Persuasive writing techniques include:

- linking your ideas with words that connect and develop them, such as, 'moreover', 'furthermore', 'in addition', 'on the other hand'
- using words like 'this' or 'these' to link new paragraphs with previous paragraphs
- using evidence or supporting points from personal knowledge or experience
- making your language choices expressive and lively.

ACTIVITY 2 | **A02** | SKILLS ▸ CRITICAL THINKING, INTERPRETATION

▼ ANSWERING A 'PERSUADE' QUESTION

Here is an example of a persuasive speech in answer to the following question.

▸ **How would you persuade the Governors to redecorate the school?**

I am here today to tell you that I believe there should be many changes to help students. I know that these ideas will cost a lot of money but I reckon they will greatly improve the facilities and the atmosphere.

First I believe we should redecorate the school. If we made the place look more pleasant then students will be happier and they will work better too. In particular the toilets are in urgent need of refurbishment. It would be a good idea to introduce some new subjects in the curriculum that are more relevant to the students. Teaching methods need to be looked at, so that students can have more modern ways of learning things.

You could also look into methods of making people want to come to school. Perhaps you could give special privileges to students who regularly attend. The school rules need to be looked at as many are out of date. Why not have a special area set aside for smokers, as long as they bring a letter from their parents?

What do you think of this speech? Copy and complete the table, adding points of your own.

▼ MERITS	▼ WEAKNESSES	▼ HOW YOU COULD IMPROVE IT
It is accurately written.	It does not go into much detail.	Give more reasons for the ideas.
The advice is generally clear and structured.	Some of the ideas are controversial and the writer should justify them.	Quote more evident to support the ideas.
The tone is appropriate and the words are formal (suitable for this audience).	It ends very suddenly.	Show more awareness of the audience for whom it is intended.

WRITING TO ADVISE

Most people give and receive advice almost every day. This advice is often social or moral (for example, how to deal with a personal problem). In general, in an exam, you will have to:

- give helpful opinions, suggestions or information to a specified person or group of people
- recommend a course of action to someone, perhaps guiding or warning them.

A question may be worded to combine both these possibilities, but the advice will almost always be targeted at a specific audience or reader.

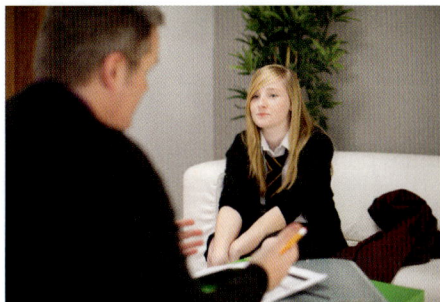

▲ Advising someone involves trying to influence them.

'Writing to advise' is linked to 'writing to argue and persuade'. If you give advice to someone, you will also be trying to influence them to follow your advice, so persuasion and reasoning play a part.

| ACTIVITY 3 | A04 | A05 | SKILLS | PROBLEM SOLVING, ADAPTIVE LEARNING, CREATIVITY, INNOVATION |

▼ ANSWERING AN 'ADVISE' QUESTION

Imagine you are an expert who gives advice on a website. Write your replies to these questions from a teenager and a parent.

> Hello,
>
> I am being bullied by some people in my form at school. They aren't hitting me, they're just calling me names and I'm fed up with it. What can I do?
>
> Mohammed

> Hello,
>
> My fourteen-year-old daughter seems to spend all her time on social media. I am really worried about her. I don't understand it. How can I help her?
>
> Mrs P

| ACTIVITY 4 | A02 | SKILLS | CRITICAL THINKING |

▼ ANALYSING AN ANSWER

Look at this exam-style question and the first part of an example student answer. How good do you think this answer is?

▶ **You have been asked to speak to younger students at your school or college, giving advice on how to cope with exams. Write the talk you would give, thinking carefully about the purpose of your talk and the audience for whom it is intended.**

> To some people, examinations are the most difficult situation to go through. Others find them easy, an opportunity to show off what they have learned. Whichever category you believe that you fall into, it really does not matter. The idea is to realise which category you fall into then understand how to conquer your weaknesses and maximise your strengths. However, what I tell you today will be useful for all of you. The first stage for any examination is to prepare for it. If you fail to prepare, you prepare to fail. It really is a simple as that...

| ACTIVITY 5 | A01 | A04 | A05 | SKILLS | PROBLEM SOLVING, CRITICAL THINKING, ANALYSIS, CREATIVITY, INNOVATION |

▼ WRITING A SPEECH

Write your own speech in answer to the question in Activity 4. Your speech should be about 350–400 words long.

LEARNING OBJECTIVES

This lesson will help you to:
- understand how to write for different audiences.

▲ 'Certain gases that trap heat are building up in Earth's atmosphere...'

WRITING FOR AN AUDIENCE

The Section B task will specify your target audience or readership. Possible tasks include writing to a school class or assembly, writing a letter to a headteacher or school governors or to a teenager abroad, and writing an article for a school or local magazine. As a writer, you need to make decisions about such things as register, style and tone, all of which will depend on your audience.

ACTIVITY 1   A01   A02   SKILLS ▸ CRITICAL THINKING, ANALYSIS, INTERPRETATION

▼ THINKING ABOUT YOUR AUDIENCE

Consider the following extracts about climate change. What audience do you think each one is written for?

1 Highlight any words or phrases that are particularly suitable for the audience.

2 Circle words and phrases that show the register of the piece of writing.

3 List the decisions that the writer has made to make the writing suitable for the intended audience.

EXTRACT A

Certain gases that trap heat are building up in Earth's atmosphere. The primary culprit is carbon dioxide, released from burning coal, oil and natural gas in power plants, cars, factories etc. (and to a lesser extent when forests are cleared). The second is methane, released from rice paddies, both ends of cows, rotting garbage in landfills, mining operations, and gas pipelines. Third are chlorofluorocarbons (CFCs) and similar chemicals, which are also implicated in the separate problem of ozone depletion ... Nitrous oxide (from fertilizers and other chemicals) is fourth...

EXTRACT B

People are seeing change all over the world. Arctic sea ice is melting earlier and forming later. Glaciers are disappearing. Heat waves, storms and floods are becoming more extreme. Insects are emerging sooner and flowers are blooming earlier. In some places, birds are laying eggs before they're expected and bears have stopped hibernating.

EXTRACT C

So what's going on?

For real, all it takes is a couple degrees
Before floods, droughts, and hurricanes are not anomalies
And all these catastrophes become our new realities
Comin' down on the world just like the Sword of Damocles.

▶

We need smarter ideas for sustainable policies
New technologies for a new green economy.
New discoveries, and new questions to ask
'Cuz we can figure out the future by examining the past.

So we sail to the Poles, and sample the extremes,
And drill into the ice, and discover what it means.
So use that brain, and make science a priority
And you can work on stopping global warming with authority.

ACTIVITY 2 | **A01** | **SKILLS** ANALYSIS

▼ USING SOPHISTICATED TECHNIQUES TO PERSUADE

Read the following extract from the Royal Society for the Prevention of Cruelty to Animals (RSPCA), which aims to persuade people to give money to the charity. Charities depend on people giving money to them so their appeals need to be very persuasive. When you have read it, copy and complete the table that follows.

Have you ever thought about how the RSPCA is truly amazing?

We've been saving animals from cruelty for nearly 200 years. We lead the world in showing how to live with animals in harmony and respect. And all because enough people in our country care about protecting animals from cruelty. Animals cannot speak out for themselves. So we do.

RSPCA inspectors have always been the most visible part of our work to prevent animals suffering. Today our 370 inspectors and animal welfare officers collect and rescue around 119,000 animals every year. It seems like people are conscious of animals' needs, and they are prepared to bring suffering animals to our attention.

Looking after pitilessly abused and abandoned animals, and finding them new homes is just part of the daily task we face. For instance, our 24-hour cruelty and advice line receives over 3,000 calls on average, every day, that's one call every 29 seconds. And each week our inspectors have to investigate around 2,750 complaints about suspected cruelty to animals. Multiply that by weeks in a month, and then by every month in a year.

The RSPCA could not survive without public support. Thank you for helping to make the RSPCA truly amazing!

▶

HINT

Always think about the purpose of your writing. The words in this charity appeal have been carefully chosen:

- to make you feel the horror of animal cruelty
- to stress the positive effect that the RSPCA has on animal welfare
- to emphasise the importance of RSPCA inspectors.

▼ QUESTIONS TO CONSIDER	▼ EXAMPLES FROM THE TEXT
What words in this piece emphasise the cruel way in which some animals are treated?	1 'pitilessly abused' 2 3
What words emphasise the positive aspects of the RSPCA's work?	1 'harmony and respect' 2 3
What words and details emphasise the strengths of the RSPCA inspectors?	1 'the most visible part of our work' 2 3

ACTIVITY 3 — A02 — SKILLS ▶ CRITICAL THINKING, ANALYSIS, INTERPRETATION

▼ WRITING TO A FRIEND

Sometimes the context for advice or persuasion is much more personal. The following extract is by a teenager who has been told by a friend that she is going alone to meet someone she only knows from a social networking site. She is writing to persuade her friend not to go. Would you expect her style (or register) to be informal? Why might it use some conversational features?

Dear Ella,

Please don't shout at me for writing this letter, but I doubt if you would let me talk directly to you. I know I am being uptight and intruding on your private life but I am sick with worry, since you told me that you were going to meet this 'boy'. We have always been close friends and you have always trusted me in the past. So listen to me now. What you are doing is plain stupid. Insane, even.

▶ Find an example of each of the following techniques in this letter:

- ■ informal style
- ■ personal pronouns
- ■ variety of sentence structure
- ■ emotional language

This letter uses different techniques from the RSPCA charity appeal. Link the statements about techniques on the left with the correct explanation for each one on the right.

▶

TECHNIQUE	EXPLANATION
1 The style is very informal and uses conversational language such as 'uptight' and 'plain stupid'.	A This is to make the friend feel guilty and also to reassure her.
2 It uses a variety of personal pronouns.	B This is to emphasise what the writer is saying.
3 It uses a variety of sentence structures, including commands and sentences with no verbs.	C This makes the letter more personal and establishes a direct link with the friend.
4 It appeals to the friend on various emotional levels.	D This is appropriate because it is written to a close friend.

▲ Writing to a friend will use a personal style and structure.

ACTIVITY 4 A04 A05 SKILLS ▶ PROBLEM SOLVING, ADAPTIVE LEARNING, CREATIVITY

▼ WRITING IN A SERIOUS STYLE

The extract about the RSPCA in Activity 2 could be easily adapted to be a speech, a leaflet or a part of an article. Write a brief piece in a similarly serious and adult style on a charity of your choice.

LEARNING OBJECTIVES

This lesson will help you to:
- understand how an appreciation of form can help you to write what is needed.

HINT

It is unlikely that you will be asked to write a very chatty letter to a close friend in the exam, because the examiners want to see that you can write with a good command of standard English.

HINT

These examples are all in similar fonts because you are not expected to try to imitate any of the visual features of the form in your exam. For example, if you are writing an article you would not need to imitate the visual appearance of a large headline.

GENERAL VOCABULARY

out in the sticks in the countryside or rural area; not near a city or town

FORM

The form of a text is the set of conventions that distinguish one type of text from another. Think about what makes a review different from a news article. Form is partly a matter of layout or appearance, partly the approach to the content, and partly the style or the way that the piece is written.

For example, in terms of the content or subject matter, the form of a feature article requires that all the content is clearly relevant to the topic, organised in a logical and clear way. In comparison, the form of a personal letter allows complete freedom to write about anything of interest to both the writer and reader (though there are still certain conventions) and not necessarily in any particular order. In terms of style, a feature article usually needs to be reasonably formal, whereas a personal letter can, of course, be very casual and colloquial.

ACTIVITY 1 **A01** **SKILLS** CRITICAL THINKING

▼ IDENTIFYING FORM

Look at the following openings of various pieces of writing.

EXTRACT A

What's in a name?

Names, common as many of them are, are like little codes: they tell people certain things about us, about where we come from.

EXTRACT B

Hi Pierre,

I expect the weather over there in Lyon is loads better than here in Canada. You don't want to be out in the sticks here I can tell you.

EXTRACT C

Dear Sirs,

I write concerning the recent plans for improvements in the local environment.

EXTRACT D

Thrills, spills and a gender twist

If you are a fan of Liam Hearn's books you won't be disappointed by the latest adventure.

Now copy and complete the following table, writing down the things that you notice about the layout and content in extracts A–D.

	▼ TYPE OF FORM	▼ FEATURES OF THE FORM
A		
B		
C		
D		

IDENTIFYING FORM BY ITS PHYSICAL LAYOUT

In many cases, the layout is the most obvious indication of form. However, it is unlikely to be the most important aspect of form.

KEY POINT

Distinguishing one form of writing from another goes beyond the sort of layout differences that one can see at a glance.

NEWSPAPER AND MAGAZINE ARTICLES	■ Short paragraphs ■ Conform to a series of conventional lengths, for example, short articles of 600–800 words; full-length features of around 1,500 or so words ■ Use headlines and subheadings ■ Short introductory summaries
FILM AND BOOK REVIEWS	■ Most commonly around 300–700 words, though can be longer ■ Tend to have a punchy or clever headline and sometimes subheadings
LETTERS	■ If official or business, writer's address top right and date below; addressee's address top left ■ Begin with 'Dear…' ■ Short paragraphs ■ End with 'Yours sincerely', 'All best wishes' or similar, depending on level of familiarity with the reader
SPEECHES	■ Begin with a form of greeting, for example, 'Ladies and gentlemen…' ■ End with a form of farewell, a conclusion suitable to a spoken address rather than a written one: this could take the form of thanks to the audience for listening

IDENTIFYING FORM BY ITS CONTENT

It is the combination of the layout and content that makes forms identifiable. Even without the layout of a letter, the words, 'Dear John', at the start of a piece of writing would identify it as a letter. Similarly, when you read a summarising opening sentence such as, 'Yesterday evening, the Prime Minister announced that there would be a referendum…', you recognise it as the start of a news article.

FORM: NEWSPAPER ARTICLES

HINT

You are not expected to lay out an article as it would appear in print, such as in columns and with large fonts for headlines. You are being tested on the way that you use language, not the visual layout. You should still include paragraphs or headings if appropriate, though.

- Headlines tell you what the article is about in a concise, attention-grabbing way. For example, it might use wordplay or alliteration and leave out any words that are not vital to the meaning.
- A standfirst or summary sub-heading gives more detail, engaging the reader further.
- Opening paragraphs summarise the gist of the piece, which is very different from the opening of short stories or letters.
- Experts or people involved are often quoted as evidence and to add weight to an argument.

THE TRUTH ABOUT LYING: IT'S THE HANDS THAT BETRAY YOU, NOT THE EYES

By analysing videos of liars, the team found there was no link between lying and eye movements.

ADAM SHERWIN

It is often claimed that even the most stone-faced liar will be betrayed by an unwitting eye movement.

But new research suggests that 'lying eyes', which no fibber can avoid revealing, are actually a myth.

Verbal hesitations and excessive hand gestures may prove a better guide to whether a person is telling untruths, according to research conducted by Professor Richard Wiseman.

ACTIVITY 2   **AO4**   **AO5**   **SKILLS** PROBLEM SOLVING, ADAPTIVE LEARNING, CREATIVITY

▼ WRITING AN ARTICLE

Write a short article that contains the features listed, you could write about aspects of climate change, changes in nutritional advice or an interesting discovery arising from research.

HINT

If you cannot remember the facts, then try inventing some. The aim here is to practise the form of your writing, rather than to focus on accuracy.

FORM: FILM AND BOOK REVIEWS

- Titles of reviews are usually catchy to engage the reader and indicate the reviewer's opinion.
- A sub-heading gives more details of the reviewer's opinion.
- Ratings give an opinion on how good the book, film or event is.
- An engaging opening paragraph sometimes uses figurative language to give the reader a taste of what the film or event is like.

THE HORSE AS HERO

War Horse, by Michael Morpurgo, is a powerful and emotive story about the trenches of the First World War from an entirely original perspective. It is one of the best books of this year for younger readers.

Most readers will know that millions died in the horrors of the 'war to end wars'; few will know that six million horses were also killed in the atrocious carnage. The tale tracks the experiences of Joey, the much-loved horse of a young recruit named Albert, who is separated from him…

▲ What was the last film you enjoyed watching?

| ACTIVITY 3 | A04 | A05 | SKILLS ▷ PROBLEM SOLVING, ADAPTIVE LEARNING, CREATIVITY |

▼ WRITING A REVIEW

Write a brief review of a book or film you have enjoyed, using the features listed on the previous page and appropriate language.

FORM: LETTERS

▼ LAYOUT OR PHYSICAL FORM

- Writer's address and the date go in the top right corner.
- Addressee's name and address go on the left, lower down.
- Start with 'Dear...'.
- Can use a subject line to draw the reader's attention to the topic.
- End with 'Yours faithfully' if started with 'Dear Sir or Madam'. If started with the addressee's name, end with 'Yours sincerely'. If informal, could end with 'All the best' or 'With love'.

▼ CONTENT

- Formal letters normally begin with the reason for writing ('I write concerning the...').
- Informal letters often begin with a thought for the addressee, such as, 'I hope all is well with you'.
- Formal letters contain information and make points. They may also express thanks or make a complaint.
- Informal letters usually contain personal news and plans.
- The last paragraph before signing off usually expresses hopes or good wishes, for example, formally, 'I hope you will give this matter your serious consideration' or, informally, 'all the best until then'.

KEY POINT

Formal letters require adherence to certain rules but there is still scope for your own choices.

| ACTIVITY 4 | A01 | A04 | A05 | SKILLS ▷ CRITICAL THINKING, ANALYSIS, PROBLEM SOLVING, CREATIVITY, INNOVATION |

▼ WRITING A LETTER

Write a letter, to the governors of your school, requesting that they improve the school in two ways that you think are important. In this case, you should use the opening greeting, 'Dear Governers'.

FORM: REPORTS

A report is a response to a request for detailed information about a place, institution, event or other project. It differs from a newspaper article because it requires extensive research into the background and often then gives a recommendation as to what should happen next. Governments commission numerous reports on all aspects of modern life as the basis for forming policy and making decisions. For example, a town council might need a report on the roads in a part of the town or the way that schools are fulfilling the needs of the community.

ACTIVITY 5 | AO1 | AO4 | AO5 | SKILLS ▶ CRITICAL THINKING, ANALYSIS, PROBLEM SOLVING, CREATIVITY, INNOVATION

▼ WRITING A REPORT

Write a response to the following question.

▶ **Your school or borough has been allotted a significant amount of extra funding to improve its facilities, which would be enough to pay for some new buildings. You have been asked to write a report on the state of facilities, in either your local community or your school, in one of the following areas:**

- ▪ **sports**
- ▪ **leisure**
- ▪ **arts**
- ▪ **provision for pedestrians and cyclists.**

FORM: BLOGS

A blog, short for 'web log', is a cross between a diary and a personal magazine. They vary from those written and designed by professional journalists and other writers, which resemble online newspapers, to very informal ones written by students or young people. They are found on many sites on the internet.

This is an example of a blog post from a blogger who reviews computer games.

> Still only available as an early alpha build on Steam, but already immensely popular, Dean Hall's bleak, utterly unsentimental zombie survival game is unbearably tense and atmospheric. Players are pitched together into a stark landscape, and must survive for as long as possible, ransacking buildings for guns and food and avoiding the undead. But just as in all the best zombie fiction, it's not the rotting monsters you often have to worry about, it's the other survivors. Each server houses up to 40 players, all desperately scavenging for the same meagre supplies. And if you kill another participant, you can take their stuff. There is a clear benefit to adopting a 'shoot first' policy.

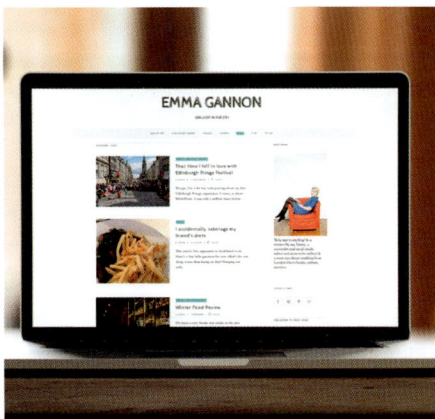

▲ A popular lifestyle and fashion blog

ACTIVITY 6 | AO4 | AO5 | SKILLS ▶ PROBLEM SOLVING, ADAPTIVE LEARNING, CREATIVITY

▼ WRITING A BLOG POST

Write a blog post on a hobby or interest that you would like to share with others. Try to use standard English, but you may need to tailor your language to the needs of your audience and use more informal language.

FORM: INFORMATION GUIDES

These are leaflets designed to offer the reader a brief guide to a place, a process, a system and so on. Read the following question and think about the information that you might need to include in the guide that you write.

▶ **Write a brief guide to your home town, village or district for new residents or a visitor.**

HINT

Remember that you can introduce a statistic with phrases such as, 'It is believed that...' or 'One expert has said that...'.

As well as providing information, you should organise this information logically using subheadings and bullet points. Include some facts, statistics and opinions, any of which could be quotations. They do not need to be completely accurate you can invent things. However, remember that this is supposed to be non-fiction, so keep it realistic.

ACTIVITY 7   **A01**   **A04**   **A05**   SKILLS ▸ CRITICAL THINKING, ANALYSIS, PROBLEM SOLVING, CREATIVITY, INNOVATION

▼ WRITING AN INFORMATION LEAFLET

Write an information leaflet in response to the question on page 158, planning it first using something like the following table.

Introduction	
Paragraph 2	The neighbourhood.
Paragraph 3	The wider town or environment.
Paragraph 4	Things worth seeing and doing.
Conclusion	

Alternatively, you could choose to use a spider diagram to help you plan.

Sports facilities — Local politics — Places of interest — Buildings — My home town — Shopping — Things to do — Local people — Famous people — Surrounding attractions

ACTIVITY 8   **A02**   **A04**   SKILLS ▸ ANALYSIS, ADAPTIVE LEARNING, CREATIVITY

▼ EXTENDED DESCRIPTION

An information guide can include some descriptive writing. The main aim is to bring the topic to life with some vivid phrasing and interesting word choices.

Re-read the information that you wrote for Activity 7. Have you included any extended descriptive sections? Could you add some now? Look back at some of the extracts in this book to remind yourself of some examples of good descriptive writing.

LEARNING OBJECTIVES

This lesson will help you to:
- select the right vocabulary to make your writing more precise, clear and effective.

VOCABULARY FOR EFFECT

Vocabulary choice improves with reading and practice. When an author's use of vocabulary is excellent, it makes the text engaging and interesting and it makes the writer appear skilful and authoritative. It is a matter of choosing individual words and the phrases into which they are combined. When thinking about vocabulary choice, it can be helpful to subdivide it into different aspects: register, variety, impact, the context of word, decoration or colour and signposting.

REGISTER

The register of a text is the way in which vocabulary is chosen for a particular audience. For example, if you are writing a letter to a friend or giving a talk to your class, you will use a more informal register than if you are writing a formal letter to the school governors or headteacher.

VARIETY

Variety can be achieved by finding alternative ways of saying similar things or making similar points. For example, you could use synonyms instead of repetition. Using the same word more than once can make your writing feel uninteresting and repetitive. Most words offer you plenty of synonyms to choose from. For example, to avoid repeating the word 'important', you could use 'significant', 'necessary', 'needed', 'vital', 'crucial', 'non-negotiable' or 'top priority'.

Using different synonyms is not just for the sake of variety – words of similar but not identical meaning may suit the content better than others. For example, the word 'imaginative' has different associations to 'ingenious', even though they are not far apart in terms of their meaning.

SUBJECT VOCABULARY

synonyms words that share the same meaning as other words; for example, 'quick' might be a synonym for 'fast'

ACTIVITY 1 | **AO1** | SKILLS ANALYSIS

▼ FINDING AND CHOOSING SYNONYMS

Use your own knowledge, a thesaurus or dictionary to find several synonyms each for the following common words: 'bad', 'terrible', 'good', 'brilliant', 'idea', 'interesting'.

ACTIVITY 2 | **AO1** | SKILLS ANALYSIS

▼ LOOKING FOR SYNONYMS

Find more synonyms for the following words: 'happy', 'unhappy', 'success', 'failure', 'do', 'go', 'achieve'. Make sure the words are grammatically equivalent (that is, if you are looking for a synonym for an adjective, you find other adjectives).

ACTIVITY 3   **A04**   **A05**   **SKILLS**   ANALYSIS, INNOVATION

▼ REPETITION AS A RHETORICAL TECHNIQUE

Repetition can be a good rhetorical technique if it is used skilfully, but if it is used badly it can weaken the impact of your writing. Re-write the following text, replacing the words 'point' and 'people' with different synonyms and trying to make the sentences more interesting.

> Social networking does have many good points. One is that it helps friends stay in touch; another point is that you can talk to people whenever you like, and this helps people in many ways; a third point is that people can introduce friends to other people very easily.

WORDS IN CONTEXT

Words do not create much impact on their own. They react with those around them in the mind of the reader. A chain of words may be linked by their subject matter if, for example, they are taken from the specialist vocabulary of the topic. A chain of words could also be linked by tone or feeling: for example, a group of positive words and phrases, or a group of words and phrases that create a dramatic effect. If you look through any of the texts featured in this book, you will find examples of different word chains.

IMPACT

Your vocabulary choice can be crucial in creating impact, especially in text that is intended to be heard, such as a speech. For example, whether you are aiming to describe or persuade, techniques such as onomatopoeia and alliteration can add force to a sentence. For example, 'lead us towards a *dark* and *desperate* situation' uses alliteration to draw attention to the adjectives describing the nature of the situation.

EMOTIVE LANGUAGE

Using emotive language can certainly add impact to your argument. For example, you may be writing about climate change and want to shock your reader into action. To do this, you need to emphasise the scale of the problem by choosing a more powerful word than 'problem'. For example, you could use 'catastrophe', 'disaster' or 'calamity'.

Compare the following sentences. Which one do you think has a greater impact?

> If we ignore alternative energy sources now, we will soon be facing a problem.

> If we ignore alternative energy sources now, we will soon be facing a catastrophe.

KEY POINT

Using words for impact has to be judged carefully. If a word is too weak then there is not enough power in the sentence, but if a word is too strong you risk sounding melodramatic.

CONNOTATIONS

You can guide your reader's reactions by thinking about the connotations of your vocabulary choice. Look at the table on the next page. Each of the suggested adjectives could be used to finish the sentences, as they have similar meanings, but they have different connotations that may affect your reader's response.

▲ Which adjective would you use to complete the sentence 'Having a job outside work makes me...'?

▼ SENTENCE	▼ ADJECTIVE	▼ CONNOTATIONS
'Having a job outside school makes me...'	exhausted	extreme physical fatigue
	drained	emptiness, suggesting that there is nothing left in the speaker
	sleepy	childishness that should not be taken too seriously
'Computer games are often...'	ruthless	lack of feeling or regard for others
	barbaric	uncivilised
	brutal	uncaring violence

The words in the table are also emotive words, meaning that they trigger an emotional response and therefore engage the audience. Such words are essential in storytelling, as well as in writing to argue and persuade.

Using words with particular connotations can be very effective in arguing for or against a statement. For example, if you are arguing in favour of euthanasia, you could describe it as 'a humane method'. However, if you are arguing against it, you could describe it as 'a licence to murder'. The connotations of the words 'humane' and 'murder' will influence the way in which your audience thinks about the subject.

Look at pages 160–163 to remind yourself of other ways in which vocabulary can be used for effect.

ACTIVITY 4	**AO4**	**AO5**	SKILLS ▶ PROBLEM SOLVING, ADAPTIVE LEARNING, CREATIVITY

▼ PERSUASIVE VOCABULARY

Write an opening paragraph for the following exam-style question, focusing on vocabulary to persuade the reader.

▶ **The editor of your school newspaper has asked for contributions in response to the topic:**

'Computer games are good for you as well as fun.'

You can write in favour of the statement or against it. Remember to choose vocabulary for its impact and for its connotations, and think carefully about the purpose of your response and the audience for whom it is intended.

DECORATION OR COLOUR

In writing to describe, you often appeal to the reader's senses by including details such as sounds, smells, feelings and tastes. In other forms of writing, where you may not use description (for example, when you are writing to argue), you can introduce similar sensory effects by using figurative language.

This is why a writer might say that an unpopular idea went down 'like a lead balloon', or that a good leader is a 'knight in shining armour'. Although both of these phrases are clichés, they still enliven the writing, and more original phrases will have a greater effect.

SUBJECT VOCABULARY

clichés phrases that are used so often that they start to lose their impact

Decorative language can also be used in informative writing. An information guide such as the one that you wrote in response to Activity 7 on page 159 can be livened up and made more interesting for the reader by using some of the following techniques.

▼ TECHNIQUE	▼ EXAMPLE
Make the description vivid	Varied adjectives and adverbs.
Exaggerate	'…has some of the finest views in the south-west…'
Use humour	This might include **puns,** or exaggerated or unusual vocabulary.
Invent quotations, within reason	'The manager of the local football club says that it is "the ideal place for a new sports pitch"…'
Use **irony** or **litotes**	'…perhaps not the most inviting of buildings…'

SUBJECT VOCABULARY

pun an amusing use of a word or phrase that has two meanings, or of words that have the same sound but different meanings
irony using words to convey a meaning that is completely opposite to their apparent meaning
litotes ironic understatement used to mean something by saying its opposite

SIGNPOSTING

Try to use 'signposting' vocabulary so that your points are more clearly structured. This is especially useful in speeches, where the paragraphing has to be heard, not seen. Some examples are given in the following table.

▼ PURPOSE	▼ EXAMPLES
To order ideas	'Firstly', 'secondly', 'moreover', 'furthermore', 'in addition', 'finally'…
To introduce reasons or consequences	'Therefore', 'as a result', 'consequently'…
To give alternatives	'On the other hand', 'nevertheless', 'however', 'in contrast'…
To develop ideas	'To develop this further', 'what this means is', 'in support of this'…

ACTIVITY 5 **A01** **A04** **A05** **SKILLS** ▸ ANALYSIS, ADAPTIVE LEARNING, CREATIVITY

▼ USING VOCABULARY FOR EFFECT

Re-write the information guide that you wrote in response to Activity 7 on page 157. Try to improve its readability by including more vocabulary for effect.

LEARNING OBJECTIVES

This lesson will help you to:

- understand how you can control sentences for greater impact.

SENTENCES FOR EFFECT

Consciously structuring your sentences will help your writing to make an impression on readers.

SENTENCE OPENINGS

The simplest way to ensure variety in your sentence structure is to think about the first words of each sentence and try to make them different from the others. Less experienced writers often start their sentences in similar ways, but the following table lists some different methods of opening sentences.

▼ TYPE OF WORD	▼ EXAMPLES
A pronoun I, you, he, she, it, we, they, my, your	'I write to you as a concerned…'
A preposition above, behind, between, near, for, with	'In all of our towns, there are…'
A present participle (or -ing word) thinking, watching, caring, making	'Looking at the state of the parks in our area…'
An adjective huge, beautiful, terrible, strange	'Noisy, threatening lorries rumble past…'
An adverb (usually end in -ly) happily, unfortunately, unhelpfully	'Alarmingly, the facts are…'
A conjunction (subordinate clause + main clause) if, although, because, when, while	'Although there are limits to the amount of money available…'

ACTIVITY 1   **A04**   **A05**   SKILLS ▶ PROBLEM SOLVING, ADAPTIVE LEARNING, CREATIVITY

▼ VARYING YOUR SENTENCE OPENINGS

Using at least five of the styles of sentence opener in the table, write different openings for an answer to this exam-style question.

▶ **Write an article explaining how you think we could improve our efficiency in recycling.**

STRUCTURING SENTENCES

LONG COMPLEX SENTENCES

Complex sentences, containing one or more subordinate clauses, are good for conveying information or ideas, so try using them in explanations and arguments. They give an impression of fluent thinking, although you should be careful not to let a sentence ramble as you may lose your reader's attention. The following text is an example of a complex sentence. What impression does it give?

> While some people think that global warming is a natural phenomenon that has happened many times before in the Earth's history, others, looking hard at the scientific evidence, are convinced that we are mainly responsible.

Many subordinate clauses begin with adverbial conjunctions, such as 'because', 'if', 'while', 'when', 'so that', 'after', 'before' and so on. These conjunctions play an important part in putting your ideas in order and linking thoughts together in a complex sentence.

ENDING FOR IMPACT

You can structure your sentences to ensure that the main point is emphasised. The last words of a sentence tend to stand out because they are read or heard most recently, so it is a good technique to place important words at the end of a sentence. Compare the following sentences and their endings.

> The government can just ignore it, despite all the work and research.

> The final insult is that, after all the work and research, the government can just ignore it.

The second sentence places the main point of the sentence at the end, where it is emphasised, and is therefore a bit more powerful than the first.

THE LONG AND THE SHORT

Short, punchy, single-clause sentences can add impact to an argument, or add variety or surprise to a description or piece of information. Short sentences are particularly effective when they follow a longer multi-clause sentence.

For example, if you used a long and complex sentence to explain a particular point, you could follow it with a simple statement such as 'They are right' or 'We need it now' to emphasise the point.

▲ A waste of time?

ACTIVITY 2 | A04 | A05 | SKILLS ▶ CRITICAL THINKING, ANALYSIS

▼ WRITING TO MAKE AN IMPRESSION

Look at the following question.

▶ **'Television is mostly a waste of time and distracts us from better things we could be doing.' Write an argument giving your views on this statement.**

Write an introduction, using the skills that you have just learned, to make an impression on the reader.

THE IMPORTANCE OF PUNCTUATION

Punctuating sentences correctly is not just for the sake of showing that you can do it. It also directly affects the impact you have on the reader.

One of the errors that many students make is using the comma splice, which is the name given to a comma used where there should be a full stop, a semi-colon or colon, or a comma with a conjunction. For many readers, the comma splice interrupts fluent reading.

▼ THE COMMA SPLICE	▼ CORRECT ALTERNATIVES
The school sets too much homework, this is why a lot of students are demotivated.	...too much homework. This is why...
	...too much homework: this is why...
	...too much homework, which is why...

LEARNING OBJECTIVES

This lesson will help you to:

■ understand how to write effective openings and conclusions to your writing.

OPENINGS AND CONCLUSIONS

One of the benefits of planning is that you are less likely to write a weak or uncertain opening because you have thought about what you are going to write. A mistake that students can make if they have not planned their response is to simply repeat words from the question with a phrase such as, 'In this article I am going to write about…'. Since your reader already knows this, it is a waste of time and is uninteresting.

OPENINGS

When you read a text, you probably expect the opening to be interesting, and to grab your attention in some way. The following table lists some effective techniques that you can use to improve your openings. Which technique you use will depend on the task.

▼ TECHNIQUE	▼ EXAMPLE
A rhetorical question	'How often do you take action when you feel something ought to be done?'
An arresting or controversial statement	'It's not children who need educating about recycling – it's the grown-ups who ought to know better.'
A surprising or shocking fact or statistic	'The unreleased energy contained in the average dustbin each year could power a television for 5,000 hours.'
A relevant quotation	'We live in a disposable society. It's easier to throw things out than to fix them.'
A short and relevant anecdote	'I have found it saves money to reuse the plastic containers…'

HINT

Remember that your statistics do not have to be accurate in the exam; they just have to sound plausible. However, if you are writing for homework, you should check that your statistics are correct.

KEY POINT

The pressure of getting started can often lead to a bland opening, written just to get something on the page. It pays to resist this pressure and think carefully about your first words.

ACTIVITY 1　**A04**　**A05**　**SKILLS** ▶ PROBLEM SOLVING, ADAPTIVE LEARNING, CREATIVITY

▼ USING DIFFERENT KINDS OF OPENING

Write two possible openings to a response to the following question.

▶ **Write an article arguing for or against the proposal that the smacking of children should be made illegal.**

ACTIVITY 2 | A01 | A02 | SKILLS ▷ CRITICAL THINKING, ANALYSIS

▼ EFFECTIVE OPENINGS

The following extracts are the openings of some of the texts in this book. Read each one and then write down the features that make them effective openings.

EXTRACT A

As a teenager I used to be obsessed with American proms, for which I blame the film *Grease*.

EXTRACT B

Social networks are massively addictive.

EXTRACT C

'I have a dream… I have a dream that one day this nation will rise up and live out the true meaning of its creed.'

EXTRACT D

'Paper has more patience than people.'

CONCLUSIONS

An effective conclusion will leave the reader with a strong impression and should make them remember the point that you have made. A weak conclusion will leave them with less to remember. Different techniques can be used to achieve a strong conclusion, as shown in the following table.

▼ TECHNIQUE	▼ EXAMPLE
A positive, upbeat note	'This is surely a recipe for success.'
A warning	'If we do not act soon, then it may be too late to save…'
An appeal for action	'We must act now – and act quickly – to save our heritage.'
A question for people to think about	'Couldn't that be the best outcome of them all?'
A vivid image	'Just a single light, shining in the dark.'
A link with the opening, though not repeating the wording	'Perhaps the question that we asked at the outset was the wrong question. Perhaps we should ask instead…'

ACTIVITY 3 | A04 | A05 | SKILLS ▷ PROBLEM SOLVING, ADAPTIVE LEARNING, CREATIVITY

▼ USING DIFFERENT KINDS OF CONCLUSION

Look back at the two openings that you wrote in Activity 1. Write two possible conclusions to the pieces, using different techniques.

ACTIVITY 4 | A02 | SKILLS ▷ ANALYSIS, REASONING

▼ EFFECTIVE CONCLUSIONS

Find three examples of conclusions from extracts in this book and explain why they are effective.

LEARNING OBJECTIVES

This lesson will help you to:
- understand the importance of planning
- improve your planning techniques.

IDEAS AND PLANNING

It is very helpful to plan before writing. Once you have a plan, you will feel more confident that you can write a successful piece and this confidence will show in your writing. Since you have about an hour for Section B, you can spend 5–10 minutes planning.

PLANNING TECHNIQUES

▲ Spider diagrams can be useful for planning.

You can plan using spider diagrams, thought clouds, lists and so on: it doesn't matter what you use as long as it works for you.

A good idea to start with is to jot down the three primary things about any piece you write: the **purpose**, the **audience** and the **form**. You can base some ideas on this triplet. For example, refer to the audience, especially when writing a speech; state your purpose clearly; and use appropriate language for the form. Jotting down your ideas will also help ensure that you do not forget them.

Once you have planned, the next thing to do is to generate some ideas. One idea per paragraph is a good start.

ACTIVITY 1   **AO4**   **SKILLS**   PROBLEM SOLVING, REASONING, ADAPTIVE LEARNING, CREATIVITY

▼ STRATEGIES FOR PLANNING

If you can think of two contrasting approaches to the topic, it will help you to make relevant points. Consider the following question.

▶ **Write an article for a local or school magazine on the topic: 'Not enough attention is paid to the problem of stress in the lives of modern teenagers'.**

A student has used the following table to plan their response to this question. If you choose to use this method, you do not need to fill out all the rows: five or six should be enough for the essay that you write in the exam. You will know when your plan is detailed enough, because at that stage you should feel that the essay will be straightforward to write.

▼ POINT	▼ APPROACH 1	▼ APPROACH 2
Time perspective	The past – was life less stressful and how? Working hours? Less competition? More stability in work and communities?	The present and the future – we are healthier, but are we under more pressure in hearts and minds? If so why? Less family stability?
Views of different groups		Group B: Working class young people – more worried about the future of the planet and their own future etc.?
Anecdotes to tell	Things that involved you or a friend.	Something that involved someone you have heard of.
Different aspects of the subject	Types and causes of stress: work, health.	
How to tackle problem	Step 1: understand causes.	
Gender angle	Boys.	Girls.

▶

Possible benefits or problems		
Timeframe	Stage 1.	
What to do now – warning for future?	Can't avoid stress but must organise life so that each individual is not overloaded.	

ACTIVITY 2 **AO4** **SKILLS** PROBLEM SOLVING, REASONING, ADAPTIVE LEARNING, CREATIVITY

▼ PLANNING A REPORT WITH RECOMMENDATIONS

> ▶ **Your local council wants to improve provisions for teenagers in the neighbourhood. Write a report for the council explaining how, in your view, the local facilities might be improved.**

Plan the report first. You could include:

- ■ what facilities exist at present
- ■ your ideas about how they can be improved
- ■ ideas about providing new facilities.

Consider the following plan. What would you do differently?

Introduction
- ■ facilities which are widely believed to be inadequate
- ■ many ideas are being discussed
- ■ motivate and engage teenagers: anecdotes or statistics of recent problems

Main point 1: Present facilities
- ■ present state: what we have now (e.g. not enough land)
- ■ poor conditions: e.g. football pitch / tennis court (quote expert views)

Main point 2: Improvements suggested
- ■ youth centre: redecorate with help of teenagers
- ■ repair sports pitch: apply for sponsorship from sports company
- ■ provide more computers and video games in local library

Main point 3: New facilities
- ■ bowling alley: give an estimate of how much money this could generate
- ■ café to be managed by volunteers

Conclusion
- ■ summarise the benefits of suggestions

HINT

Some exam questions will contain prompts of this kind. They give a useful place to start structuring your answer. In terms of the previous planning table, the three main points opposite would fit the 'time perspective' approach. Notice that, although this is mainly a piece of writing to explain, it clearly gives opportunities to inform, to describe and to persuade.

ACTIVITY 3 **AO4** **SKILLS** PROBLEM SOLVING, REASONING, ADAPTIVE LEARNING, CREATIVITY

▼ PRACTISE YOUR PLANNING

> ▶ **Write a speech for your class or year group, in which you try to persuade them to participate in the school's extra-curricular activities.**

Plan your response to this question. You could try using the planning table or another strategy, such as spider diagrams or lists. Consider your own experiences and how you could use them to persuade others that the extra-curricular activities at your school are valuable.

LEARNING OBJECTIVES

This lesson will help you to:
- understand how the methods and techniques discussed in this chapter can combine to make a good answer.

EXAM-STYLE QUESTION

A01 **A04** **A05**

SKILLS CRITICAL THINKING, ANALYSIS, PROBLEM SOLVING, CREATIVITY, INNOVATION

HINT

Think of planning first. Notice that the question asks you to argue and persuade: 'argue' means that you should present your own views and explain why others are wrong; 'persuade' means that you need to think about your audience and how to encourage them to think the way that you do.

PUTTING IT INTO PRACTICE

In the exam in Section B you will have one question to answer. You should aim to spend one hour planning and writing your response to the transactional writing question.

'Schools have a duty to continually improve conditions for students.'

You have been asked to give a speech in which you express your views on this statement.

Your speech may include:
- who should have responsibility for improvements
- whether improvements would help students
- any other points you wish to make.

Think carefully about the purpose of your speech and the audience for whom it is intended.

(30 marks)

ACTIVITY 1 **A04**   **SKILLS** PROBLEM SOLVING, REASONING, ADAPTIVE LEARNING, CREATIVITY

▼ IDEAS AND PLANNING

Using the following table to help you, make your own plan for the exam-style question.

▼ PARAGRAPH PLAN	▼ TECHNIQUES TO USE
■ Intro: mention poor conditions – suggest there is an answer.	■ Rhetorical questions.
■ Para 1: argue link between environment and work (Ofsted, etc.).	■ Direct address to reader.
■ Para 2: what some people think (to counter).	■ Alliteration – 'dreary dining rooms'.
■ Para 3: persuasive questions.	■ Imperatives – short final sentence.
■ Para 4: argue what is minimum needed now – joint action needed.	■ Connectives – 'moreover', 'firstly', so on.
■ Para 5: What are current plans to improve?	■ Use 'us' and 'we'.
■ Conclusion: politicians, etc.	■ Variety of sentences.
	■ Facts and statistics.
	■ Some informal vocab.

SAMPLE ANSWER

Read through the following answer to the exam-style question and the comments.

For how much longer must students in school put up with dilapidated classrooms, sub-standard social areas and dreary dining rooms? Starting with a rhetorical question is a good way to engage the audience from the start.

a poor quality environment leads to poor quality work Repetition of 'poor quality' makes this point more powerful.

INTRODUCTION

For how much longer must students in school put up with dilapidated classrooms, sub-standard social areas and dreary dining rooms? Ambitious and hardworking students like your children and students deserve better.

DEVELOP IDEAS

The first reason why conditions must improve is that a poor quality environment leads to poor quality work. Substandard work restricts students' chances of

With an under-qualified workforce, the whole nation will suffer. The student is using a formal register and referring to large scale ideas, which adds weight to the argument. linked statements to develop a strong point.

Cluttered classrooms, foul toilet facilities and inadequate outdoor space Here, the student has chosen adjectives carefully as emotive language.

over 60% of schools operate out of shoddy buildings. Statistics make the argument sound more assured and well-researched.

you The focus has shifted away from facts, to the audience. Using second person is highly persuasive and makes the issue more personal.

The minimum that our children deserve is this: attractive, airy buildings with no hiding-room for bullies; adequate indoor and outdoor recreational space; appealing eating areas, offering a variety of good value, high quality meals and snacks; sufficient hygienic and well-maintained toilet facilities so that no-one wastes time in queues. A list of detailed, well thought out ideas adds momentum to the argument here.

Our children's future depends upon it. Ending with a short sentence and emotive language is a powerful way to conclude.

EXAMINER'S COMMENTS
This argument is well-written and highly persuasive due to judicious use of techniques such as rhetorical questions, statistics and repetition. The formal register and statistics adds weight to the points made. Sentence structures have been chosen for effect, and often help to build momentum.

---

achieving good qualifications. With an under-qualified workforce, the whole nation will suffer.

Ofsted reports repeatedly expose the grim quality of Britain's school premises. Cluttered classrooms, foul toilet facilities and inadequate outdoor space are all too commonly reported: over 60% of schools operate out of shoddy buildings. It is time that the school authorities took action.

Some people think that it is not worth providing decent facilities for children. They think that youngsters won't take care of expensive resources. But how are children ever to learn to value such resources, if they never encounter them?

MOVE ONTO PERSUASION

Have you ever asked yourself why school are so shoddily equipped? Do you want your children to be educated in buildings as dreary as the ones you attended? Or are you prepared to stand up and demand that something is done?

The citizens of a rich and modern state deserve up-to-date conditions in which to study and work. Your children are the future citizens of such a state and if we want their best efforts and loyalty to the nation, we must show them that we value them. How better to do this than to provide them with schools fit for the 21st century? The last Labour government started the Building Schools for the Future project. What a pity that the money ran out in the recession.

We're coming out of that now. If we all pull together we can make change happen. The minimum that our children deserve is this: attractive, airy buildings with no hiding-room for bullies; adequate indoor and outdoor recreational space; appealing eating areas, offering a variety of good value, high quality meals and snacks; sufficient hygienic and well-maintained toilet facilities so that no-one wastes time in queues. Surely you would not settle for less for your children? Let us demand from our politicians that they tell us what plans they have to improve schools. If they cannot answer satisfactorily, then we will not elect them.

CONCLUSION

Undoubtedly we are agreed that something must be done. Indeed, we are agreed on what must be done. Politicians will try to block us by pleading poverty and putting off the time for action. Do not be deflected. If we act now to insist on upgraded school conditions, our children will thrive; if we do not, they will suffer and may never forgive us. Ladies and gentlemen, use your influence now. Our children's future depends upon it.

ACTIVITY 2   **AO1**   **AO4**   **AO5**   **SKILLS** CRITICAL THINKING, ANALYSIS, REASONING

▼ MARKING AN ANSWER

Using the following mark scheme, assess sample answer and give it three marks: one for AO1, out of 10, one for AO4, out of 12, and one for AO5, out of 8.

MARK SCHEME FOR AO1 (UP TO 10 MARKS)

Level 3: 5–6 marks
- Selection and interpretation of the given bullet points is appropriate and relevant to the points being made.
- Offers a reasonable number of relevant points.
- Shows secure appreciation of information and ideas.

Level 4: 7–8 marks
- Selection and interpretation of the given bullet points is appropriate, detailed and fully supports the points being made.
- Offers a good number of relevant points.
- Makes well-focused comments about information and ideas.

Level 5: 9–10 marks
- Selection and interpretation of the given bullet points is apt and is persuasive in clarifying the points being made.
- Offers a wide range of relevant points.
- Presents well-focused comments with perceptive references to information and ideas.

MARK SCHEME FOR AO4 (UP TO 12 MARKS)

Level 3: 5–7 marks
- Communicates clearly.
- Generally shows clear sense of purpose and understanding of the expectations/requirements of the intended reader.
- Appropriate use of form, tone and register.

Level 4: 8–10 marks
- Communicates successfully.
- Shows a secure realisation of the writing task according to the writer's purpose and the expectations/requirements of the intended reader.
- Effective use of form, tone and register.

Level 5: 11–12 marks
- Communication is perceptive and subtle with discriminating use of a full vocabulary.
- Task is sharply focused on purpose and the expectations/requirements of the intended reader.
- Sophisticated control of text structure, skilfully sustained paragraphing as appropriate and/or assured application of a range of cohesive devices.

MARK SCHEME FOR AO5 (UP TO 8 MARKS)

Level 3: 5–6 marks
- Punctuation is accurate, with a range of marks used to enhance communication.
- A range of grammatical structuring is used accurately and effectively.
- Spelling is almost always accurate, with occasional slips.

Level 4: 7–8 marks
- Control of the full range of punctuation marks is precise, for example by the deployment of semi-colons, pairs of commas or dashes to indicate apposition or interpolation.
- Grammatical structuring is ambitious and assured, with sophisticated control of expression and meaning.
- Spelling of a wide and ambitious vocabulary is consistently accurate.

ACTIVITY 3 | A01 | A04 | A05 | SKILLS CRITICAL THINKING, ANALYSIS, REASONING

▼ MARKING AN ANSWER

Now read the following sample answer and mark it the same way that you marked the previous sample answer. Remember to give it one mark for AO1, out of 10, a second mark for AO4, out of 12, and a third mark for AO5, out of 8.

> Why is school so badly equipped? Do you want your children to be educated in buildings as boring as the ones you attended? Perhaps you should be willing to try to take some action to improve the situation.
>
> The people of a rich and modern state need up-to-date conditions in their schools. Your children are the future of this country and we need to show them that we value them.
>
> So we need schools fit for the 21st century? We've got a few, but where are the rest?
>
> What we want is: spacious buildings we're not always bumping into people; plenty of space outdoors too; good food and snacks; better toilet facilities – these are what you'd like for your children.
>
> If we do something about it we can make things happen. We need to get our politicians to improve schools, but if they don't come up with the goods, then we don't have to elect them.

KEY POINT

Include a clear and urgent call to action. The writing can be figurative, but make sure it is imperative.

ACTIVITY 4 | A01 | A04 | A05 | SKILLS CRITICAL THINKING, PROBLEM SOLVING, ANALYSIS, CREATIVITY, INNOVATION

▼ PRACTISE YOUR WRITING

The government is encouraging debate on how to tackle the problem of poor diet and lack of exercise. Write an article explaining some of the actions that they could take and arguing that they should act quickly and effectively.

▲ Poor diet and lack of exercise is a problem in the UK.

الكتبية
KOUTOUBIA

ساحة جامع الفنا
PLACE JEMAA EL FNA SQUARE

ضريح يوسف بن تاشفين
TOMBEAU YOUSSEF BEN TACHFINE TOMB

قصر البديع
PALAIS EL BADII PALACE

قصر الباهية
PALAIS EL BAHIA PALACE

متحف دار السي سعيد
MUSEE DAR SI SAID MUSEUM

SECTION C: WRITING

Assessment Objective 4

Communicate effectively and imaginatively, adapting form, tone and register of writing for specific purposes and audiences

Assessment Objective 5

Write clearly, using a range of vocabulary and sentence structures, with appropriate paragraphing and accurate spelling, grammar and punctuation

In Section C, the Assessment Objectives are worth the following amounts.
AO4 – 20%
AO5 – 10%

This chapter focuses on Section C of Paper 1 of the English Language B course. Working through these lessons and activities will help you to develop the writing skills that you will need for Section C of the Paper 1 exam.

The chapter consists of the following section:
■ Imaginative writing.

Section C is worth 30% of the total marks for Paper 1.

In Section C, you will need to be able to meet Assessment Objectives AO4 and AO5.

LEARNING OBJECTIVES

This lesson will help you to:

- understand how to follow your imagination in a way that will allow you to create a piece of writing for a reader to enjoy.

AN INTRODUCTION TO IMAGINATIVE WRITING

In Section C of Paper 1, you will have to complete one writing task from a choice of three. There will be one **discursive**, one **narrative** and one **descriptive** task to choose from. The pages in this book on Section B (pages 138–173) cover discursive writing, so this part of the chapter focuses more on narrative and descriptive writing, although it will help you to improve your writing for any purpose. You can source ideas for your writing from stories you have already heard or read, or from events about which you know something. You may know or imagine a character to use in your story, whose actions and feelings you can convey to your reader.

PLOT

SUBJECT VOCABULARY

discursive writing that discusses a topic
narrative writing that tells the story of an event
descriptive writing that describes something or someone

The plot consists of the main events of a story. You can develop a plot by listing the events that you think will take place in your story. These events, and the order in which they occur, may well change as you write and develop your characters and setting.

| ACTIVITY 1 | A01 | SKILLS | CRITICAL THINKING, TEAMWORK |

▼ WORKING ON A PLOT

Working in small groups, choose a story that you all know or that you have studied in school. Work together to list the main narrative points of the story.

STRUCTURE

▲ Emlyn Williams's *Night Must Fall* is a psychological thriller partly set in a courtroom.

Here are some key questions to ask yourself in relation to structure.

- How will you present your narrative?
- Will the end come at the end, or will you arrange things differently?
- What effect would you like to have on your reader?
- How do you think you could use structure to help you achieve the desired effect?

Works of crime fiction often follow a particular structure that is common to the genre, in which a crime is detailed early on but the perpetrator is not revealed until the end. Whilst this is quite a predictable structure, there are ways in which a writer can utilise structure to challenge and surprise the reader.

There are many examples of stories that use unconventional or non-chronological structures. For example, Emlyn Williams's play, *Night Must Fall*, concerns the actions of a murderer. The opening scene takes place in a court where the murderer is convicted. In this scene, the audience learns the identity of one victim, but not that of the second. The next scene is set before the second murder, and the audience has to follow the character that they know to be the killer through scenes with other characters, wondering who his second victim will be. The effect would be very different if both victims' identities were revealed in the opening scene.

ACTIVITY 2   **AO1**   SKILLS ▸ CRITICAL THINKING, PROBLEM SOLVING, ADAPTIVE LEARNING

▼ THINKING ABOUT STRUCTURE

Choose a story that you know well. It could be a film, book, a short story or even a fairytale.

1 Write down the way in which the story is structured. Do events run in chronological order or are they arranged differently?

2 Write down the key moments in the plot and try re-organising them into a different structure. What effect do you think this would have on the story and the reader's experience?

NARRATION

Who is telling your story? Is it told by an all-knowing narrator who knows the characters' thoughts, or is it told by one of the characters, whose knowledge and understanding of events is limited? Is it even narrated by someone unknown, who watches events without being involved.

ACTIVITY 3   **AO4**   **AO5**   SKILLS ▸ ADAPTIVE LEARNING, CREATIVITY, INNOVATION

▼ CHOOSING A NARRATOR

Working in pairs, write two versions of the first three or four sentences of a story entitled 'Runaway'. The first version should be told from the writer's point of view, while the second version should be told from the point of view of the first character that you introduce.

CHARACTER

How much do you need to know about your characters? How will this information be conveyed to the reader? Will you introduce the character upfront, so that the reader knows a lot about this character early on in the narrative, or will the reader slowly get to know the character as the story unfolds?

ACTIVITY 4   **AO4**   **AO5**   SKILLS ▸ ADAPTIVE LEARNING, CREATIVITY, INNOVATION

▼ WRITING CHARACTER

Working on your own, write an introduction to a character at the start of a story entitled 'Not yet my friend, not yet'. You must decide whether to reveal things about this character immediately and whether you want to hint at events that will happen later. Write no more than 100 words. When you have finished, exchange your piece with someone else. Read your partner's character introduction, then write a continuation of the story and character development, following on from the first part that your partner has written.

KEY POINT

With practice, you will develop a feel for imaginative writing. At first, you will have to consider the aspects of your writing separately, such as character, plot, structure and narration, but as you continue to practise you should find yourself considering these things automatically as you write. However, you should always remember to check what you have written.

LEARNING OBJECTIVES

This lesson will help you to:
- develop the confidence to consider ideas
- plan ways of handling ideas
- present ideas appropriately.

GENERATING IDEAS

Any exercise or exam question that requires you to write imaginatively will give you some sort of starter, even if it is simply a title. This is your starting point from which you will have to produce further ideas, develop them and turn them into an effective narrative that is written clearly and accurately.

GENERATING IDEAS FOR DIFFERENT PURPOSES

You may be asked to write in order to **explore**, to **imagine** or to **entertain**. Before you start trying to generate ideas, you should consider your purpose and what is expected.

- **To explore**: Think about a subject, considering its importance, especially if the question involves a particular reader or audience. What is important or significant about the subject? What do other people think about the subject? How do you react to thinking about it?

- **To imagine**: If you are asked to imagine something, the natural response is to write a narrative. Everyone is familiar with stories, whether imagined or real, and this makes telling a story a more comfortable option for many students in an exam. Remember that good story telling requires the same planning and organising as any other kind of writing.

- **To entertain**: This requires similar skills to story telling with the difference being that, in order to entertain, your story will have to amuse the reader and hold their attention. You will not be able to claim that a story is funny; you will have to tell it in a way that makes your reader smile or laugh.

Now you will need to consider possibilities, sources and other things with which you may be familiar or unfamiliar. It might help to ask yourself the question: 'What if...?'. There may be characters from stories that you know or from real life that you could adapt and manipulate or change to suit your purpose. It can be fun to realise that, in fiction, you can make your characters do things that people might not do in real life.

ACTIVITY 1 | A01 | SKILLS ▶ CREATIVITY, COOPERATION

▼ ADAPTING STORIES AND CHARACTERS

In pairs, make a list of stories known to you that you could adapt for your own story telling. Make a note of interesting characters and situations that might form the basis of a good story.

▲ There are many world-famous characters in literature that you could use in your own writing, such as Sherlock Holmes.

Sharing initial thoughts and asking quick-fire questions of one another are techniques often used to help generate ideas. When people have to respond rapidly to questions, they are sometimes surprised how easily new ideas will appear. Sometimes there can be a chain reaction and a flood of unexpected ideas will result. The important thing is to engage with the exchange of ideas and opinions. Doing something different or unusual often triggers the discovery of new ideas.

ACTIVITY 2   **AO4**   **SKILLS** CREATIVITY, TEAMWORK

▼ WHAT IF…?

In groups, try asking the question, 'What if…?' about people and situations with which you are familiar. Write down a list of key words that would provide you with the beginning of a story plan.

When you are required to write imaginatively, you may choose to use a familiar format, story elements or genre. For example, you could choose to write a fairytale, a horror story, a science fiction story about space travel, a historical story set in a particular time period, a detective story or an adventure story.

ACTIVITY 3   **AO4**   **AO5**   **SKILLS** ADAPTIVE LEARNING, CREATIVITY

▼ INTRODUCING DIFFERENT GENRES

In pairs, choose four of the types of story listed above that are familiar to you and list the main features of each type. Then decide what you would want to include in the first paragraph of each type of story. Finally, working on your own, write four introductory paragraphs, one for each story type.

KEY POINT

Consider the topic of your writing and plan carefully what you think you want to write before you start. However, once you have planned and started to write, do not be reluctant to change direction rather than continue with an idea that has lost its appeal.

▲ What genres could these be?

LEARNING OBJECTIVES

This lesson will help you to:

- understand how to create a plot that suits your purpose in writing.

PLOT

When you are planning the plot of your piece of writing, you should always consider the questions: 'What is happening?' and 'Why is it happening?'

The importance of these questions is that they make you think about what you want to present in your narrative and how that helps your purpose. You might produce a wonderful dramatic passage or a moving description but, unless these serve the purpose for which you are writing, you will not be successful. Examiners will notice this and will expect to find a sense of connected purpose as they read your work.

FIRST STEPS OF PLOTTING

Before you plot anything, you will need a clear sense of your purpose in writing. Even a simple sentence will guide you through the planning process.

| ACTIVITY 1 | A01 | SKILLS | CRITICAL THINKING, INTERPRETATION |

▼ IDENTIFYING PURPOSE

Working in pairs, list twelve stories that you know. They could be books, television programmes, films and so on. For each story, write one sentence to summarise the writer's purpose. In each case, ask yourselves what you think the writer was trying to achieve.

Sometimes a writer will set out their reasons for writing a particular book. For example, Charles Dickens introduced the purpose of his first novel, *The Pickwick Papers*, with just one sentence:

> The author's object in this work was to place before the reader a constant succession of characters and incidents; to paint them in as vivid colours as he could command; and to render them, at the same time, life-like and amusing.

KEY POINT

The plot is a key step in planning imaginative writing. Once it has been established, you can start to apply details, remembering that further ideas may come to you as you plan and write and that you should be ready to respond to these ideas. Ideas can come from thinking about and developing the events and characters in your plan, so make use of these ideas where possible.

| ACTIVITY 2 | A04 | SKILLS | CREATIVITY, TEAMWORK |

▼ STARTING TO CREATE A PLOT

1 In pairs, follow Dickens's idea for a succession of characters and amusing incidents by listing people you know. For each of these people, try to imagine an amusing incident in which they might easily become involved. Make brief notes on the incident.

2 Still working in pairs, list the really important events that you want to include in your narrative, then write one sentence for each of these points, saying why they are important for readers following your story.

DEVELOPING PLOT

Once you have established a clear sense of purpose for your writing, you can start to develop your plot further. Utilising the simple sentences and initial ideas you have used to outline your plot, you can start to expand these to create a more detailed outline of the narrative you wish to tell.

There are many ways in which you can develop ideas. Try using some of the following techniques.

- Using a photograph or an image, try applying your story idea to the subject matter or situation shown in the photograph. This can help you generate a chain of events, setting or story.
- Consider an alternative perspective from different characters to offer a differing view or approach to your idea.
- Establish a start, middle and end of your story. Once these key components have been created, use your ideas to connect them together and develop them further.
- Consider the type of plot you wish to use. Many writers experiment with time, perspective or twists to keep the reader engaged.

▲ What ideas for a plot does this photograph give you?

| ACTIVITY 3 | AO4 | SKILLS ADAPTIVE LEARNING, CREATIVITY |

▼ ADAPTING PLOTS

Using your list of plot points from Activity 2, make the following changes and note how each change alters the plot.

- Use a different narrative perspective.
- Present the plot in a different order.
- Add a shocking twist at the end.

LEARNING OBJECTIVES

This lesson will help you to:

■ understand how to order important items in a narrative and link them in the most effective way.

STRUCTURE

The structure of a piece of writing involves both the order and the manner in which components of a narrative are assembled. Ordering the components is one thing, but deciding how they will fit together within the story is another. Each of the components will have to fit somehow with the component that precedes it and the component that follows. For example, will any two components be closely linked so that you move quickly from a physical description of a character to an explanation of that character's history or an account of some of the things done by that character?

These are the kinds of decisions that you will have to make as you plan and write.

BEGINNINGS AND ENDINGS

Beginnings and endings provide the support for the rest of the narrative in much the same way as two book-ends hold up a row of books. They are both important. The introduction sets the narrative in motion and establishes the tone or mood of the piece: is it relaxed or tense, detailed or in a hurry to move on? The conclusion provides the author's final word. Is it a happy one? Is the writer anxious to finish? Is the fate of major characters something that the writer is pleased with? Would the writer want to return to this topic, or to this character?

Look at the opening of Graham Greene's *Brighton Rock* and think about what this opening tells you about the rest of the story.

▼ FROM *BRIGHTON ROCK* BY GRAHAM GREENE

Hale knew they meant to murder him before he had been in Brighton three hours. With his inky fingers and his bitten nails, his manner cynical and nervous, anybody could tell he didn't belong – belong to the early summer sun, the cool Whitsun wind off the sea, the holiday crowd.

Whitsun A date in the Christian calendar, seven weeks after Easter.

▲ A scene from the film adaptation of Graham Greene's *Brighton Rock*

This is the opening of a psychological drama where a desperate man, all alone, is filled with the terror of knowing that someone wants to murder him. This is the first, shocking thing that the reader is told about him. Immediately, Greene goes on to describe him in way that confirms what he has just told the reader: that this man no longer belongs to life (that is, to the sun, the wind or the crowds of holiday-makers).

ACTIVITY 1   **A04**   **A05**   **SKILLS** ▶ ADAPTIVE LEARNING, CREATIVITY, INNOVATION

▼ IDENTIFYING PURPOSE

In pairs, create a list of points that make up the plot of a story. Write the opening sentences of this story, so that a character and his or her situation are introduced quickly and suddenly, so that the reader will be shocked. Now write a second opening to the same story. This time, link the two ideas more slowly, to give your reader more time to fully understand events. How does this change in structure affect the impact on the reader?

Now look at the end of an equally famous novel. In *Nineteen Eighty-Four*, George Orwell tells the story of a dystopian world where the population is under the complete control and supervision of a powerful and mysterious government Party, headed by Big Brother. The narrative follows Winston Smith as he seeks to rebel against Big Brother and the Party. His rebellion is short-lived however as he is captured and brainwashed to conform and love the Party.

▼ FROM *NINETEEN EIGHTY-FOUR* BY GEORGE ORWELL

The voice from the telescreen was still pouring forth its tale of prisoners and booty and slaughter, but the shouting outside had died down a little. The waiters were turning back to their work. One of them approached with the gin bottle. Winston, sitting in a blissful dream, paid no attention as his glass was filled up. He was not running or cheering any longer. He was back in the Ministry of Love, with everything forgiven, his soul white as snow. He was in the public dock, confessing everything, implicating everybody. He was walking down the white-tiled corridor, with the feeling of walking in sunlight, and an armed guard at his back. The long-hoped-for bullet was entering his brain.

He gazed up at the enormous face. Forty years it had taken him to learn what kind of smile was hidden beneath the dark moustache. O cruel, needless misunderstanding! O stubborn, self-willed exile from the loving breast! Two gin scented tears trickled down the sides of his nose. But it was all right, everything was all right, the struggle was finished. He had won the victory over himself. He loved Big Brother.

KEY POINT

Try to structure your sentences, paragraphs and whole narratives while bearing in mind the likely responses of your readers as you link the points that you make.

This is an uncomfortable and powerful conclusion for a number of reasons. The sentences and information sound detached, emotionless and impersonal as things happen quickly and outside of Winston's control showing him to be broken and defeated. The use of the pronoun 'he' instead of his name distances Winston from the rebellious character that the reader has grown to know throughout the story.

This is a particularly effective conclusion as it acts to bring the narrative to an end in a manner that shocks the reader and, most importantly, inspires a range of further thoughts and questions.

LEARNING OBJECTIVES

This lesson will help you to:

- develop the skill of drawing the reader into the narrative so that they will appreciate being entertained.

▲ 'The Mole had been working very hard all the morning'…

NARRATION

A narrative has to lead the reader. If the reader does not like the narrative, it is very easy for them to stop reading.

Non-fiction writing involves a greater level of sharing the writer's purposes in writing, such as to inform someone who needs to know something or to discuss a topic in which the reader is interested. However, a fictional narrative is designed to entertain someone who can choose to stop reading if they are not enjoying the experience of reading. The narrator has to present something that will trigger a reader's interest and satisfaction.

Kenneth Grahame's *The Wind in the Willows* was written for children in 1908. Read the following extract from the beginning of the story, paying attention to the way in which Grahame seeks to engage the reader.

▼ FROM *THE WIND IN THE WILLOWS* BY KENNETH GRAHAME

The Mole had been working very hard all the morning, spring-cleaning his little home. First with brooms, then with dusters; then on ladders with steps and chairs, with a brush and a pail of whitewash; till he had dust all over his black fur, and an aching back and weary arms. Spring was moving in the air above and in the earth below and around him, penetrating even his dark and lowly little house with its spirit of divine discontent and longing. It was small wonder, then, that he suddenly flung down his brush on the floor, said, 'Bother!' and, 'O blow!', and also, 'Hang spring-cleaning!' and bolted out of the house without even waiting to put on his coat.

| ACTIVITY 1 | A01 | SKILLS | CRITICAL ANALYSIS, ANALYSIS, INTERPRETATION |

▼ ENGAGING THE READER'S INTEREST

In small groups, list the ways in which Grahame begins this narrative. These could include things such as the image of someone hard at work, the details of Mole's equipment, and so on. For each of these techniques used by Grahame to engage the reader's interest, explain in one sentence how you react to them.

| ACTIVITY 2 | A01 | SKILLS | CREATIVITY, TEAMWORK |

▼ BEGINNING A STORY

In pairs, make a list of stories that you have enjoyed. They do not necessarily have to be stories from books or films. They could be stories that you have simply heard from other people. For each story, write down one sentence explaining how the story begins. Note whether the story starts by focusing on a character, by describing something like the setting, or by presenting some action. You may discover a way of starting a story that is new to you, so be prepared to learn new techniques.

FIRST- AND THIRD-PERSON NARRATIVES

SUBJECT VOCABULARY

first person written from the perspective of one person – that is, using 'I'; this differs from the second person, which directly addresses the reader ('you'), and the third person ('he', 'she' and 'it')

third person using the third person – that is, 'he', 'she' and 'it'; this differs from the first person ('I') and the second person, which directly addresses the reader ('you')

The three paragraphs that follow are written in the **first person**. First-person narratives provide a sense of immediacy as we listen to someone who was there and saw for themselves what actually happened and what was actually said.

I first began to take notice of the family when I ran into the mother on the way to the shops. She smiled and reached out her arm to touch my shoulder then allowed her hand to rest for a moment on the lapel of my jacket.

'Will you thank your wife for me?' Over her shoulder I could see the two little ones. Margaret had taken them in when their cat had been run over and looked after them until their mother had returned from the vet.

'That's OK,' I said. 'They were no trouble.' I nodded towards her children, who were about to catch her up. 'We enjoyed looking after them.'

The next three paragraphs are written in the **third person** and are more detached, as if the writer is observing from a distance rather than being involved. This can give the impression that the writer is giving a more balanced or reliable view of things, and is not affected by the things that he or she writes about.

There had been rumours about the disused mine for years. Tom and his friend had played around the entrance when they were small, but, understandably, when their parents had found out a fuss had been made and the owners were obliged to seal it up.

Still the rumours had continued. As the boys grew older, and their circle of friendship had widened, they had encountered other boys from further afield who had also heard the rumours. At school and at home there had been hand tools that they had learnt to use: hammers, chisels, crowbars and spades. At school there had been adventure stories about children their own age.

They met one morning at what had been the mine entrance, carrying tools borrowed from garden sheds and garages, tools belonging to parents who would not have agreed to lend them for this particular purpose.

What difference do you think could be made by choosing one of these two narrative styles? How might the impact on the reader change, depending on whether the story is narrated in the first or third person?

ACTIVITY 3 **A04** **A05** **SKILLS** ADAPTIVE LEARNING, CREATIVITY, INNOVATION

▼ CHOOSING BETWEEN FIRST AND THIRD PERSON

In pairs or on your own, write a different version of each of the two narratives that you have just read. For the first narrative, which is currently written in the first person, use the third person. You could start with the words, 'He first began to...' For the second narrative, use the first person, writing perhaps from the point of view of one of the boys involved or one of their parents.

KEY POINT

Remember that, as the writer of a narrative, you will have to decide the character of the narrator. Is it you, a character in the story, or someone who is detached from the story and treats events like a newspaper reporter?

LEARNING OBJECTIVES

This lesson will help you to:
- think about how to create and use characters in your writing.

CHARACTERS

Characters influence readers in several ways: through your direct awareness of what they think, do and say; through their influence on other characters; and through what the author tells you about them.

Characters are not just the people in a story. One of them may be the narrator of the story. They may be the people in the story, about whom readers learn from the author, in a third-person narrative. A character may never actually appear in a story, but they may still be of importance and the reader may learn about them from the narrator or from other characters.

ACTIVITY 1　　A01　　SKILLS > CRITICAL THINKING

▼ LEARNING ABOUT CHARACTERS

In pairs, read the following excerpts from pieces of imaginative writing and identify how you learn about each of the characters. Do you learn about them through their own thoughts and actions, through the narrator's descriptions and judgements or through another character's eyes?

- He thought she was stunning. You could tell when he spoke about her and when he waited after school, when most of us boys had set off for the park. You could tell when we asked him about her. Most telling was the cruel moment when someone said that she had been running after one of the boys in the other class.

- I noticed them gradually, as they crawled out of the rotten woodwork onto the paving slabs. What use they were I could never tell and so, before they could reach the dog's bowl, I lifted my foot and ground them into the concrete. Mary wouldn't have liked it but then she was not there to see what I had done.

- He was the biggest rabbit in the litter. Since they had arrived in the straw, under the lamp, he had quickly learnt to barge his brothers and sisters to one side so that he always got the best feed. Now that they were weaned the others simply moved aside when he wanted a drink or the best spot in the warm straw bed.

◀ 'He was the biggest rabbit in the litter...'

ACTIVITY 2 | A01 | SKILLS CRITICAL THINKING

▼ QUESTIONS TO ASK ABOUT CHARACTERS

Try answering the following questions about each of the characters in Activity 1.

- Who are they?
- What are they?
- What are they doing?
- What are they trying to achieve?
- How do they interact with each other?

REVEALING CHARACTER

An author has to decide whether characters should be revealed by someone such as the narrator, who passes on what they know or feel about them, or by the characters themselves, so that readers can see the characters in action and make up their own minds about them.

Sometimes the reader needs to know something about a character that the character would be reluctant to reveal themselves. Then the author, or another character, might need to tell the reader.

> She was far too modest to tell anyone about her bravery, how she had forced her way into the burning house to rescue her neighbours' children. When she forgot to put on her gloves you could see the scars.

Sometimes the reader is better convinced when they can see an event for themselves, rather than being told about it.

> She put down the phone and rushed outside. She looked over to the other neighbours' houses but there were no lights to be seen. Somehow she found the strength to force open the door and make her way in. Moments later she emerged with a small child whom she laid carefully on the grass, away from the house. By now a red glow showed itself from all the upstairs windows and smoke was streaming from the door. From some distance away came the sound of a siren. The girl paused, took a deep breath and turned back into the smoke.

ACTIVITY 3 | A04 | A05 | SKILLS CREATIVITY, INNOVATION

▼ INTRODUCING CHARACTERS

Working on your own, write an opening section for a story containing introductions to two characters. One character should be introduced by the narrator or another character, whereas the second character should introduce themselves.

KEY POINT

You learn about characters by what they say and do, by the reactions of other characters and by what you are told by the author.

LEARNING OBJECTIVES

This lesson will help you to:
- use speech to reveal character.

MONOLOGUES AND DIALOGUES

Monologues represent the thoughts or speech of a single person or character, whereas dialogues are exchanges between more than one person or character. These serve different purposes in imaginative writing: monologues can be more fluid, like your thoughts, whereas dialogues can portray arguments, love or perhaps progress towards a resolution of some question.

The following extracts are taken from Susan Hill's novel, *I'm the King of the Castle*. When Edmund Hooper is about 11 years old, his father tells him that another boy is coming to live in their house, along with his mother who is to be their housekeeper. Edmund's mother had died a few years before. The story continues.

> Hooper began to mould plasticine between his hands, for another layer to the geological model, standing as a board beside the window. He thought of the boy called Kingshaw, who was coming.
>
> 'It is my house,' he thought, 'it is private, I got here first. Nobody should come here.'

Hooper's words here form a **monologue**. They are private words, whether spoken or thought. Through them Hooper reveals his determination that no one should share the house with him. No one else can know about these thoughts and the author has given the reader a private view, as it were, into the boy's jealous determination.

Soon the boys are left together.

> He walked round the table, towards the window. Kingshaw stepped back as he came.
>
> 'Scaredy!'
>
> 'No.'
>
> 'When my father dies,' Hooper said, 'this house will belong to me. I shall be master. It'll all be mine.'
>
> 'That's nothing. It's only an old house.'

Here the story moves on with a **dialogue**, and the reader can see the very beginning of the bullying and rivalry that will result in a death. This failure of the boys to co-operate can easily be presented in a natural situation such as this one, more so than using someone's private thoughts.

SUBJECT VOCABULARY

monologue the speech or thoughts of one person alone

dialogue the speech between two or more people involved in a conversation

▲ Monologues can be used to create the complexity of individual character.

ACTIVITY 1   **A04**   **A05**   **SKILLS** ADAPTIVE LEARNING, CREATIVITY, INNOVATION, TEAMWORK

▼ USING MONOLOGUES

In pairs, briefly introduce four characters using monologues. Your characters will find themselves:

- alone at night, unable to sleep
- in a crowd
- with someone who refuses to speak to them
- in a situation of your own choice.

Speech and private thoughts provide a writer with useful tools for introducing characters. What people say and think when they are alone, or when they think that they are alone, can be very revealing about their character. Satirical magazines such as *Private Eye* make good use of this technique. One early novel in the English language, *Pamela* by Samuel Richardson, uses thoughts from a private diary to reveal important information.

ACTIVITY 2   **A04**   **A05**   **SKILLS** ADAPTIVE LEARNING, CREATIVITY, INNOVATION, TEAMWORK

▼ USING DIALOGUE

In pairs, briefly introduce four characters or groups of characters through dialogue. Your characters will find themselves in the following situations.

- A home owner confronting a stranger in his or her back garden.
- A group of friends trying to persuade a bouncer or security guard to let them into a night club.
- A group of magistrates questioning someone who is on trial or who is giving evidence.
- A teacher asking a student why their homework has not been done.

ACTIVITY 3   **A04**   **A05**   **SKILLS** ADAPTIVE LEARNING, CREATIVITY, INNOVATION

▼ USING PRIVATE THOUGHTS

In pairs or on your own, use a character's private thoughts or words that have been overheard to introduce one or more of the characters. Try not to tell your reader what you think of your character or characters. Instead, try to show what they are, using their words. You could use the following words as a starting point.

> They couldn't believe their luck. There, on the table in front of them, was the diary. It had been left open and there on the first pages were some of the words they had hoped to find.

KEY POINT

You are affected by what people say. In your writing, help your reader to sense what characters' words suggest about their personality.

LEARNING OBJECTIVES

This lesson will help you to:
- use your senses to guide your descriptive writing.

DESCRIPTIVE WRITING

Descriptions can be written for their own sake or to accompany narratives, instructions, explanations and argument. They rely on an engagement of your senses and your imagination.

USING THE SENSES

It is through your five senses that you know the world around you. The more that you can engage your reader's senses, the more effective your writing will be.

Were you woken by an alarm clock or by the sound of a parent's voice this morning? Was the first thing that you saw a bright light shining in your face? Was the first thing you felt someone pulling back the blankets? Did you smell toast? Was the first thing you tasted toothpaste, some fruit juice or a boiled egg?

▲ Are your senses acute or dull in the morning?

| ACTIVITY 1 | A04 | A05 | SKILLS ▸ CREATIVITY |

▼ USING YOUR SENSES

Working on your own, try to remember and list the first things that you heard, saw, felt, smelt and tasted after waking up this morning. Use this list as the basis of a description of the first half hour of your day.

SHOW, NOT TELL

Sometimes, you can describe things more convincingly by 'showing' the reader rather than telling them.

| ACTIVITY 2 | A02 | SKILLS ▸ ANALYSIS, COLLABORATION |

▼ SHOWING OR TELLING?

In pairs, consider which of these pairs of sentences you find more convincing:

1 **A:** He removed his coat from a hook behind the door.
  B: He lifted one arm and eased his coat from the hook behind the door.

2 **A:** On the horizon a car appeared.
  B: From the horizon something hurried towards them along the road.

3 **A:** They heard the squeal of angry brakes and were thrown forward against the opposite seats.
  B: The driver applied the brakes suddenly.

4 **A:** The engine died.
  B: For no reason he could think of, the engine stopped.

ACTIVITY 3 | A02 | SKILLS CRITICAL THINKING, ANALYSIS

▼ CREATING EFFECT

In pairs, identify the words and phrases that are used to create effective description in the following passage adapted from *The War of the Worlds*. In H.G. Wells's story of an invasion by creatures from Mars, there is a description of one of their spaceships that serves to enhance the drama of its discovery. When the novel was dramatised and broadcast like live news on American radio, it caused widespread panic as listeners thought they were listening to a news bulletin.

▼ FROM *THE WAR OF THE WORLDS* BY H.G. WELLS

The Thing itself lay almost entirely buried in sand, amidst the scattered splinters of a fir tree it had shivered to fragments in its descent.

The uncovered part had the appearance of a huge cylinder, caked over and its outline softened by a thick scaly dun-coloured incrustation. It had a diameter of about thirty metres. He approached the mass, surprised at the size and more so at the shape, since most meteorites are rounded more or less completely. It was, however, still so hot from its flight through the air as to forbid his near approach. A stirring noise within its cylinder he ascribed to the unequal cooling of its surface; for at that time it had not occurred to him that it might be hollow.

Suddenly he noticed with a start that some of the grey clinker, the ashy incrustation that covered the meteorite, was falling off the circular edge of the end. It was dropping off in flakes and raining down upon the sand. A large piece suddenly came off and fell with a sharp noise that brought his heart into his mouth.

And then he perceived that, very slowly, the circular top of the cylinder was rotating on its body. It was such a gradual movement that he discovered it only through noticing that a black mark that had been near him five minutes ago was now at the other side of the circumference. Even then he scarcely understood what this indicated, until he heard a muffled grating sound and saw the black mark jerk forward an inch or so. Then the thing came upon him in a flash. The cylinder was artificial – hollow – with an end that screwed out! Something within the cylinder was unscrewing the top!

KEY POINT

An imaginative choice of words can enhance a description. For example, what is the difference in effect between 'the cat *sat* on the mat' and 'the cat *sprawled* on the mat'?

ACTIVITY 4 | A01 | A04 | A05 | SKILLS ANALYSIS, ADAPTIVE LEARNING, CREATIVITY, INNOVATION

▼ IDENTIFYING DESCRIPTION

1 In pairs, list the verbs and verbal adjectives that help to convey the descriptive elements in the extract from *The War of the Worlds*. There are 20. Then list the 17 ordinary adjectives that Wells uses.

2 Use the lists in order to write your own description of 'The Thing'.

VOCABULARY FOR EFFECT

Sometimes you may say that you are 'trying to find the right word'. Sometimes it is not until you stumble across the right word, by chance perhaps, that you will realise that you have found it.

CHOOSING THE RIGHT WORD

This sense of 'the right word' is a strong one and, just as we can realise this when you are writing or speaking, so you can appreciate it when you listen to someone else or read what they have to say.

Read the two versions of the same account that follows.

EXTRACT A

Before a visit to the dentist when I was about fourteen, I liked ice cream. Then I had a tooth removed, under a general anaesthetic.

Soon I was dreaming that I was eating an ice cream. The ice cream tasted of tomatoes. I had never liked tomatoes. For six months afterwards I didn't fancy ice cream until I made myself buy one and found that it tasted all right.

EXTRACT B

Before a visit to the dentist when I was about fourteen, I was unable to resist ice cream. Then I had a tooth removed, under a general anaesthetic.

Soon I was dreaming that I was eating an ice cream. Unfortunately the ice cream tasted of fried tomatoes and, worse still, smelled of fried tomatoes. I had never liked tomatoes, in fact I loathed them. For six months afterwards I was unable to face ice cream until I forced myself to buy one and discovered, much to my relief, that it tasted of ice cream.

▲ 'The ice cream tasted of tomatoes...'

ACTIVITY 1 | **A02** | **SKILLS** ▶ INNOVATION

▼ THE EFFECTS OF DIFFERENT WORDS

In pairs, list the words that have been changed between Extract A and Extract B, starting with *liked* (in Extract A) and *was unable to resist* (in Extract B). Then, for each change, write one sentence explaining the effect of the change.

ACTIVITY 2 | **A04** | **A05** | **SKILLS** ▶ CREATIVITY, INNOVATION

▼ CHOOSING THE PERFECT WORD

Working on your own, describe in one paragraph something that has surprised you. It could be a particular sight or scene or an event that you have witnessed. Try to use some *mots justes*. Exchange your description with someone else and try to identify your partner's *mots justes*.

SUBJECT VOCABULARY

mots justes a French phrase, meaning words that are apt, or just right

CREATING IMAGES

Writers often use images, or things that can be seen or visualised, as reminders of concepts or events, as a narrative progresses. In this way, associations between things allow the writer to provide quick links or reminders for the reader which nevertheless do not impede the story.

Read the following piece of imaginative writing.

> They were not used to lighting their own bonfires, but one of them had smuggled a box of matches out of the house. Ignoring precautions, they enjoyed seeing the flames leap, from the first match to the paper stuffed under the brush wood, then flare up through the heavier branches until the flames roared skywards over the wood and waste material that had been piled high.
>
> When a stiff breeze suddenly blew amongst them they watched horrified as the flames licked across to the garden shed which held their toys. Within minutes the roof was a blanket of flame and the toys had gone for ever.

Here, a box of matches becomes an image of danger and fear, a reminder in the characters' adult lives of something that can go badly wrong and cause danger and destruction.

ACTIVITY 3 | **A04** | **A05** | **SKILLS** ▸ CREATIVITY, INNOVATION

▼ USING IMAGES TO CONVEY MEANING

Working on your own, choose one of the following objects and write a paragraph in which you turn it into an image of something important:

- ■ a pen
- ■ a pair of shoes
- ■ a memory stick.

HINTING, SUGGESTING, UNDERSTATING

Consider the following instructions or comments.

- ■ 'Keep an eye on him.'
- ■ 'Your homework is dreadful.'

How do you think you would respond to these instructions or statements? Do you think you would respond differently if they were re-phrased as follows?

- ■ 'Just try to keep an eye on him.'
- ■ 'Your homework is rather disappointing.'

In the second list, the writer is trying to reduce or soften the impact of their words. The first instruction becomes a suggestion that perhaps you should keep an eye on someone. The second comment is amended so that, rather than sounding angry, the teacher is trying to make you regret letting them down.

KEY POINT

You readily use subtle forms of words when you speak to other people. With a little thought you can be just as flexible when writing.

ACTIVITY 4 | **A04** | **A05** | **SKILLS** ▸ ADAPTIVE LEARNING, CREATIVITY, INNOVATION

▼ USING SUBTLE LANGUAGE

Working on your own, extend each of the four instructions or comments that you have just read so that they make it clear what is going on. You could follow the pattern of the example sentence below.

> I don't think this is going to work; the glue has already set.

Try to use subtle words and phrases to do so, so that you suggest what is going on rather than stating it.

SENTENCES FOR EFFECT

Sentences have various ways of being organised: short, compound or complex. All these types produce different effects.

SENTENCE TYPES

doing wheelies Balancing a bicycle on its rear wheel while riding it.

dog collar An informal description of the white collar worn by the clergy of some Christian churches.

▲ A mountain biker demonstrating a wheelie

HINT

Look back at previous sections about the effect of different sentences on pages 22–23, 38–39 and 164–165.

In her novel, *The Risk of Darkness*, Susan Hill describes a young woman priest walking home. At the time of the novel's setting, the sight of a woman priest was a novelty in England.

A boy bounced past her on a bicycle doing wheelies over the cobbles. Jane smiled at him. He did not respond but when he had gone by, turned and stared over his shoulder. She was used to it. Here she was, a girl, wearing jeans, and a dog collar. People were still surprised.

The first sentence is a simple one containing only one main verb. It is also quite loose, as the main verb is found at the start of the sentence. This sentence could be stopped after just five words and it would still make sense. What do you think is achieved by including the rest of the sentence?

▶ **In pairs, find the other two places in the extract where a sentence could be stopped early. What effect does the writer achieve by building up the sentences in this way?**

ACTIVITY 1 **A01** **SKILLS** ANALYSIS, CREATIVITY

▼ DEVELOPING SENTENCES

Decide how you could develop the following sentences. Write down the purpose for extending each one, then add to it.
- The door opened.
- They could see the dog.
- The streets were always the same.

What sort of sentences have you produced? Are they loose, periodic or balanced? Are they simple, compound or complex?

Look again at the paragraph from *The Risk of Darkness*. The third and fifth sentences grow in a similar way to the first sentence, but what about the other sentences? They are all simple, periodic sentences, but are related to the more complicated sentences that they follow. Look again at the third sentence.

He did not respond but when he had gone by, turned and stared over his shoulder.

Here there is much detail added to the basic sentence and the boy's reaction to Jane is made clear. Her reaction is conveyed in only five words.

She was used to it.

ACTIVITY 2 | A01 | SKILLS > ANALYSIS

▼ THE EFFECT OF DIFFERENT SENTENCE TYPES

In pairs, decide the effect of revealing Jane's reaction in this simple sentence without further detail. What effect is achieved in the sixth sentence?

OTHER WAYS OF ORGANISING SENTENCES

You have seen the way in which strong effects can be created when sentences of different types are carefully placed together. Now you are going to look at other ways of organising sentences. Read the following piece of imaginative writing.

> It was icy, bitter cold. The washing hung frozen on the lines and icicles reached down from gutters that were filled with water that could no longer flow, held in place by unbelievably low temperatures. He looked for his gloves. He had left them to one side, by the door, but the space on the shelf was empty now and only the marks which he had brushed in the dust remained to remind him that his memory was not playing tricks.

Instead of showing a reaction to something, as with the short sentences in Hill's paragraph from *The Risk of Darkness*, these long, complex sentences develop the ideas in the short sentences that they follow. Of course, the pairs of sentences here also develop a wider idea – the drama of this character and the bitter cold he faces.

ACTIVITY 3 | A04 | A05 | SKILLS > CREATIVITY, INNOVATION

▼ DEVELOPING AN IDEA USING SENTENCE TYPES

Working alone, decide on an idea that you would like to develop in one paragraph. Write down that idea in one sentence and then start. If you are writing on paper use only every third line to give yourself room to try out words and make improvements to what you have written as you make progress. Your paragraph should be a minimum of four sentences.

ACTIVITY 4 | A04 | A05 | SKILLS > CREATIVITY, INNOVATION, COLLABORATION

KEY POINT

While you are writing, be prepared to stop occasionally and ask yourself whether the words you have written will achieve your purpose or purposes.

▼ USING DIFFERENT SENTENCE PATTERNS

In pairs or in groups, try to develop an idea using different patterns of sentences, investigating what might serve your purposes and focusing on what you were aiming to achieve at the outset.
Remember, you have to decide your purpose before you start to write, because you must bear it in mind while you are writing.

LEARNING OBJECTIVES

This lesson will help you to:
- take greater control over your writing
- think about the use of the senses when writing
- make clear what you want to say about characters, actions and locations.

PUTTING IT INTO PRACTICE

In the exam, you will need to demonstrate the following points in your imaginative writing.
- Ideas that are communicated effectively and imaginatively. This is what you will have to plan before you start.
- Writing that is clear and accurate. This is what you will have to check after you finish.

EXAM-STYLE QUESTION

A04

A05

SKILLS CRITICAL THINKING, ANALYSIS, CREATIVITY, INNOVATION

Write a story (true or imaginary) entitled 'An Unexpected Event'. **(30 marks)**

It was a warm summer's day and we set off from the farmyard to round up some sheep. Early in the summer all the sheep were rounded up so that they could be dipped, pushed one at a time through a long narrow bath that contained an insecticide that would protect them from flies that would burrow into their flesh and lay their eggs in the wounds that they had created. The condition is called fly-strike. The sheep we were looking for had spread themselves over the moor and across to an open area of land between the road and the sea. With us we had two sheep dogs. Once we had crossed the road we sent the dogs round in wide sweeping paths to move the sheep together into a flock that we could move across the road and back to the farm.

Ahead of us we could see the dogs, their heads up as they looked from side to side for sheep that were standing still as if wondering whether to move or not. They moved on, and left us to follow, pushing the flock up towards the road. Then, as the ground sloped more steeply away beneath our feet, we could see them no longer. Below us, to our left, we could hear the sea crashing into the rocks at the foot of the cliffs. Suddenly, from ahead of us, came the blare of a fog horn.

We hadn't noticed the clouds that had come up behind us. They had yet to blot out the sun and we were more aware of the growing flock to our right that was moving slowly towards the road. Ahead of us the dogs were barking furiously now and we stepped forwards to see what was troubling them. Again the fog horn blared, this time almost above us.

Suddenly, the fog had surrounded us; damp and chill, it had been blown up behind us as the breeze had lifted. We could see nothing of dogs or sheep, but we could hear them and the rocks that were directly below us. To one side we leant on the round wall of the tower that housed the fog horn, built into the cliff. Around us sheep and dogs continued to move carefully, but we two-legged creatures were far less stable on the cliff face and so we waited until the breeze dropped and the fog slid away off the cliff and moved slowly, back down to the water.

The condition is called fly-strike. A long, detailed description is followed by a short sentence to vary pace.

we sent the dogs round in wide sweeping paths The vocabulary is fairly straight forward, but chosen precisely to create a vivid image.

Below us, to our left, we could hear the sea crashing into the rocks at the foot of the cliffs. Suddenly, from ahead of us, came the blare of a fog horn. Adding these sensory details makes the scene feel more real and also creates suspense.

Ahead of us the dogs were barking furiously now and we stepped forwards to see what was troubling them The description of the clouds, and then the dogs barking 'furiously', increases tension.

Suddenly, the fog had surrounded us; damp and chill, it had been blown up behind us as the breeze had lifted. Use of a semicolon to link together descriptions of the fog is very effective.

EXAMINER'S COMMENTS

This is a highly effective piece of imaginative writing. A vivid scene is created through precise use of vocabulary, which shows it's not always necessary to use lots of figurative language to describe effectively. The atmosphere becomes increasingly tense, showing the student has a good grasp of how to structure a piece of writing. There is a good balance of longer, more detailed sentences and short sentences for effect.

COMMENTARY

This is an explanation of how this sample answer was written. Try following this process in your own imaginative writing.

PLANNING THE PLOT

The planning of this piece is focused on the fog surrounding the two characters who were caught unawares. The rounding up of the sheep provides a context, a background or explanation as to why the characters were on the sloping cliffs where fog was more of a danger, a sense of drama that could be used to a lesser or greater extent by the writer.

As the gathering of the sheep proceeds, the task becomes a distraction for the characters as they watch the sheep, rather than the weather behind them. As the drama develops you can feel the slope of the cliffs, see the dogs disappear from sight, somewhere ahead, then you hear the waves and the sudden burst of the fog horn. The reader's senses are used to create the drama.

CHECKING

This is where you must read the passage aloud or, under exam conditions, imagine the sound of a voice reading it aloud. This is the most effective way of checking your writing. If the punctuation is poor, you will find yourself unable to read the passage fluently, and if there are lapses in the grammar then the sense of the writing will not be clear. If this happens, ask yourself, 'What is the subject of this sentence?' and 'What am I told about the subject?'. These questions should help you to clarify the sentence.

EXAM-STYLE QUESTIONS

AO4

AO5

SKILLS CRITICAL THINKING, ANALYSIS, ADAPTIVE LEARNING, CREATIVITY

KEY POINT

Engaging your audience is crucial. Remember that good writing usually involves something that the author wants to say. If the author wants something to be read, the reader must be given a reason to start and encouragement to keep reading.

Write approximately 400 words on one of the following:

EITHER

1 'Competing is good but winning is better.' Discuss.   **(30 marks)**

OR

2 Write a story (true or imaginary) entitled 'Victory'.   **(30 marks)**

OR

3 Describe a game that has made an impression on you.   **(30 marks)**

Exchange your finished piece with a partner, then read each other's work and exchange comments. Try to suggest ways of improving each other's work rather than simply finding faults.

▲ The reader's senses are used to create the drama.

EXAM PREPARATION

SUCCESSFUL REVISION

Many books offer different suggestions and advice for revision. One thing is clear: not everything works for everyone. Each person has particular ways of revising and habits of working. Look at all the advice and try out the different suggestions. Decide clearly what the knowledge, skills and techniques you need to develop, consolidate or revisit.

PLAN YOUR LEARNING AND REVISION

HOW TO PLAN A SCHEDULE

- Draw up a table to show the days and weeks before the examination.
- Decide how much time to give to the subject in each week or day.
- Work out a timetable.
- Think about the need for variety and breaks.
- Make sure your schedule is building towards a 'peak' at the right time.

HOW TO IMPROVE

- Test yourself.
- Test a friend.
- Practise answering exam questions.
- Write answers to the time limits of questions in the actual exam.
- Check that you understand all texts, looking particularly at words, meaning, plot and character.
- Revise technical terms, using the glossary on pages 202–203.
- Make sure you can apply these terms properly, spell them properly, give examples and explain how and why the techniques are used.

AIDS TO LEARNING

Write short, clear notes. Use aids such as:

- postcards
- diagrams
- flowcharts
- mnemonics (aids to memory, such as rhymes)
- computer programmes
- websites and apps.

GOOD PREPARATION

Good preparation is one of the main elements affecting how people perform in exams. This includes both attitude of mind and physical preparation.

- Check how long the exam lasts and use your time properly.
- Make sure you understand the specification and know what you have to do.

Don't be tempted to rush your initial reading. It is surprising how many exam candidates make basic mistakes because they did not read through the text in front of them properly.

USING YOUR TIME EFFECTIVELY IN THE EXAMINATIONS

Note that the time allocation of 3 hours for Paper 1 includes time to check instructions and read the paper carefully. Decide how much time you need to allocate to each question: the question paper gives suggestions. You should also aim to leave enough time for checking through at the end. An example of how to plan your time for each paper is given below.

PAPER 1: Reading and Writing

▼ READING THE QUESTION PAPER	▼ SECTION A 40 MARKS	▼ SECTION B 30 MARKS	▼ SECTION C 30 MARKS	▼ FINAL CHECKING
5–10 minutes	Planning: 5 minutes Writing: 50 minutes	Planning: 5–10 minutes Writing: 45–50 minutes	Planning: 5–10 minutes Writing: 45–50 minutes	5–10 minutes
	Duration of exam: 180 minutes (3 hours) **Total marks: 100**			

CHECK YOUR WORK

Check that you are keeping to your planned timings. Keep thinking throughout about:
- relevance, presentation, accuracy and varied vocabulary.

If you manage to leave some checking time at the end:
- make sure you have answered all questions fully and appropriately
- correct any errors in spelling or punctuation (particularly that all sentences have full stops)
- be certain to make sure everything you have written can be read easily.

RELATIONSHIP OF ASSESSMENT OBJECTIVES TO UNITS

▼ UNIT NUMBER	▼ ASSESSMENT OBJECTIVE				
	A01	A02	A03	A04	A05
PAPER 1	15%	20%	15%	32%	18%

PLANNING YOUR ANSWERS

ANSWER THE QUESTION

Do **not** just write down everything you know: this is the most common mistake made by exam candidates. Planning consists of:

- reading the question carefully and deciding what the key words in it are
- deciding the main points you wish to make is, what the question is looking for and how you intend to tackle it
- making sure that the points you want to include are appropriately positioned and structured in the answer
- giving your answer a structure: introduction, main section(s) and conclusion
- choosing examples or quotations.

THINKING ABOUT THE QUESTION

Identifying the key words in the question can help to show:

- **what** the question is looking for
- **how** you intend to tackle it.

Key words and phrases in the question show what the examiner is expecting from an answer. For example:

- **'how does the writer'** is asking you to explain methods and techniques
- **'explain'** asks you to make clear to the examiner your understanding of the text and its methods
- **'analyse'** expects you to look in detail at the writing, its methods and techniques and its effects
- **'compare and contrast'** asks for an examination of similarities and differences in any relevant aspects (for example, themes, moods, forms and language).

KEY POINTS

Write down quickly, in note form, your immediate thoughts about the subject. You may find a diagram useful for this purpose. Do not write full sentences here, or you will waste too much time.

THE CONTENT OF THE ANSWER

The examiner **does** want to know what you think: your own, personal ideas and opinions. However, a series of unsupported statements that start with the words 'I think…' is not enough, since the examiner also needs to know that these ideas are based on your analysis of the texts, your understanding of the subject matter and other evidence.

DECIDING THE STRUCTURE: INTRODUCTION, MAIN SECTION(S) AND CONCLUSION

- **Introduction**: A clear, brief introductory paragraph can make a very good initial impression, showing the examiner that you are thinking about the actual question.
- **Main section(s)**: Decide how many paragraphs or sections you wish your answer to contain.
- **Conclusion**: This may be quite a brief paragraph. It should sum up clearly and logically the argument that has gone before. Above all, it should show the examiner that you have **answered the question**!

WRITING ANALYTICALLY

When writing analytically, whether for English Language or Literature, many students find it helpful to follow the acronym:

- **P** – Point
- **E** – Evidence
- **E** – Explain.

This may help to remind you to structure your paragraphs around a point, include quotations as evidence and then explain in some detail what it is about the quotations that validates your point.

A slightly more advanced approach is to add:

■ L – Link.

This means that you should link your point to the previous and following points, giving your answer a tight and logical structure. Think P-E-E-L.

EVALUATIVE COMMENTS

When reading Section A answers that analyse aspects of a text, examiners will always give more credit for some detailed explanations of how the writer is using language, in which the student shows clearly that they have understood how language is working, than for 'technique-spotting'. In other words, you will get few marks for just saying that a writer uses short sentences and alliteration here and there; but if you can write a few lines on how a writer uses language effectively in just one sentence, you will write a better answer.

USING QUOTATIONS

When writing about texts, whether books, poems, articles or extracts, one of the most important techniques is to use quotations, where these are required and allowed. Quoting is a skill that has to be practised. Overuse of quotations is as significant a mistake as not using any at all. You should use quotations:

■ to illustrate or give an example, for example, a simile or an instance of alliteration

■ to explain why you believe something, to support an opinion or argument or to prove a point.

Quotations should be relevant, effective and short: a single word to a line or two at the most. Introduce quotations fluently into your sentence structure. Avoid writing things like, 'He says…'.

LESS CAN BE MORE

If you can, practise doing Section B-type questions, but never rush them. Just as you should concentrate on explaining in some detail how a writer creates effects for Section A, so in Sections B and C your aim should not be to show how much you can write, but to show that you can think as you write – think of ideas, paragraphing, sentence structure, vocabulary, persuasive or rhetorical techniques and so on. Try to write with care!

LAST-MINUTE REVISION

Think ahead. Revision the night or morning before an exam can be very useful, but generally only if you have done all of the work already. Last-minute revision should consist of looking at checklists, summative notes, mnemonics and any of your particular weaknesses. This can be very helpful, but make sure that you do not panic and make sure that you have done all of the actual work in the weeks before your exam.

ON THE DAY OF THE EXAM

Again, checklists and mnemonics can be useful to consult as you go into school, as might reading through a model answer or two. Always read the exam paper carefully all the way through, and look at the choices for Section C before you start Section A. Many experienced teachers would advise taking some 'mint-time' (that is, the time it would take a mint to dissolve in the mouth – and there is no reason why you should not take one just before you go into the exam room) to read and think and make some notes, before you begin the first question. This can have the effect of steadying the nerves as well as allowing you to think. (Not chewing gum, though!)

TIME WAITS FOR NO-ONE!

Your teacher may not make you practise answering exam questions against the clock, but you should do it anyway. It is invaluable practice for the real exam, which is always a race against time.

What is essential is that you divide your time up carefully in the exam: many students will find it harder to answer Section A with enough detail and accuracy than to complete reasonable answers to Sections B and C, so if you could allow more time for Section A, then aim to complete Sections B and C in about 50 minutes each. Remember that the Section A questions are marked against detailed mark schemes of what should be in the answers (your teacher can show you examples), whereas Section B and C questions are marked on more general guidelines. Also remember that your answer does not have to be a certain length, which means that you can gain good marks with a carefully written answer of 400 words.

Good luck!

adjective a word that describes a noun or pronoun

adverb a word that describes a verb or an adjective

alliteration the use of several words together that begin with the same sound or letter

atmosphere the feeling that an event or place gives you

bias not fair; a particular point of view influenced by one's own or someone else's opinions

broadsheet a newspaper printed on large sheets of paper, especially a serious newspaper

chronologically organised in linear time

clause a group of words that make up part of a sentence, built around a finite verb

clichés phrases that are used so often that they start to lose their impact

conjunction a word that joins parts of a sentence

connotation an idea linked to a word; an idea that has become associated with a word

contrast where two objects, people or ideas are placed next to each other to highlight their differences

denotation what something literally is or shows

descriptive writing that describes something or someone

determiner a word used before a noun in order to show which thing is being referred to

dialogue the speech between two or more people involved in a conversation

diction the writer's choice of words

direct address using second person pronouns 'you' or 'your'

direct speech words spoken by a character in a novel, play or poem

discursive writing that discusses a topic

dynamic verb a verb that describes actions or events that are happening , e.g. 'I go'

emotive language language that produces an emotional reaction

explicit expressed in a way that is very clear and direct

first person written from the perspective of one person – that is, using 'I'; this differs from the second person, which directly addresses the reader ('you'), and the third person ('he', 'she' and 'it')

flashback when the narrator of a story jumps out of the present in order to describe an event which happened in the past (often in the form of memories)

hyperbole exaggerating for effect

imperative verbs verbs that give an instruction or command

implicit suggested or understood without being stated directly

infer read between the lines

interjection a word used to express a strong feeling

ironic using words to convey a meaning that is completely opposite to their apparent meaning

juxtaposition putting two very different things close together in order to encourage comparison between them

litotes ironic understatement used to mean something by saying its opposite

metaphor describing something by comparing it to an image which it resembles, in a way that says the object *is* the image

mnemonic a device used to aid memory – usually in the form of a saying or rhyme

modal auxiliary verb a verb that helps another verb express a meaning, e.g. 'can', 'would', 'should'

monologue the speech or thoughts of one person alone

mots justes a French phrase, meaning words that are apt, or just right

narrative the story or plot, or writing that tells the story of an event

narrator a character that tells the story in a novel, play, poem or film

noun a word that represents a person, place, object or quality

objective based on facts, or making a decision that is based on facts rather than on your feelings or beliefs

onomatopoeia where a word sounds like the noise it makes

periodic sentence a sentence that is not complete until the final word or clause

personal pronoun a word used instead of a noun, such as 'I', 'you' or 'they'

personification when something which is not human is made to seem human by attributing human qualities to it

persuasive able to make other people believe something or do what you ask

phonological relating to the sound structure of words

premodified a noun with a description before it, e.g. 'the big blue car'

preposition a word that is used before a noun or pronoun to show time, place or direction

pronoun a word that is used instead of a noun

pun an amusing use of a word or phrase that has two meanings, or of words that have the same sound but different meanings

quotation marks punctuation marks used to indicate where you have quoted a text

quotations words from a text

referend the thing or idea to which a word refers

register the type or style of vocabulary used according to the situation

repetition saying the same thing more than once to highlight its importance

retrospective written in the past tense; looking back at events that have already occurred

rhetorical device using language in a certain way to achieve an effect

rhetorical question a question that you ask as a way of making a statement, without expecting an answer

rule of three where three things are linked or something is repeated three times in order to emphasise them and ensure they are memorable

setting the place where something is or where something happens, and the general environment

simile a description that says that an object is *like* an image

stereotypes fixed and generalised ideas about particular types of people or groups

superlative a word that expresses the highest or a very high degree of a quality, e.g. 'cleverest' or 'most practical'

synonym a word that shares the same meaning as another word; for example, 'quick' might be a synonym for 'fast'

syntax the way in which words and phrases are arranged into sentences

third person using the third person – that is, 'he', 'she'and 'it'; this differs from the first person ('I') and the second person, which directly addresses the reader ('you')

topic sentence the first sentence in a paragraph, often used to explain the key idea

transactional non-fiction writing for a purpose: to inform, explain, review, argue, persuade or advise

travelogue a book that describes a travel experience

unbiased fair; not influenced by one's own or someone else's opinions

verb a word that describes actions

verbose excessively wordy or long-winded

INDEX

NOTES

The publisher would like to thank Rebecca Watkins for her contribution of additional material.

The authors and publisher would like to thank the following individuals and organisations for permission to reproduce photographs:
(Key: b-bottom; c-centre; l-left; r-right; t-top)

123RF.com: 197, Cathy Yeulet 162, demain1975 179bl, foodandmore. 8, Ilker Celik 47c, instinia 52l, Jan Gorzynik 55, Le Gal Michel 32, meinzahn. 15; **Alamy Stock Photo:** Aurora Photos 119, Eitan Simanor 125, Everett Collection Historical 137, Freddie Jones 188l, Images-USA 129, Janice and Nolan Braud 96, keith morris news 136, louise murray 98, Pacific Press 128, Rose-Marie Murray 130; **Emma Gannon:** 158; **Fotolia. com:** bit24 133, chelle129 18c, christianchan 168, cook_inspire 190, Coprid 13, Focus Pocus LTD 188r, jovannig 45, jsco 47t, Jurgen Falchle 134, martinlisner 150, Monkey Business 132, shock 21; **Getty Images:** Abraham Nowitz 174, Alfred Gescheidt 178, Atlantide Phototravel 24, 138, Bob Thomas / Popperfoto 27, Caroline Purser 173, China Photos / Stringer 68, ColorBlind Images 42, Dave Hogan 61b, Getty Images / Staff 105, Hero Images 142, Jeff Overs 72b, JTB Photo 2, Lauren Nicole 165, MARCEL MOCHET 59, mbbirdy 194, Meiko Arquillos 192, Roberto Machado Noa 56, Stringer 62, sturti 149, Zigy Kaluzny-Charles Thatcher 6; **Pearson Education Ltd:** Gareth Boden 34, 146, Gareth Boden 34, 146, Malcolm Harris 186, Tudor Photography 82; **Shutterstock.com:** 1983497 131, 158 (main), Africa Studio 52r, Aleksey Stemmer 18b, Alessia Pierdomenico 61t, AND Inc. 37, Andre Coetzer 90, brackish_nz. 18t, Charlotte Purdy 53t, D. Kucharski K. Kucharska 184, Dr. Morley Read 127, Dragon Images 47b, Dudarev Mikhail 135, Ermolaev Alexander 153, Ermolaev Alexander 153, Florin Stana 111, Galyna Andrushko. 117, Gelpi JM 53b, iDigital Art 181, iofoto 179br, LifePhotoStudio. 157, Luisma Tapia 179bc, magicinfoto 140, Martin Christopher Parker 38, Maxisport 41, Mikadun 101, Mikhail Pogosov. 83, Morphart Creation. 107, PCHT 29, Regien Paassen 118, Sorbis 16, Stephen Coburn 176, Suzanne Tucker. 72t, tsyhun 74, Vinterriket 23; **The Kobal Collection:** Brighton Rock (1947), FILM Copyright © 1947 STUDIOCANAL FILMS LTD. ALL RIGHTS RESERVED 182; **TopFoto:** The Granger Collection 33

Cover images: *Front:* **Getty Images:** Atsushi Hayakawa
Inside front cover: **Shutterstock.com** Dmitry Lobanov

All other images © Pearson Education

We are grateful to the following for permission to reproduce copyright material:

Text
Extract on pages 6–7 from A WALK IN THE WOODS: REDISCOVERING AMERICA ON THE APPALACHIAN TRAIL by Bill Bryson, copyright © 1997 by Bill Bryson. Used by permission of Broadway Books, an imprint of the Crown Publishing Group, a division of Penguin Random House LLC. All rights reserved.; Extract on pages 10–11 from It's SO over: cool cyberkids abandon social networking sites, Copyright Guardian News & Media Ltd 2017; Extract on pages 11–12 from David Derbyshire, Social websites harm children's brains, Daily Mail; Extract on pages 14–15 from Lucy Maddox, Myth of the teenager, Does the stroppy adolescent exist?, article first appeared in Prospect Magazine; Extract on page 27 from *Titanic Voices,* Copyright Amberley Publishing; Poetry on page 32 from 'This is Just to Say' by William Carlos Williams, from THE COLLECTED POEMS: VOLUME I, 1909–1939, copyright ©1938 by New Directions Publishing Corp. Reprinted by permission of New Directions Publishing Corp, also copyrighted and reprinted here by kind permission of Carcanet Press Limited; Extract on pages 59–60 from Taking On

The World by Ellen MacArthur (Penguin Books 2003) Copyright Ellen MacArthur, 2003. Reproduced by permission of the author c/o Rogers, Coleridge & White Ltd., 20 Powis Mews, London W11 1JN; Extract on page 63 from Martin Luther King, I Have a Dream, Copyright 1963 Dr. Martin Luther King, Jr., Copyright renewed 1991 Coretta Scott King; Extract on page 65 from THE DIARY OF A YOUNG GIRL: THE DEFINITIVE EDITION by Anne Frank, edited by Otto H. Frank and Mirjam Pressler, translated by Susan Massotty, (Viking, 1997) copyright © The Anne Frank-Fonds, Basle, Switzerland, 1991. English translation copyright © 1995 by Doubleday. Used by permission of Doubleday, an imprint of the Knopf Doubleday Publishing Group, a division of Penguin Random; House LLC. All rights reserved.; Extract on pages 66–67 from The Letters of DH Lawrence Volume II 1913–1916 by D H Lawrence reprinted by permission of Pollinger Limited (www.pollingerltd.com) on behalf of the Estate of Frieda Lawrence Ravagli; Extract on page 69 from Mongolia: Telegraph Travel Book Award 2001, Telegraph Media Group Limited 2001; Extract on pages 70–72 from *A passage to Africa* , Little, Brown Book Group Ltd.The material by George Alagiah is reproduced by permission of the author c/o The Hanbury Agency Ltd, 53 Lambeth Walk, London SE11 6DX. Ltd.Copyright © 2001 George Alagiah. All Rights Reserved; Extract on page 74 from Social Media Addiction Is a Bigger Problem Than You Think, *Computer World* (Elgan. M), Used with permission of Computerworld Copyright© 2016. All rights reserved; Extract on page 75 from Are humans definitely causing global warming, Copyright Guardian News & Media Ltd 2017; Extract on page 77 from A Review of Star Wars: Episode vii, Copyright Guardian News & Media Ltd 2017; Extract on page 78 from Vladimir Slamecka, Information processing, Acquisition and recording of information in digital form "Reprinted with permission from Encyclopædia Britannica, © 2016 by Encyclopædia Britannica, Inc."; Extract on page 79 from "rap". Reprinted with permission from Encyclopædia Britannica, © 2016 by Encyclopædia Britannica, Inc.; Extract on pages 92–93 From Cider with Rosie by Laurie Lee Reprinted by permission of David R. Godine, Publisher, Inc. Copyright © 1980 by Laurie Lee Reproduced with permission of Curtis Brown Group Ltd, London on behalf of The Beneficiaries of the Estate of Laurie Lee; Extract on pages 96–97 from *The Hungry Cyclist*, Reprinted by permission of Harper Collins Publishers Ltd, Kevill-Davies, T.; Extract on pages 97–98 from The Explorer's Daughter, Penguin (Harbert, K), copyright Kari Herbert 2004, by permission of Aitken Alexander Associates Ltd; Extract on pages 106–108 Approximately one thousand two hundred (1,200) words from 'How the Poor Die' as featured in SHOOTING AN ELEPHANT AND OTHER ESSAYS by George Orwell, with an Introduction by Jeremy Paxman (Penguin Books, 2009). This collection first published 2003. Published in Penguin Classics with an Introduction 2009. This collection copyright © The Estate of Sonia Brownwell Orwell, 2003. Introduction copyright © Jeremy Paxman, 2009. Reprinted by permission of Houghton Mifflin Harcourt Publishing Company. All rights reserved; Extract on pages 113–114 From pp. 72–78, Touching The Void by Joe Simpson. Copyright 1989 by Joe Simpson Published by Jonathan Cape. Reprinted by permission of The Random House Group Limited and HarperCollins Pubishers; Extract on pages 118–119 from *Between a Rock and a Hard Place by Aron Ralston*, Reprinted with the permission of Atria, a division of Simon & Schuster, Inc. Copyright © 2004 Aron Ralston. All rights reserved.; Extract on pages 124–125 from "The Great Railway Bazaar" by Paul Theroux. Copyright © Paul Theroux, 1975, 2008, used by permission of The Wylie Agency (UK) Limited.; Extract on pages 126–127 from Notes From An Author, National Geographic Traveller (UK) / Paul Rosolie; Excerpt on page 128 Reproduced with permission of Curtis Brown Group Ltd, London, on behalf of Malala Yousafzai Copyright Malala Yousafzai 2013 Taken from Masala Yousafzai's Speech to the United

Nations; Extract on page 129 from I KNOW WHY THE CAGED BIRD
SINGS by Maya Angelou, copyright © 1969 and renewed 1997 by Maya
Angelou. Published by Little, brown Book Group. Used by permission of
Random House, an imprint and division and of Penguin Random House
LLC. All rights reserved.; Extract on page 130 from Lovely Prom Dress,
Angel. Your Carriage To Absurdity Awaits, The Sunday Times/News
Syndication; Extract on page 131 from Why All This Selfie Obsession,
The Independent; Extract on page 132 from Teenage Kicks, – The Value
of Sport in Tackling Youth Crime by Camilla Nevill, Matt van Poortvliet,
p.11. Commissioned by the Laureus Sport for Good Foundation
from and in collaboration with New Philanthropy Capital, http://www.
thinknpc.org/publications/teenage-kicks/ ; Extract on page 133 from
schoolfoodplan.com/plan, used under public sector information licensed
under the Open Government Licence (OGL) v2.0; Extract on page 134
from Review of Gravity, Telegraph Media Group Ltd 2013; Extract on
page 135 From THE MEN WHO STARE AT GOATS by Jon Ronson.
Copyright © 2004 by Jon Ronson. Reprinted by permission of Simon
& Schuster, Inc. All rights reserved, reproduced by permission of Pan
Macmillan via PLSclear; Extract on page 136 from My Family moved
from Pakistan to the UK 40 Years Ago–How Far We've Come, by Sarfraz
Manzoor, Copyright Guardian News & Media Ltd 2017; Extract on page
137 from The Correspondence of W.E.B. Du Bois, Volume I. Copyright
© 1973 by the University of Massachusetts Press. Extract on page 151
from RSPCA, Reproduced with permission of the RSPCA, 2016.

Select glossary terms have been taken from The Longman Dictionary of
Contemporary English Online